Policing and Crime Prevention

❖

DEBORAH MITCHELL ROBINSON

Editor
Valdosta State University

M. L. DANTZKER

Series Editor

Prentice
Hall

Upper Saddle River, New Jersey 07458

Library of Congress Cataloging-in-Publication Data

Policing and crime prevention / Deborah Mitchell Robinson, editor.
   p. cm. — (Prentice Hall's policing and . . . series)
   Includes bibliographical references
   ISBN 0-13-028436-X
   1. Crime prevention—United States. 2. Law enforcement—United States. 3.
Police-community relations—United States. 4. Community policing—United States. I.
Robinson, Deborah Mitchell. II. Series.
   HV7431 .P634 2002
   363.2'3'0973—dc21

                                                                    2001036233

Publisher: Jeff Johnston
Executive Editor: Kim Davies
Production Editor: Marianne Hutchinson, Pine Tree Composition
Production Liaison: Barbara Marttine Cappuccio
Director of Production and Manufacturing: Bruce Johnson
Managing Editor: Mary Carnis
Manufacturing Manager: Cathleen Petersen
Creative Director: Cheryl Asherman
Cover Design Coordinator: Miguel Ortiz
Cover Designer: Marianne Frasco
Cover Image: Siedes Preis/Photo Disc
Marketing Manager: Jessica Pfaff
Assistant Editor: Sarah Holle
Editorial Assistant: Korrine Dorsey
Composition: Pine Tree Composition
Printing and Binding: Phoenix Book Tech

Pearson Education LTD.
Pearson Education Australia PTY, Limited
Pearson Education Singapore, Pte. Ltd.
Pearson Education North Asia Ltd.
Pearson Education Canada, Ltd.
Pearson Educación de Mexico, S. A. de C. V.
Pearson Education—Japan
Pearson Education Malaysia, Pte. Ltd.

10 9 8 7 6 5 4 3 2 1
ISBN 0-13-028436-X

Contents

❖

SECTION III
POLICING AND CRIME PREVENTION PROGRAMS AT WORK

SECTION IV
POLICING AND CRIME PREVENTION CAPSTONE

Acknowledgments

---◆---

This book is dedicated to Doug, my husband and best friend. This, my first book, is a result of your never-ending patience, support, and most importantly, your love. I love you Sweetie.

I would like to thank my Mom and Dad for their assistance and support. I would also like to thank the Senior Editor of the Policing series, Dr. Mark Dantzker, for his advice and guidance with this project. Prentice Hall has been a great publisher to work with and I hope this will be the start of a long and prosperous relationship.

Introduction

❖

The concept of crime prevention is as old as policing. In modern society, crime prevention is a major issue, especially important to police agencies and their officers, the very individuals to whom the American public turns for protection. Crime prevention is a multifaceted concept, ranging from an individual's responsibility for locking doors to society's responsibility for the suppression/prevention of terrorism. It takes on many forms, from the identification and modification of physical structures and environments to the modification of individual attitudes toward personal safety. Crime prevention is an ever-changing concept, mirroring the continuous and inevitable changes in society. From these changes a myriad of crime prevention definitions, techniques, strategies, and programs have emerged, more or less effective in varying degrees. It is generally accepted that there will always be laws, crime, and a need for policing and crime prevention.

Many crime prevention ideologies today share a common bond to the model of Crime Prevention Through Environmental Design (CPTED), created in 1971 by C. Ray Jeffery. The basic premise of this model is that "through environmental design, areas may be made safer and the quality of life may be enhanced for individuals living in or using those areas" (Robinson 1998a, p. 32). This idea has implications for all communities throughout the country. "By focusing attention on the physical environment, the CPTED model concerns itself with offense areas," those areas where crimes are committed (Robinson 1998b, p. 45). Under this model, all citizens in a community can participate in crime prevention techniques by adjusting the environment to reduce crime.

Many crime prevention programs have been created by police agencies. These programs, or strategies, have been developed as policing policies, many under the heading of "community-oriented policing." Community-oriented policing strategies may take on any of several focuses within the community: specific areas and groups may be targeted, or general strategies may be adopted to prevent crime throughout the entire community. By focusing on the environmental aspects of the community, "the frequency of certain types of criminal behavior may be reduced through identification and modification of the environmental conditions under which such offenses occur" (Robinson 1998a, p. 32). Many police agencies employ a combination of community-oriented policing programs, using specifically targeted strategies within a broader, general strategy.

The purpose of this text is to give the reader an introduction to policing and crime prevention, as well as the interaction between them. With the increase in policing technology, crime prevention has become a major part of local, state, and federal policing. Research into the area of crime prevention has also allowed for developing, implementing, and testing various crime prevention programs for effectiveness. Crime prevention is becoming a major part of many academic curricula in criminology and criminal justice and has become important in police academy training. Many police departments are creating specific crime prevention units with the purpose of establishing relations within the community. Both policing professionals and the general public understand that crime prevention is not only a desired aspect of policing but also a necessity. A successful crime prevention strategy involves both police officers and ordinary citizens.

Throughout this text, the need for police-community interaction to build a successful crime prevention program is emphasized. It is important that everyone understands the need for each individual to accept a stake in preventing crime, as well as participation in that prevention.

This text is divided into four sections, containing a total of ten chapters. Section I is titled "Historical Aspects of Policing and Crime Prevention." In Chapter 1, author C. Frank Simons discusses the U.S. Department of Justice's "Operation Weed and Seed" crime prevention program and its current level of success. Simons traces the recent developments in crime prevention to the early 1900s, when police officers began to understand that effectiveness may be best measured by the absence of crime rather than by the number of arrests. Operation Weed and Seed is best described in the words of the Attorney General of the United States, Janet Reno, in her testimony before the Senate Appropriations Committee on April 22, 1993:

> The Weed and Seed Program is one of those good ideas that began as an interagency pilot program in a few cities and is now firmly established. Weed and Seed has the comprehensive objective of weeding out crime from designated neighborhoods, moving in with a wide range of crime and drug programs, and then seeding these neighborhoods with a comprehensive range of human service programs that stimulate revitalization.

In Chapter 2 titled "Cooperation and Coordination in Improving Crime Prevention Strategies," authors John R. Pike and Laura S. Gaultney provide an analysis of crime prevention strategies that may be employed by policing agencies. These strategies include turf protection, pride, intelligence dissemination, professional courtesy and ethics, public relations and trust, Reverse 911, combined resources, crossing jurisdictional lines, and resource indexing. The authors examine these issues and how each relates to the prevention of crime. Many of these issues are common sense, but common sense seems to take a backseat when governmental agencies are concerned, even when the goal is cooperation and coordination.

In Chapter 3, titled "Public versus Private Security: Whom Do We Trust?", author Pamela Ann Sexton-Alyea identifies the issues relating to the decision to choose between public and private security agencies. Sexton-Alyea discusses the media and how it has presented both types to the public. The techniques public and private security agencies use to address crime prevention are also discussed. Issues in choosing a specific policing agency include (1) armed versus unarmed guards, (2) salaries of private and public officers, (3) age of the officers, (4) level of education of the officers, (5) number of employees, and (6) union versus nonunion officers.

Section II of the text is titled "Policing and Crime Prevention in the Academic Setting." This section includes crime prevention techniques and strategies in elementary, secondary, and higher education. In Chapter 4, "Crime Prevention Through Environmental Design (CPTED) in Elementary and Secondary Schools," author Matthew Robinson examines the role of crime prevention in the American K–12 school system. In the wake of recent violent attacks and mass murders in schools, crime prevention has become an important issue for both teachers and education administrators. Robinson discusses how CPTED—which involves numerous alterations to the physical, psychological, and social environments of buildings, individuals, and groups—is being used in U.S. elementary and secondary schools. As the goals of CPTED are to reduce criminal victimization as well as lower perceptions of risk and fear of crime, Robinson documents the degree to which such crime prevention strategies achieve their intended objectives.

In Chapter 5, "The Bibb County Model for Community Policing in Schools," author Michael S. Dorn outlines the proven policing approach that has been used by the Bibb County, Georgia, Board of Education Campus Police Department to reduce crime on all the county's school campuses. Dorn discusses the success of this department and the techniques used to thwart six planned school shootings, one planned school bombing, and one planned double suicide. The Bibb County Model was developed with significant involvement by students, parents, teachers, the clergy, the media, and the general public; it is widely used as a national model for community-based crime prevention through school-police partnerships. As a direct result of the success of this program, Dorn is involved in training more than five-thousand educators and public safety officials yearly and has produced two international safety videos.

In Chapter 6, "Creating That Invisible Shield," authors James W. Rowe and Deborah Mitchell Robinson discuss designing, planning, and instituting an "invisible shield" to protect university and college campus communities. Rowe and Robinson analyze how traditional and nontraditional crime prevention techniques are employed by campus police officers and departments in protecting their institutions and satisfying the requirement that they meet or exceed the standards of protection expected by their students, their administrators, and the courts. Rowe and Robinson present a list of options from which the reader may select and possibly adapt a combination of programs and approaches that will best meet his or her needs and satisfy the campus community policing approach within his or her geographic location, be it rural or urban, public or private.

Section III of the text is titled "Policing and Crime Prevention Programs at Work." In Chapter 7, "Crime Prevention in Public Housing," author Brian McDonough examines the increased attention given to crime in public housing by the media, governmental agencies, and criminal justice researchers. McDonough focuses on Curries Woods in Jersey City, New Jersey, a public housing development that has seen its share of rising crime and social disorder activity. With the use of governmental funding to combat the rampant drug and violent crime problems within public housing, the Jersey City Housing Authority and Jersey City Police Department have worked closely together to develop proactive strategies to reduce and eliminate drug trafficking and violent crime. McDonough discusses the myriad of crime prevention strategies implemented that aided the transformation of a crime-infested high-rise project into a more secure, gated townhouse community. These strategies included the following: community redesign using CPTED techniques; development of resident entry monitoring stations staffed by trained resident monitors; community-police problem-solving meetings; resident-management police conferences; a resident-oriented Citizen Police Academy; a continuous deployment of Jersey City Police Community Service Officers; hiring of an off-duty site-based officer using PHDEP (Public Housing Drug Elimination Program) funding; and consistent enforcement of the "One Strike and You're Out" Public Housing Policy.

In Chapter 8, "Shadows of the Street: Policing, Crime Prevention, and Gangs," author Gordon A. Crews examines the role of crime prevention with regard to juvenile gangs. Crews discusses the characteristics of gangs, their impact in schools, and how crime prevention programs targeted toward gang activities must be realistic because, unfortunately, many communities still deny the presence of juvenile gangs. Crews advocates a community-oriented policing approach to preventing gang violence, in which the community and the police each have specific roles and responsibilities in preventing juvenile gang activity. This approach involves everyone in the community, from community leaders to police officers to citizens.

In Chapter 9, "Policing Domestic Violence," author Susan T. Krumholz presents an in-depth examination of the role of police in responding to domestic violence, including an examination of the history of domestic violence laws. Krumholz discusses the establishment of the first Family Violence Intervention Units in the 1960s, the lawsuits against the police in the 1970s, specific studies of arrests in the 1980s, and how those events have shaped police policies with regard to domestic violence. Krumholz concludes the chapter by presenting models currently implemented by police departments in their attempt to prevent domestic violence.

In Section IV, "Policing and Crime Prevention Capstone," the final chapter of the text reviews the preceding chapters. Authors M. L. Dantzker and Deborah Mitchell Robinson recap the various issues. They present a final discussion related to policing and crime prevention and offer insights into the future of crime prevention strategies, as well as the role the police will play in these strategies.

Collectively, the chapters in this text present the most up-to-date information regarding policing and crime prevention. Many issues related to crime prevention are discussed, including an analysis of several crime prevention programs currently in use. Upon completion of this book, the reader will have gained a broad understanding of the roles that police and citizens play in crime prevention, thus advancing the campaign to prevent—and ultimately eliminate—crime.

Deborah Mitchell Robinson, Ph.D.

REFERENCES

JEFFERY, C. R. (1971). *Crime prevention through environmental design.* Beverly Hills, CA: Sage Publications.

ROBINSON, D. M. (1998a). A case study of student fear of crime on a small southeastern university campus: Is it justified? In L. J. Moriarty & R. A. Jerin (Eds.), *Current issues in victimology research,* (pp. 31–42). Durham, NC: Carolina Academic Press.

ROBINSON, D. M. (1998b). A comparative analysis of environmental characteristics related to criminal victimization in activity areas of interstate highway interchanges and local highway intersections. *Journal of Security Administration, 21* (1), 45–57.

About the Authors

Gordon A. Crews is presently an Associate Professor and Head of the Department of Criminal Justice at Jacksonville State University in Jacksonville, Alabama. He serves on the board of directors for the Southern Criminal Justice Association and speaks nationally on issues surrounding school violence and juvenile delinquency. He earned B.S. and M.S. degrees in Criminal Justice, a graduate certificate in Alcohol and Drug Studies, and a Ph.D. in Education/Criminal Justice from the University of South Carolina. His publications include journal articles dealing with school violence, youth involvement in occult and satanic practices, and various law enforcement issues. His books include *Faces of Violence in America* (1996; Simon & Schuster), *The Evolution of School Disturbance in America: Colonial Times to Modern Day* (1997; Praeger), and *A History of Correctional Violence: An Examination of Reported Causes of Riots and Disturbances* (1998; American Correctional Association). His most recent book is titled *Chasing Shadows: Confronting Juvenile Violence in America* (2001; Prentice Hall).

    Michael S. Dorn is the School Safety Specialist for the Office of the Governor in the Georgia Emergency Management Agency. He is responsible for research and development relating to school safety for the State of Georgia. He has twenty years of law enforcement experience and served as the Chief of Police for the Bibb County, Georgia, Board of Education Campus Police Department for ten years. He earned B.A. and M.S. degrees in Quality Service Management from Mercer University and is a graduate of the FBI National Academy 181st Session. He is widely recognized as an authority on school safety and has presented speeches at more than one hundred state, national, and international professional conferences.

Laura S. Gaultney is currently employed with the Georgia Department of Juvenile Justice as a Regional Staff Development Training Coordinator. Prior to this position, she was a juvenile probation officer for 13 years. She earned B.S. and M.S. degrees in Criminal Justice from Valdosta State University. She is a Peace Officer Standards and Training (P.O.S.T.) certified instructor in the State of Georgia and teaches at the Georgia Public Safety Training Center. She also teaches for the Georgia Police Chiefs' Association, the Georgia Sheriffs' Association, the Georgia Corrections Association, and the Office of Juvenile Justice and Delinquency Prevention.

Susan T. Krumholz is currently an Assistant Professor and Coordinator of Criminal Justice at the University of Massachusetts at Dartmouth. She earned a B.A. degree from Keene State College, a J.D. from Seattle University (formerly University of Puget Sound School of Law), and an M.S. degree in Criminal Justice and a Ph.D. in Law, Policy, and Society from Northeastern University. Her research interests include domestic and intimate violence and restorative justice. She has published in the *Encyclopedia of Women and Crime,* the *Journal of Offender Rehabilitation,* and *Overcrowded Times.*

Brian McDonough is a lieutenant with the Jersey City, New Jersey, Police Department, with twenty-one years of policing experience, and is currently Commander of the Housing and Crime Prevention Police Unit. During his career he has served in various capacities, most notably with the Narcotics Unit. A decade of experience in antinarcotic work resulted in the arrest of 4,500 narcotic offenders and the execution of 100 criminal and narcotic search warrants. He earned a B.S. degree in Criminal Justice from Jersey City State College and is pursuing an M.S. degree from John Jay College of Criminal Justice. He is employed by the Jersey City Housing Authority in an off-duty capacity, responsible for overseeing, giving direction, coordinating, monitoring, and evaluating the Housing Authority's PHDEP. He served as the coordinator for two National Institute of Justice research projects: the "Crime Prevention Program in Public Housing" (1995) and the "Measuring Crime in Public Housing" research project (1998). He has also participated in several HUD-sponsored seminars that included "Youth Violence Prevention Conference," "One Strike Policy and You're Out," and "Crime Prevention Through Environmental Design."

John Pike began his career in policing in 1970 as a patrol officer with the Columbus, Georgia, Police Department. After rising to detective, he joined the Georgia Bureau of Investigation (GBI) in 1975 as a special agent. He spent seventeen years in management, narcotics, and field investigations with the GBI, retiring in 2000 as a regional Special Agent in Charge. He earned a B.S. degree in Criminal Justice from Columbus State University and an M.S. degree in Criminal Justice from Valdosta State University. He is a P.O.S.T. certified instructor in the State of Georgia and teaches at the Georgia Police Academy.

Deborah Mitchell Robinson is an Associate Professor of Criminal Justice at Valdosta State University in Valdosta, Georgia. She earned a B.S. degree in Public Relations from the University of Florida and M.S. and Ph.D. degrees in Criminology from Florida State University. She teaches in a variety of areas, including criminal law and procedure, victimology, criminological theory, and statistics, and has developed a Crime Prevention Through Environmental Design (CPTED) course at Valdosta State. She is a P.O.S.T. certified instructor for the State of Georgia and an adjunct instructor for the Georgia Police Academy. She has presented numerous professional papers in the area of crime prevention and has published in the areas of crime prevention, victimology, and sexual deviance in the *Encyclopedia of Criminology and Deviant Behavior,* the *Journal of Security Administra-*

tion, and a chapter in *Issues in Victimology Research.* She is currently working to assess the impact of community-oriented policing strategies of several police agencies on police officers and the communities they serve in South Georgia as well as CPTED strategies in public housing communities.

Matthew B. Robinson is an Assistant Professor of Criminal Justice at Appalachian State University in Boone, North Carolina, where he teaches in the areas of criminological theory and crime prevention. Most recently, he has published in the *Encyclopedia of Criminology,* the *Encyclopedia of Criminology and Deviant Behavior,* the *American Journal of Criminal Justice,* the *Howard Journal of Criminal Justice,* the *Journal of Contemporary Criminal Justice,* and the *Journal of Criminal Justice Education.* He recently published his first book, *Justice Blind: Ideals and Realities of American Criminal Justice* (2002; Prentice Hall).

James W. Rowe Sr. retired in August 2000 as the Chief of Police and Director of Public Safety for the University of Lowell, Massachusetts, Police Department. He has had a long and distinguished career as a police officer, joining the Dover, New Hampshire, Police Department in 1963 and retiring in 1983 as a captain. He earned a B.A. degree from St. Anselm College and an M.P.A. degree from Golden Gate University. He is past president of the New Hampshire Police Association and the Massachusetts Association of College and University Public Safety Directors. He is currently the Executive Editor of *Knight Stick* magazine, a consultant on policing and security matters, an Adjunct Professor of Criminal Justice at New Hampshire Technical Institute, and a deputy sheriff for the Strafford County, New Hampshire, Sheriff's Office. He and his wife Patricia have three sons: James Jr., the head trainer for the Boston Red Sox; Paul, a deputy sheriff; and Justin, a New Hampshire State Trooper.

Pamela Ann Sexton-Alyea is currently employed at the Tallahassee Regional Headquarters of the Florida Department of Law Enforcement (FDLE), in the Criminal Justice User Services Bureau, as a criminal justice information technician. She graduated *summa cum laude* in 1995 from Florida State University, earning a B.S. degree in Criminology and Criminal Justice. Prior to her employment at FDLE, she was an assistant to the director of operations at Maxwell Security Services, Inc., a private security guard firm, as well as Director of Operations for Baldwin and Associates Private Investigations firm. She holds a private investigator (PI) license for the State of Florida. She is married with four children.

C. Frank Simons began his career in policing in 1973 as a police officer for the Columbus, Georgia, Police Department. He is a former Chief of Police for the Perry, Georgia, Police Department and is currently the Chief of Police for the Valdosta, Georgia, Police Department. He has the distinction of taking both departments to state and national accreditation. He also served as director of the Abraham Baldwin Agricultural College, Georgia, Regional Police Academy for nine years. He earned a B.S. degree in Political Science from Georgia Southwestern College and an M.S. degree in Criminal Justice/Police Administration from Troy State University.

1

The Evolution
of Crime Prevention

C. Frank Simons

❖

"For centuries, crime—a universal phenomenon—has troubled and challenged societies of the world. How can crime be reduced and legal and social justice be attained? This question has confronted every civilized nation, and yet none has been successful in solving this complicated social phenomenon" (Mathias, Rescorla, and Stephens, 1980, p. 1). Crime, in one form or another, touches each of our lives on a daily basis. If you are fortunate enough not to have been a direct victim, you are still affected by the threat and cost of crime, as well as by the emotional consequences of realizing that crime is all around you.

An entire industry has developed around the fear of crime. From the manufacture of "burglar bars" for the windows and doors of your home to sophisticated alarm systems, closed-circuit television surveillance, and armed bodyguards, the fear of crime is all around us. We all pay the cost of crime, either as direct or indirect victims. Although you may have avoided being the target of a specific crime, you have still been victimized by the inflated price you pay to cover expenses that occur as the direct result of theft. Even the cost of insurance, which we purchase to protect us from financial loss, must be adjusted upward to cover the growing number of crime-related claims. Crime is indeed all around us.

WHY IS CRIME PREVENTION SO DIFFICULT?

Before we can develop a workable plan to prevent crime, it is helpful to first understand why a particular act is identified as a crime and prohibited by society.

Early codes suggest four important observations: 1. Most laws are products of prevailing social, political, and economic conditions; 2. Some laws articulate long-established customs and traditions and can be thought of as formal restatements of existing mores; 3. Some laws reflect efforts to regulate and coordinate increasingly complex social relations and activities; and 4. Some laws display prevailing ethical and moral standards and show close ties with religious ideas and sentiments (Barlow, 1978, p. 15).

Any discussion about the development of early criminal codes should include an explanation of the basic concepts that define criminal activity. An understanding of the early concepts of *mala in se* and *mala prohibita* help demonstrate how our system of criminal laws developed. *Mala in se* simply means the act is wrong on its face. Examples are murder, robbery, and rape. Offenses that are thought of as *mala prohibita* are wrong because they encompass activities that, though not intrinsically wrong, are prohibited as the result of society's viewpoint. Gambling, pornography, drug abuse, and other so-called victimless crimes fall into this category.

Mala prohibita offenses reflect societal values. Their classification as prohibited activity may change as the mores and values of society change. The treatment of drug abuse as criminal is a good example of how our system of laws can change as our population embraces new or different ideas. Although private, nonmedical use of certain drugs such as marijuana is prohibited (*mala prohibita*) in most states and jurisdictions, many in our culture are beginning to rethink this prohibition. Just as alcohol was once prohibited and possession of alcohol was deemed to be "criminal," the issue of marijuana possession for personal use is currently under review in some states. Some members of our society promote the view that drug addiction is really an illness and therefore a medical problem; as such, it should not be sanctioned with any criminal penalties. Similar arguments are advanced for addictions to gambling and pornography.

The increasing acceptance of pornography in our society demonstrates the impact of changing values. Simple possession of pornography is not usually considered a crime, though the sale or distribution of it is deemed illegal in most states (Klotter & Kanovitz, 1981, p. 66). It is often difficult to even define pornography, as demonstrated in 1964 when Supreme Court Justice Stewart, in a ruling concerning the motion picture *Lovers*, offered the following: "I shall not attempt further to define the kinds of material I understand to be embraced within that short-hand description (i.e., hard-core pornography); and perhaps I could never succeed in intelligibly doing so. But I do know it when I see it, and the motion picture involved in this case is not that" (Chase & Ducat, 1979, p. 1284).

The acceptance of gambling casinos in many states illustrates the way changing values affect our views of "right" and "wrong." Although most states prohibit private gambling, many states have legalized it on a limited basis or, in the case of state-sponsored lotteries, now promote the activity. Removing criminal sanctions from these types of offenses signifies a societal change in how we view the activity and what we are willing to accept. The acts are therefore excluded from the list of activities we prohibit. "In the minds of some, law is based on ethical beliefs, and criminal codes are a sort of catalogue of sins. But others have argued that there is much in our criminal codes that bears no obvious connection with ethics or morality" (Barlow, 1978, p. 15).

New and developing technologies and their potential use and misuse contribute to an ever-expanding debate about the criminality of certain behaviors. The current controversy over the use of computers and the Internet illustrates how changing technology affects the definition of criminal behavior. Cyberstalking is a relatively new offense, but there are already seminars conducted nationwide on how to investigate and deal with this new crime. Identity theft takes on a new meaning in the cyberworld with the growth of e-commerce.

Current laws are often ill-prepared to deal with this rapidly changing technology. Is it, or should it be, wrong to download an artist's music to your computer from the Internet without paying the artist or the music production company for the product? Is this an ethical issue, or is it an act that is so wrong as to subject offenders to a criminal punishment? Citizens debate these questions daily as state legislatures review the issues and courts attempt to define the law. Even though many seek simple solutions to the problems of crime prevention, the social landscape continues to change rapidly as we endeavor to define crime and debate how to prevent it.

Identifying unacceptable behavior and defining criminal prohibitions are only parts of the process of crime prevention. To have any significant effect, laws must be enforced. The determination of the proper role of police and the correct methods of law enforcement vary depending on an individual's philosophy and political views. The purpose and intent of legislation and the impact it has on various populations is increasingly being subjected to suspicion and examination. As the United States becomes more multicultural, the tasks expected of police in the fight against crime are becoming progressively more difficult to accomplish. Previously, the United States has been considered a cultural "melting pot," where individual differences blended into the dominant culture. "Multiculturalism, on the other hand, assumes that society should be able to accommodate the uniqueness and differences associated with multiple cultures" (Wright, 2000, p. 230), whereas the concept of "police" can be very different, depending on which part of the world served as the backdrop for a person's socialization. One indication of the multicultural nature of our society is the diversity of views held by citizens relative to the role of police officers and the tasks they are asked to perform.

An example of this diversity is the present debate about racial profiling—is it real or simply a perception? Is the police officer your friend or an oppressor? Can you rely on the police to protect you, or do you need to be protected from the police? Questions such as these multiply the inherent difficulties surrounding the issues of policing and crime. Those at the greatest risk of victimization may be unwilling to rely on local police to protect them. The issue is trust: Can local police be trusted to deal fairly with individuals in our society who are viewed as economically and politically powerless? Why is trust at the center of the debate?

Local police must address these issues. They must believe that people in a multicultural society can trust police, and police must act in a trustworthy manner. They must also demonstrate this trustworthiness to the population they serve. For meaningful crime prevention to occur, the citizenry and local police must work hand-in-hand. Both extremes of the spectrum have been tried, from the earliest attempts to prevent crime in the time of the "hue and cry" when the citizen was the local police, to the more recent professional model in which police officers are expected to control crime alone. Neither approach produced a totally acceptable outcome. The community and the police must work together if any significant crime prevention is to occur.

Mistrust extends beyond the cop on the beat. A larger issue is the question of acceptance of our new multiculturalism by the United States as a whole. Is there a hidden agenda when state and federal legislatures pass laws and create criminal penalties that impact particular or specific groups of citizens more harshly or more frequently? Are state and federal laws, which provide greater penalties for crack cocaine as compared with powder cocaine, racially biased in their construction and enforcement? Is the death penalty itself racist? Is it simply the application of the death penalty that is skewed? Is the death penalty ever an appropriate or acceptable device for preventing or controlling crime and protecting society? The controversy surrounding these and other difficult questions relative to criminal legislation and its enforcement is intense and complicated. These issues must be dealt with and resolved so that citizens can believe the law itself is fair and that police officers will apply it fairly. Only then can real trust be established and a meaningful cooperative effort occur between citizens and police.

Policing hasn't always appeared this difficult. At its root, the most basic intent of criminal legislation, policing, incarceration, and the death penalty is crime prevention. It encompasses a simple logic: The threat of discovery, apprehension, and punishment is intended to persuade a potential criminal to forgo illegal conduct. It is all about crime prevention. If there were no crime, laws and punishments would cease to exist. And this is where the simplicity ends.

How the deterrence of crime can be accomplished has been the subject of debate from the earliest times. It is generally considered that the prevention of future crimes was first contemplated in conjunction with the punishment of current offenders around the year 500 B.C.

Henry Fielding was one of the innovators of crime prevention in Great Britain during the 1700s and is credited with initiating the first crime prevention measures of his day. His intent was not only to stamp out current crime but also to prevent future outbreaks of crime. Fielding held that three steps were necessary to accomplish this. The first step required the development of a strong police force. Next, it was necessary to organize an active group of citizens. Third, action had to be taken to remove some of the causes of crime and the conditions in which it flourished (Vetter & Territo, 1984). Fielding's model is still viable in today's world, where many modern crime prevention programs promote an enhanced version of the same method. From the establishment of the constables of the Massachusetts Bay Colony in the 1600s to our most recent efforts, crime and crime prevention have been a major concern for Americans.

Most of our previous thinking has been about the prevention of the prohibited act itself. How can we stop the next murder, robbery, or assault or prevent the next act of drug abuse? It has only been in relatively recent times that we have begun to view the prevention of crime as something more than stopping the commission of a particular act. What if we could identify the cause of crime? Much like a medical approach, if we can identify the cause of the disease and remove it, the disease (crime) would not develop. By taking this approach, we remove the casual conditions and prevent the next specific act (Harpold, 2000).

Harpold (2000) argues, in his article "A Medical Model for Community Policing," that there are six types of neighborhoods that exhibit various levels of well-being: the integral, the parochial, the diffuse, the stepping-stone, the transitory, and the anomic. Analyzing a community using the six different identifiers allows the analyst to draw basic conclusions about the health of the neighborhood in terms of its susceptibility to criminal activity.

1. The integral neighborhood is composed of law abiding citizens who demonstrate a high level of pride, visibly interact, and have a link to outside organizations which helps them solve problems. There is a strong internal support system in the neighborhood.

2. The parochial neighborhood is characterized by homogeneous values and cultures, and residents seek to insulate themselves by taking care of their own problems without involving the police.

3. Although the members of the diffuse neighborhood may have much in common, they rarely interact, therefore limiting their ability to quickly perceive and react to problems.

4. In the stepping-stone neighborhoods, residents tend to move in and out quickly. They are likely to become involved in community roles and assume leadership roles; however, there is little consistency in the leadership of the neighborhood.

5. Residents who have very little in common or move frequently characterize transitory neighborhoods. They lack a consensus and cohesion. When neighbors isolate themselves, it becomes more difficult to improve deteriorating conditions.

6. The anomic neighborhood is characterized by isolation and alienation, where residents have accepted criminal victimization as a way of life. Problem solving in these communities is made more difficult by the lack of a defined leadership. (Harpold, 2000).

Police in the different types of neighborhoods also recognize the different levels of health and crime in their neighborhoods. "In healthy neighborhoods, residents fix windows quickly; in deteriorated neighborhoods, it takes a little longer. In the worst neighborhoods, broken windows give way to boarded-up and abandoned buildings. Police agencies recognize that when broken windows remain unfixed, crime problems left untreated fester and develop into cancer. Its symptoms manifest in repeat calls for service" (Harpold, 2000, p. 24).

THE CORNERSTONES OF CRIME PREVENTION

Understanding crime prevention and the development of crime prevention strategies requires an understanding of the roles of the citizen and the police, who must work in sync, if any crime prevention strategy or program is to be successful.

Citizen Involvement

The prevailing and most basic philosophy about crime prevention is to place the citizen at the core of the effort. This concept is as old as the idea of prevention itself, but the task has been found difficult to accomplish. Every citizen must contribute to the prevention of crime, or the effort is destined to fail. In the earliest days, under the Anglo-Saxon system of Alfred the Great, the citizen was expected to participate in both crime prevention and crime control. Under the "frankpledge" system, each man was required to be responsible for, and to, his neighbors. Upon hearing the "hue and cry" alarm, each qualified citizen was required to pursue the offender until his capture. Failure of any man who was not legally excluded from this obligation to participate in the pursuit of the offender was considered a serious breach and would subject him to heavy fines (Phelps, Swanson, and Evans, 1979).

The requirement that citizens participate in helping to create safe neighborhoods is still recognized today. The 1974 National Advisory Commission on Criminal Justice Standards and Goals declared that citizen involvement in crime prevention is not only desirable but also necessary. The President's Commission on Law Enforcement and Administration of Justice in 1967 and the National Commission on the Causes and Prevention of Violence in 1969 both noted that citizen involvement in crime prevention was essential. The National Commission noted, in part, that "informed private citizens, playing a variety of roles, can make a decisive difference in the prevention, detection and prosecution of crime" (Vetter & Territo, 1984, p. 557). From the traditional neighborhood watch approach to the more radical "taking it to the streets" approach, citizens must be involved. Citizen involvement is a cornerstone of crime prevention.

Community Policing

While questions relating to multiculturalism, profiling, and fairness issues are being debated, a paradigm shift in the government's approach to traditional crime prevention and policing has been taking place. Citizen participation in crime prevention is made more attainable with the shift in thinking about how policing is achieved. "Community-oriented policing" is a term often used today but is still misunderstood by many. Some call for a single definition of the term, as if there were a specific program or one particular method of achieving its implementation.

Community-oriented policing is not a specific program. It is an approach to policing that calls for an organizational structure and strategy to provide police services at the neighborhood level (Wright, 2000). It requires moving away from the belief that criminal sanctions, enforced by the police or the government, can, by themselves, be successful in preventing crime and realizing that police alone cannot prevent crime. The causes of crime are much too complicated for this simplistic approach to prevention to be successful. Community policing seeks to forge a partnership with citizens to solve community problems related to crime and neighborhood deterioration (Wright, 2000). Individual citizens, working together in a community, in conjunction with the police and other branches of government, are necessary to address both the cause of crime and the prevention of crime.

Community-oriented policing is a concept that holds that the police should be a part of the community and the community must unite to address the causes of crime and its prevention. The multicultural aspect of the United States and our historical failure to prevent crime makes community-oriented policing imperative. Police, working in conjunction with the community, is the second cornerstone in crime prevention.

Challenges to Successful Community Policing

For a community-oriented policing effort to be successful, it must contain at least three elements. First, it must have the support of the police management. This support must go beyond the lip service that top administrators sometimes give to a project because an elected official or community activist has promoted it. This effort requires rethinking about how police conduct business from a management perspective. Second, the rank and file of police must understand the effort and be willing to accept changes in the way they react to the public. Unfortunately, besides being hampered by a natural resistance to change, the conversion to community policing may be thwarted by the very administration attempting to install it.

Police agencies are often complex in their structure, but they can be categorized as either open or closed. Open systems respond well to their environment and can adapt as necessary to any change they may encounter. They are capable of engaging in self-organizing behavior. The opposite is true of closed systems. Traditional police departments that closely follow the closed model give a priority to stability, control, centralization, and command; they are resistant to change and therefore prone to maintain the status quo (DeParis, 2000). In this case, the organization itself will preclude the adoption of a new concept such as community-oriented policing. The rank and file officers must be made to understand that a change in the organization is occurring and they have permission to participate in that change.

The third requirement is that the other branches of the local government must understand their role and support the total project. A better name for "community policing" may be "community government." If the police are going to have any real success in their efforts to gain the trust and cooperation of the residents, other divisions of local government must be willing to participate. The city's or county's public works department, engineering department, parks and recreation department, and other governmental branches must be willing to help the police solve the community's problems.

Once the community is comfortable talking with police officers and voicing its concerns, issues besides those typically identified as crime problems will arise. They may be absentee landlords, the streetlight on the corner that hasn't worked in the past three years, the vacant house at the end of the street that is being used as a drug house, or maybe the overgrown vacant lots that concern residents and promote crime in their neighborhood. These and other similar issues will require a community government approach. Government participation, outside the ranks of the police, is the third cornerstone of crime prevention.

Problem-Oriented Policing and Scanning Analysis Response Assessment

Two additional components that contribute to a successful community policing strategy are problem-oriented policing (POP) and scanning analysis response assessment (SARA). A brief definition of POP is a view of crime as a symptom of the real problem. To simply solve a crime and not address its cause produces little effect. Additional crimes of a similar nature are likely to occur. The standard approach to addressing crime usually revolves around the symptom, not the cause. In his 1979 article, Herman Goldstein argued that "the most commonly proposed improvements to policing fall far short of the mark. Most improvements focus on the means of policing (staffing, equipment, structure) rather than the ends of policing (the effectiveness of police response to crime and disorder problems)" (Sampson & Scott, 2000, p. 1).

The police officer on the beat must be able to recognize how the general problems he or she is dealing with today may relate to past and future criminal activity in the same neighborhood. The officer will then be armed with the knowledge to become proactive rather then simply reactive. By employing a problem-oriented approach, the pieces of the puzzle begin to fall into place and the true causes of the crime may be identified and addressed. If we discover and eliminate the root of the problem, we are more likely to have a significant impact on the overall crime picture in the neighborhood.

SARA allows officers to address crime in particular areas of a community (Wolfer, Baker, and Zezza, 1999). The scanning aspect includes a review of current crime statistics, crime prevention surveys, and crime-specific planning. The analysis of the data allows the police officers to understand the actions and interactions among offenders, victims, and the crime scene before developing appropriate responses to crime problems. Analysis is important relative to several factors generally relied upon in the investigation of crimes. One theory holds that property crimes are typically committed within a relatively short travel distance from the offender's residence (Wolfer, Baker, and Zezza, 1999). In gaining an understanding of which crimes are being committed in a certain area, police will have a better opportunity to predict the location of future crimes and the possible location and identity of the offenders.

Even though POP and SARA represent successful strategies in the fight against crime, many communities have developed additional programs. Oxnard, California, for example, has expanded the effort by establishing the "five Cs" of advanced community policing. "The five C's stand for collaboration, cooperation, commitment, compassion, and concern. Understanding these terms and using this system every day has brought increased community participation and pride, closer relationships between the community and law enforcement, a reduction in crime, and a sense of peace and safety in the community" (Rodriquez, 2000, p. 14). The five Cs model of crime prevention is designed to advance the principles of community-oriented policing by linking the community and police together in a stronger relationship.

When police officers become more involved with the communities they serve and begin to understand the differing cultural views of the people in their communities, they may better serve the residents and are more likely to avoid the mistrust and suspicion police officers often face. Mistrust and suspicion will be replaced with trust and cooperation. Cooperation with the police is essential to successful crime prevention.

UNDERSTANDING THE CAUSES OF CRIME

What are the causes of crime? It is a simple question without a simple answer. Is crime a product of a person's environment or is it an inherited/genetic trait? Does the amount or quality of the offender's education affect that person's willingness to engage in criminal behavior? What roles do poverty and opportunity play? Do socialization processes determine who will become a career criminal and who will avoid criminal behavior?

Although some theories hold that the cause of crime is genetic, others maintain that genetics play only an insignificant role. Contemporary beliefs hold that there is little doubt the environment is the principal determinant and cause of criminal behavior. Under this theory, poverty, high unemployment, poor education, overpopulation, and deviant group norms are all considered as contributing causal factors of crime (Bartol & Bartol, 1986). In mankind's attempt to determine the cause of crime, we have embraced such widely varying theories as heredity, the impact of a person's environment, and evolution. In 1876, Cesare Lombroso published a work maintaining that criminal behavior was the result of evolution. "The criminal, Lombroso believed, represented a separate species that had not yet evolved sufficiently toward the more 'advanced' homo sapiens; this species was genetically somewhere between modern humans and their primitive origins in physical and psychological makeup" (Bartol & Bartol, 1986, p. 22).

In their 1983 work, Haskell and Yablonsky argue there is no one accepted cause of crime. They maintain that researchers must consider the following concepts and issues:

1. A relationship of factors is not necessarily a causal nexus. The fact that a preponderance of criminals and delinquents come from broken homes does not necessarily mean that a broken home must cause delinquency and crime.
2. No single theory explains all crime and delinquency. Different patterns of crime and delinquency require different explanations. The sexual psychopath, the burglar, and the violent gang youth would not tend to emerge from the same causal context.
3. Primary and secondary causes should not be confused. The lack of social workers or poor school facilities is not a primary cause of delinquency; however, a broken home may be a primary causal factor.
4. One cannot logically isolate one single cause of crime or delinquency.
5. In examining causal explanations based on research with offenders, we have the problem of separating the causal force from the impacts of the administration of justice (arrest, jail, courts, prison) (p. 464).

Curt and Anne Bartol observe in their 1986 book, *Criminal Behavior: A Psychosocial Approach,* that criminal behavior may be linked more to solving problems than being related to any of the usually discussed causes of poverty, class, education, or genetics. They ask us to contemplate unlawful conduct as subjectively adaptive rather than simply deviant. This view holds that unlawful conduct is a response pattern a person has found to be effective, or thinks will be effective, in certain circumstances. "Engaging in criminal behavior might be one person's way of adapting or surviving under physically, socially, or psychologically dire conditions. Another person might decide that violence is necessary to defend honor, protect self, or reach a personal goal. In either case, the person is choosing what he or she believes is the best alternative for that particular situation" (Bartol & Bartol, 1986, p. 77–78).

As one can see, there are many theories on the causes and origins of criminal conduct. It is therefore understandable that discovering the magic bullet of "crime prevention" is a difficult task. Just as there are likely to be numerous causes of deviant behavior and criminal conduct, there have been a variety of approaches to crime prevention. Because no individual approach is apt to produce the desired results, a combination of possible solutions appears to have the best chance of influencing future criminal conduct. Understanding that the causes of crime are complex and affected by the world around us is the final cornerstone in our effort to prevent crime.

OPERATION WEED AND SEED

The multifaceted approach proposed by Operation Weed and Seed, under the sponsorship of the U. S. Department of Justice, appears to see crime as a symptom of other larger problems. Like the problem-oriented policing method, it addresses the entire issue rather than just the symptom. "Operation Weed and Seed, a U.S. Department of Justice community-based initiative, is an innovative and comprehensive multi-agency approach to law enforcement, crime prevention, and community revitalization" (U.S. Department of Justice [USDOJ], 2000, p. 1). "The Weed and Seed concept began with three pilot programs in major U. S. cities and grew to more than 200 full-fledged projects in less than nine years" (Branson, 2000, p. 82).

The apparent success of the effort is likely the result of its broad-based approach and its understanding of the difficulty of defining the causes of crime. If we agree that there is, indeed, no one explanation for the cause of crime, then it is reasonable that any serious attempt to prevent crime must be multifaceted and address all the known or suspected causes. Admittedly, it is a huge task, but the Weed and Seed program is taking just such an approach.

"The U.S. Department of Justice launched Operation Weed and Seed in 1991 to demonstrate that a large array of resources can be mobilized in a comprehensive, coordinated effort to control crime and drugs and to improve the quality of life in similar targeted high-crime neighborhoods. The initiative's name was drawn from its two-pronged strategy: to 'weed out' violent offenders through intensive law enforcement and prosecution and to 'seed' the neighborhood with prevention, intervention, treatment, and revitalization services" (Roehl et al. 1996, p. 2). As stated by the Executive Office of Weed and Seed (1999, p. iv).

> Weed and Seed is the Department of Justice's premier community-based crime prevention program. It is a coordination strategy that works to make a wide range of public and private sector resources more accessible to communities. Under the leadership of U.S. Attorneys, the strategy brings together federal, state and local crime-fighting agencies, social service providers, representatives of public and private sectors, prosecutors, business owners, and neighborhood residents, linking them in a shared goal of weeding out violent crime and gang activity while seeding the designated area with social services and economic revitalization. Weed and Seed is foremost a strategy, in which the grant is one among many tools to help prevent, control, and reduce violent crime, drug abuse, and gang activity in designated high crime neighborhoods across the country. The Weed and Seed strategy includes four basic elements: law enforcement, community policing, prevention/intervention/treatment, and neighborhood restoration. This community-based initiative is an innovative and comprehensive multi-agency approach to law enforcement, crime prevention and community revitalization.

So How Does It Work: Grassroots Approach

The road to success through Operation Weed and Seed starts with the affected communities. It is truly a "grassroots" effort. "At some point during our education we're taught the theory of democracy. It goes something like this: citizens clearly articulate their vision for the community they share, and government administrators listen carefully to what citizens want. That's the way it's supposed to be" (Smith, 2000, p. 12). The community leadership—

either elected officials or other people in the community who have the overall betterment of the community in mind—must begin the effort.

First, support for a communitywide effort must be established. There is no universally accepted "right" way to form a Weed and Seed community. Each community is recognized as having a unique set of problems and kind of leadership. Part of the overall success of the program appears to be the development of skills necessary to unite the different elements of the community in order to identify and overcome the problems with which it is confronted.

> [To] implement an effective Weed and Seed strategy within a community, you need to develop and capitalize on the relationships between people and agencies. During the developmental stages, time is required to get to know people with whom you don't normally work with day-to-day and understand issues facing other agencies. By doing this, you develop a network which is more informed than any individual player is, and which in turn can collectively act more powerfully and completely (Morey, 1999, p. 1).

Area support must include both residents and nonresidents, area leadership, and business leaders, as well as elected officials in local government who can help achieve success. Because this is a grassroots effort, the local organizational committee is given discretion as to how the individual program between the affected parties is necessary for success. Training materials for Weed and Seed steering committees attempting to create success promote the use of the MEEGA principle, which holds that "effective leadership for conducting Weed and Seed strategies is structured at the local level. A consensus in neighborhoods is to motivate, engage, energize and guide the actions (MEEGA) of a group of individuals, constituents, stakeholders, volunteers and personnel, to successful results" (Weed and Seed Steering Committee, 2000).

When a new organization is being created, like most new organizations, it is likely to experience "growing pains." Divergent ideas among the residents and leaders relative to identifying community problems, deciding how they should be addressed, determining who will be eligible to serve in this new program, and deciding on the form and structure of the various subcommittees to be created must be reconciled with organizational differences. Initially, these issues may be divisive, producing stress among the program participants. Many new Weed and Seed initiatives experience a "storming," or conflict, phase in their program development. The Executive Office of Weed and Seed is prepared to deal with these problems through program and on-site assistance to overcome organizational difficulties. The result of these difficulties may prove to be beneficial to the overall health of the program as participants begin to understand how issues are viewed differently by others. Learning the art of compromise is necessary to the development of a comprehensive, successful strategy.

Next, the physical boundaries of the area to be addressed must be determined. This area is referred to in Weed and Seed documents as the "target area." Target areas should consist of readily identifiable neighborhoods that demonstrate the type of community problems to be addressed through the program. When selecting the target area, community leaders may review the type of problems being exhibited and how they can be addressed through this unique program. Issues usually under review include the overall crime picture and the specific types of crimes that present themselves as community problems. Substandard housing, the unavailability of affordable housing and related problems, few business or employment opportunities within the neighborhoods, and the lack of treatment and intervention programs available to the community may also be identified as problems. The scope of the issues being addressed must also be considered as the program boundaries are being decided.

Once the physical boundaries have been determined, a strategy must be developed to respond to the identified problems. As previously stated, the variety of problems and issues to be addressed must be considered when attempting to identity the target area. However, the leadership at this initial stage of the program formation should be careful not to impose its will on the residents of the target area. For this effort to be successful, the residents of the community must take part in the program design and selection of issues to be addressed. Community residents are likely to resist any neighborhood plan that has been developed without their significant input. Additionally, because it is their neighborhood, they may be far better prepared to know what the real problems are and to offer workable solutions. The goals of an Operation Weed and Seed program will likely not be successful without community input and participation.

One successful approach to gaining community support and input is to coordinate and widely advertise a series of organizational community meetings to be conducted over a period of time and hosted in several different locations within the selected target area. A full explanation of the Weed and Seed program and the opportunity it represents should be given to those in attendance, and their ideas and participation should be requested. Government and community leaders in attendance should be prepared to listen to all criticism, whether legitimate or unfounded. Target areas are selected because they have identified problems. It should be expected that those bearing the greatest impact of the problems have formed their own ideas as to their cause and possible solutions. Their thoughts may or may not be correct, but in order to gain the trust and respect of the community residents, it is necessary to solicit and respond to their concerns. The issues brought forward by the community should be reduced to a manageable list by combining like projects, eliminating duplication, recognizing those goals unobtainable or too broad for the project, and consideration of other project limitations.

In addition to soliciting their thoughts about problem areas, it is also necessary to solicit the residents' active participation in the program. A key to success is to retain and continue the grassroots nature of the project. Target area residents must be part of the decisions being made about their neighborhoods. Interested and motivated residents should be integrated into the leadership of the project. The new leadership, which now includes the residents, should participate in narrowing the task to be accomplished and developing a strategy to address the target area issues.

To make this task more manageable, a steering committee must be formed, composed of interested area citizens and leaders in business, government, and the community who are able to assist in bringing resources to the target area. The membership of the steering committee will develop a strategy to address the identified problems and to gain any necessary local and federal support. Although the initial strategy usually depends heavily on federal support, the plan should provide for discovering and expanding local financial resources both to continue and expand the project.

Once the target area and projects to be addressed are identified and the strategies to respond to the issues have been developed, the overall program strategy is presented to the Executive Office for Weed and Seed (EOWS) for review and acceptance. The description of the target area, the strategy for responding to goals of the program, and the proposed budget are then submitted to EOWS for its approval. Upon satisfying the requirements of EOWS, the initiative will be awarded official recognition as a Weed and Seed site, and the project is ready to begin applying its strategy. With the acceptance of the steering committee's strategy, the local program may apply for funding through EOWS. For the fiscal year 2000 funding cycle, EOWS has made available $125,000 for each continuation site, plus $50,000 in additional grant funds for Special Emphasis Initiatives and $50,000 in Asset Forfeiture Funds for joint police operations, including qualifying community policing activities (USDOJ, 2000). The program requirements call for a minimum of $40,000 to be directed to the development and continuation of at least one "safe haven" in the target area. The term *safe haven* is discussed later in this chapter.

Funding is supplied under the terms of a grant provided through EOWS. It is intended to initiate the strategy, and it is expected that the local Weed and Seed effort will locate local funding through collaboration and joint projects for continuation of the strategy at the conclusion of the federal funding cycle.

Two separate program committees may be used to manage the strategy that has been accepted by EOWS. A "Weed committee," which generally involves police and prosecution partners, is formed to focus on crime-related issues, whereas a "Seed committee," composed of area residents and individuals who represent community resources necessary to address prevention and revitalization issues, is created. These two committees work together with the steering committee to accomplish the overall goal of the Weed and Seed Initiative to eliminate violent crime, drug trafficking, and related crime from the target area and to provide a safe, crime-free environment for law-abiding citizens (Roehl et al., 1996).

Safe havens, as mentioned earlier in this chapter, are a key element of the Weed and Seed strategy, and all sites are required to have at least one safe haven. A minimum of $40,000 of grant funds must be allocated for the safe haven(s). "A Safe Haven is a multiservice center where a variety of youth and adult services are coordinated in a highly visible, accessible facility that is secure against crime and illegal drug activity. It is a place where youth and other residents can access needed services, develop relationships, find opportunities to be productive and successful, and enhance skills" (USDOJ, 2000, p. 6). The safe haven is expected to be a place safe from criminal and drug-related activity, which is available both to youths and adults. It should be open and accessible after regular work and school hours. "The Safe Haven should provide a variety of services and supportive programs, e.g., educational, cultural, recreational, health, and justice-related, with emphasis on coordinated delivery of these services" (USDOJ, 2000, p. 6).

EOWS will fund up to $50,000 for one or two Special Emphasis Initiatives that address the following topics: gun abatement, truancy prevention, conflict resolution, justice innovations, community economic development, antigang initiatives, prevention through the arts, mentoring, anti-drug/alcohol abuse strategies, environmental activities, computer learning centers, victim services, and reentry programs for offenders. The remaining available funds may be used to support the site strategies that address the issues and problems identified by the steering committee and the target area residents. Issues such as community blight, unemployment and employment training, child care for latchkey kids, tutoring for school-age children, and adult literacy may be addressed through Weed and Seed. Additionally, crime and traffic-related issues receive greater attention through the police department's enhanced relationship with target area residents. Cooperation with area residents gives police officers an improved opportunity to interrupt and dispel street crime.

Community Acceptance of Additional Police Activities

A 1996 National Institute of Justice (NIJ) research brief on an evaluation of Operation Weed and Seed reported that additional police attention has not always been seen in a positive light. According to the research, increased police activities are most often viewed positively by communities who felt ignored and besieged by crime. However, at other sites, the announcement of proposed "weeding" activities was met with concern and negative reaction from community leaders and civil rights activists. Their primary concern was the targeting of predominantly minority communities for additional police attention.

Overall, however, the program is viewed in a positive light. The NIJ (1996) brief reported that the "Weed and Seed program helped spread and reinforce the idea of community policing, which was a positive experience for both the community and police agencies. It also helped demonstrate that enforcement can be enhanced by close contact with the community and that enforcement and service are not necessarily incompatible policing functions" (p. 14).

Drug Education for Youth

No crime prevention program would be complete without a component intended to address youth and their problems. The Drug Education for Youth (DEFY) Initiative is such a program. The Department of the Navy and the Department of Justice, using the Executive Office of Weed and Seed, offers the DEFY program to sponsoring U.S. attorneys who operate Weed and Seed programs within their jurisdictions. "The DEFY program began as a special initiative of the Secretary of the Navy in 1992 when the Secretary of the Navy's Drug Demand Reduction Task Force (DDRTF) was established. The DEFY mission is to be a catalyst for increasing community participation and commitment to youth. DEFY produces 9–12 year-olds who have the character, leadership, and confidence to engage in positive, healthy lifestyles as drug-free citizens" (Drug Education for Youth [DEFY], 2000, p. 2).

The purpose of DEFY is to provide leadership training and life skills through teaching team-building, conflict resolution skills, goal setting, and self-confidence. The DEFY program consists of four-year-long components divided into two phases. The first phase consists of either a residential or nonresidential leadership camp that includes classroom instruction, physical fitness activities, physical challenge, and field trips. During the first phase, participants receive instruction that teaches and fosters positive life traits. The individual skills taught include the following:

1. Relationships and conflict management
2. Substance abuse prevention
3. Physical fitness
4. Hygiene, Nutrition, First aid, and Safety
5. Self-confidence
6. Gang awareness and deglamorization

7. Citizenship and leadership
8. Goal setting
9. Physical challenge

The experience is intended to be enjoyable, as well as to provide the necessary in-struction for the desired learning. All candidates for Phase II adult mentors must be intro-duced to the children during the leadership camp. The second phase of the program continues throughout the remainder of the year and teams the children with adult mentors who work through a structured program to reinforce the leadership and drug-free skills taught during the camp phase. Parents or guardians are encouraged to participate through-out the year to further develop the skills being taught and to foster a commitment to a drug-free life. The last component of the program is outplacement. During this part of the program, the children continue to receive support and encouragement from a DEFY adult in a community-based, youth-activity program.

Although DEFY began with the Secretary of the Navy, it is considered an inclusive program and is open to partnerships with most national programs that deliver a positive, protective, youth-oriented preemption program. DEFY partners include the Department of the Air Force, the Southwest Border and New York and New Jersey High Intensity Drug Trafficking Areas (HIDTA), and Drug Awareness Resistance Education programs. It is also partnered with the Department of the Treasury, the Bureau of Alcohol, Tobacco, and Firearms, and the Department of Transportation (DEFY, 2000).

The Drug Education for Youth program appears to bring the Weed and Seed pro-gram full circle. Although other aspects of Weed and Seed concentrate on crime preven-tion and removing the obstacles to being crime free, the DEFY program concentrates on building the character, leadership, and confidence necessary for children to mature into adults who will contribute to a crime-free community. "The success of the DEFY program continues to grow. The 1999 DEFY Camps served approximately 200 more youth than the 1998 season. With 75 Weed and Seed sites offering the DEFY program in their communi-ties, more than 2,600 children were given the opportunity to participate in this increas-ingly popular mentoring program" (DEFY, 2000, p. 6).

CONCLUSION

When considered in conjunction with the information presented in the first part of this chap-ter, the emerging picture of the Weed and Seed program appears to indicate that the initia-tive has attempted to take the most successful portions of our past attempts at crime pre-vention and combine them into one successful effort. Much like the early determination of unacceptable behavior (*mala prohibita*), target area residents' involvement in a Weed and Seed community can identify those events occurring in their community that require im-mediate attention and direct the necessary resources to correct the problem. Borrowing from the Anglo-Saxon frankpledge system, area residents are taking responsibility for their neighbors, much as they did in the days of "hue and cry."

Although the program certainly does not expect individual citizens to literally "take up the chase," the Weed and Seed program gives citizens a modern-day opportunity to take joint responsibility for the safety of their community. The concepts of community-oriented policing are important to the success of the program with the inclusion of expanded involvement between the police and residents. The trust issues discussed earlier can be addressed through a dialogue and daily involvement between the police and citizens. Problem-oriented policing and scanning analysis response assessment can be more efficiently applied with the cooperation of the community. The community's attempt to bring new businesses and commercial ventures, when appropriate, to the area and the repair or removal of dilapidated houses and buildings in the target area addresses the "health" of the neighborhood. The issue of community pride and the impact it has on the susceptibility to crime is evident in the residents' desire to remove the eyesores and improve the livability of the area.

Through a closer relationship with the police, citizens may be better able to understand issues related to criminal sentencing guidelines and why some crimes are punished more harshly than others. This understanding offers an opportunity to dispel citizens' suspicions that the guidelines and enforcement practices are intentionally racially or ethnically biased or that some other conspiracy is at work. Interaction with other appointed and elected government officials will allow citizens to gain a better grasp of how local government operates and how to better accomplish their goals for their community.

The Weed and Seed approach appears to embrace Haskell and Yablonsky's (1983) argument that there is no one accepted cause of crime and that a multifaceted approach is necessary for successful crime prevention. The National Institute of Justice reported in a July 1999 release that an evaluation of Operation Weed and Seed found it to be a positive catalyst for communities, and, in most cases, it decreased crime and helped promote social and economic revitalization. Through an understanding of what we have learned throughout the history of crime prevention, the Weed and Seed initiative provides the opportunity to make a significant difference in those neighborhoods willing to accept the challenge and take charge of their community (NIJ, 1999).

The opening paragraph of this chapter stated that crime and crime prevention have been with us throughout history. We have sought the solution to this problem continuously and unsuccessfully since the beginning of civilization. We have variously identified the cause of crime as evolutionary, genetically based, the failure of organized religion, the result of demonic possession, medical, a product of a person's socialization, and as simple conflict resolution by the offender. It is apparent that we have not yet discovered why some people are prone to commit criminal offenses and others are not. Until we can read the criminal mind, we will continue to search for ways to prevent the criminal act.

We have accepted that crime is with us always and that vigilance is our best approach to avoid victimization. A vigilance that is not only personal but includes neighborhoods and communities gives us the best chance of preventing the crime that touches our lives daily. In our search for prevention, we return again and again to a community-based model.

REFERENCES

BARLOW, H. D. (1978). *Introduction to criminology*. Boston: Little, Brown and Company.
BARTOL, C. R., & BARTOL, A. M. (1986). *Criminal behavior: A psychosocial approach* (2nd ed.). Englewood Cliffs, NJ: Prentice-Hall.

BRANSON, H. K. (2000). Weed and seed in Honolulu: The key is community input. *Law and Order, 48*(9), 82–86.

CHASE, H. W., & Ducat, C. R. (1979). *Constitutional interpretation: Cases, essays, materials* (2nd ed). St. Paul, MN: West Publishing Co.

DEPARIS, R. J. (2000). How contemporary police agencies can adapt to the community policing mission. *The Police Chief, LXVII*(8),108–114.

DRUG EDUCATION FOR YOUTH: 1999 recap. (2000). *Weed and Seed In-Sites, VIII*(l), 6-7.

EXECUTIVE OFFICE OF WEED AND SEED. (1999). The Weed and Seed strategy. In *Weed and Seed Best Practices, Fall*(2), (p. iv). Washington, DC: United States Department of Justice, Office of Justice Programs, Executive Office of Weed and Seed.

HARPOLD, J. A. (2000). A medical model for community policing. *FBI Law Enforcement Bulletin, 69*(6), 23-27.

HASKELL, M. R., & YABLONSKY, L. (1983). *Criminology: Crime and criminality* (3rd ed.). Boston: Houghton Mifflin Company.

KLOTTER, J. C., & KANOVITZ, J. R. (1981). *Constitutional law* (4th ed.). Cincinnati, OH: Anderson Publishing Co.

MATHIAS, W., RESCORLA, R. C., & STEPHENS, E. (1980). *Foundations of criminal justice*. Englewood Cliffs, NJ: Prentice-Hall.

MOREY, M. P. (1999). Network and linkages among Weed and Seed sites: The power is in the partnerships. In *Weed and Seed Best Practices, Fall*(2), (pp. 1–4). Washington, DC: United States Department of Justices, Office of Justice Programs, Executive Office of Weed and Seed.

NATIONAL INSTITUTE OF JUSTICE. Study shows Weed and Seed works. Retrieved August 25, 2000, from the World Wide Web: http://www.ci.shreveport.1a.us/dept/police/news/news9921.htm

PHELPS, T. R., SWANSON, C. R., Jr., & EVANS, K. R. (1979). *Introduction to criminal justice*. Santa Monica, CA: Goodyear Publishing Company, Inc.

RODRIQUEZ, G. (2000). Life after SARA: An advanced model of community policing. *Weed & Seed In-Sites, VIII(2),* 14.

ROEHL, J. A., HUITT, R., WYCOFF, M. A., PATE, A., REBOVICH, D., & COYLE, K. (1996, October). National process evaluation of Operation Weed and Seed. *National Institute of Justice Research in Brief* [online serial]. Retrieved July 31, 2000, from the World Wide Web: http://www.ncjrs.org/txtfiles/weedseed.txt

SAMPSON, R., & SCOTT, M. S. (2000). *Tackling crime and other public-safety problems: Case studies in problem-solving*. Washington, D.C.: U.S. Department of Justice.

SMITH, D. R. (2000). The way it's "supposed" to be: Residents drive the Weed and Seed strategy. *Weed & Seed In-Sites, VIII*(3), 12–13.

UNITED STATES DEPARTMENT OF JUSTICE. (2000). *Weed and Seed fiscal year 2000 program guide and application kit*. (Available from the Office of Justice Programs, 810 Seventh Street, NW, Washington, D.C. 20531).

VETTER, H. J., & TERRITO, L. (1984). *Crime and justice in America: A human perspective*. St. Paul, MN: West Publishing Co.

WEED AND SEED STEERING COMMITTEE. (2000, February). Training presented at the meeting of the Valdosta Weed and Weed Steering Committee, Valdosta, GA.

WOLFER, L., BAKER, T. E., & ZEZZA, R. (1999). Problem-solving policing: Eliminating hot spots. *FBI Law Enforcement Bulletin, 68*(11), 9–14.

WRIGHT, B. S. (2000). Policing in a multicultural society. In W. G. Doerner & M. L. Dantzker (Eds.), *Contemporary police organization and management: Issues and trends* (pp. 229–250). Boston: Butterworth-Heinemann.

2

Cooperation and Coordination in Improving Crime Prevention Strategies

John R. Pike

Laura S. Gaultney

Cooperation and *coordination* are two terms that conjure up images of people working together toward a common goal. Today, police agencies and officers work together toward the common goal of crime prevention—right? Although common sense would suggest this to be true, these two terms do not always apply to policing and crime prevention. Police agencies, although having similar overall goals in enforcement, have a separate and distinct authority which often prevents the appropriate dissemination of pertinent data relating to crime prevention and control.

The data presented in this chapter are not theoretical but are based on actual field experience and observations dating back to 1970. The issues will be dealt with from a commonsense perspective, showing practical, proven strategies which will improve crime prevention and subsequent crime solving methods. The goal is to broaden the reader's understanding of the inner workings of federal, state, and local police agencies.

Crime prevention is becoming a major issue in policing. Cooperation and coordination among police agencies are the keys to any successful crime prevention strategy. This chapter identifies the following nine areas within the criminal justice system that present possible solutions to problems that impact successful policing initiatives:

1. Turf protection
2. Pride
3. Intelligence dissemination
4. Ethics and professional courtesy between agencies
5. Public relations and trust
6. Resource indexing
7. Combined resources
8. Crossing jurisdictional boundaries
9. Reverse 911

TURF PROTECTION

In all probability, the most persistent problem that hampers the police community and stymies effective enforcement procedures is that of turf protection. When a police agency tries to ensure that its jurisdiction, either over a geographic area or a field of perceived expertise, is not infringed upon by another agency or its representative, it is called turf protection. It is an effort to maintain total control of the defined area. Although there are no ethical justifications for turf protection, there are various explanations as to why it abounds.

Turf protection can exist in federal, state, or local jurisdictions, but is more likely to exist within local jurisdictions where city-county police rivalries are present. How overlapping jurisdictions appear to foster those rivalries will be discussed later in this chapter. Pettiness and turf protection appear to be commonplace among many jurisdictions that have overlapping authority, and often it requires a mediator of sorts (a federal or state agency, a local or federal prosecuting attorney) to place a matter of contention in proper perspective, thus creating an atmosphere of cooperation that allows for effective enforcement efforts.

Generally speaking, the mind-set of the agency head, whether a sheriff, police chief, or state/federal officer, is the underlying reason that turf protection remains. It is the command staff that instills this negative viewpoint. Once in place, the trickle-down effect begins to permeate the entire agency. For example, the sheriff answers to the county populace, whereas the police chief is accountable to the city government. Both are scrutinized by the public and want to maintain their own autonomy. Often, when either the city or county works closely with or identifies with a state or federal investigative agency, the other will refuse collateral assistance, regardless of the severity of the crime issue. This form of jealousy is counterproductive and often causes a breakdown in the effective exchange of intelligence information.

It is less likely that turf protection will exist between state and federal agencies because their investigative missions, although similar, do not conflict, thus allowing for a truer form of cooperation. Some turf protection however, does exist between the many federal agencies that have overlapping jurisdictions. As a general rule, though, the appropriate U.S. Attorney's Office resolves those conflicts before they become counterproductive. Before the issues involving turf protection can be adequately resolved, there must exist a recognition of the problem, a commitment to a solution, and an acceptance of a person or agency charged with the responsibility to mediate and direct cooperative efforts. This commitment has to be a cooperative effort by all parties involved, much like a contract.

PRIDE

Another area of concern is pride in the agency's autonomy and success as an independent agency. Many observations reveal that agencies, and ultimately the people they serve, suffer when pride prohibits the utilization of resources. These resources include availability of officers; expertise of highly trained staff, such as crime scene technicians, computer forensics specialists, undercover agents, and explosive ordinance disposal (EOD) technicians; technical equipment such as photographic video/audio monitoring and specialized vehicles; intelligence data resources; and monetary resources. When an agency believes it can "be all things to all people" without having the appropriate resources, yet still allows pride to prevent it from asking for assistance, then its work is less likely to be effective.

These resources—manpower, expertise, and specialized equipment—when not utilized will inhibit the successful outcome of the crime prevention and/or crime solving strategies. Unfortunately, among the heads of police agencies, ego tends to override judgment, resulting in competitiveness among agencies where winning may not always mean solving the problem or providing the best service possible. Even worse, if the agency head creates an image of success and can maintain that image, regardless of the success of the mission, then the public, without knowing the truth, will mistakenly adopt a positive attitude toward the agency. Again, ego can be a powerful motivator for the success or failure of a mission. This precludes outside influence. Other issues relating to pride include federal funding, a power struggle between local agencies, and local politics, all of which may have a negative impact on the successful conclusion of the mission.

INTELLIGENCE DISSEMINATION

The gathering of data and the dissemination of intelligence lead to a collective-knowledge base which positively enhances the initiative that is used for the improvement of crime prevention and crime solving stategies. Intelligence is data collected from various sources throughout an agency's jurisdiction that, after being compiled, are used to substantiate questions involving criminal conduct, crime prevention methods, and criminals. Most local police agencies have some form of collecting and networking intelligence information. This information is gathered throughout the agency and submitted in the form of intelligence reports for final compilation in a database. Once collected, its dissemination becomes the relevant and overriding issue. State and federal agencies have a tactical advantage by having access to a larger database due to their multijurisdictional assignments.

It is imperative for the success of any police agency to use any and all intelligence resources available when dealing with issues of public safety. For example, a subversive group working in a city might not be known to that city's police department or its employees unless the state's investigative agency's intelligence database is queried regarding suspected criminal conduct of such a group. The more information that is shared among the criminal justice community, the more likely it is that the system will be successful.

At a minimum, data collected should include such information as criminal history, suspects, witnesses, crime trends, high-crime areas, and methods of operation (MOs). Initial information should involve the who, what, when, where, why, and how, as well as the time frame and source of information. Moreover, any additional information about significant crime issues in a specific jurisdiction that could prove helpful should be included. For example, the database could be enhanced to show the number of cocaine arrests within a city's jurisdiction to highlight specific people and places where the sales transactions are being completed. The more data collected, collated, and disseminated, the better the agency will become in developing successful crime prevention tactics and crime solving initiatives.

ETHICS AND PROFESSIONAL COURTESY

The area of ethics and professional courtesy in the police community can be a cul-de-sac of weighing the options of solving crimes versus the territorial nature of certain agency heads within specific jurisdictions. For police professionals, public relations among fellow agencies is paramount in being able to instill confidence, good working relations, and trust that responsibilities will be completed. As mentioned earlier, intelligence dissemination is the lifeblood of the police community. This dissemination not only includes computerized data, but also informal information that is shared between the officers themselves. It is imperative that the officers maintain the highest degree of integrity. Once an officer's judgment or information is tainted, the trust so needed among the agencies is broken. Further, this provides ample incentive to promote the turf protection we have already shown to be destructive.

In any profession, it is expected that the members will adhere to a certain code of conduct. In the area of juvenile justice, the expectation is the same. Often, the rules are not exactly clear regarding what is expected in terms of ethical behavior. The Juvenile Justice System is responsible for the difficult and sensitive task of supervising juveniles, both in the community and in detention situations. This agency is responsible for the protection of juvenile rights on a daily basis. Unethical behavior is very visible in the local media and in state and national politics, especially if the matter involves the use of force by staff in controlling aggressive juveniles within a secure setting. The agency deals with the dangerous and difficult issues of sadness, truth telling, justice, goodness, right, valuing life, and individual freedom—all of which are based on ethics and morality because of human needs and the recognition of the importance of living.

Professional ethics must be acknowledged and practiced in order to carry out the responsibilities with which the agency has been entrusted. Ethics and professionalism are commonly referred to as basic principles, values, and morals. When people think of professional ethics, they often think of the following:

- **Ethics:** Knowing what is right and wrong and doing what is right. In essence, ethics are the highest standards of personal integrity, truthfulness, and honesty. Ethics involve having principles of honor and morality and living by accepted rules of conduct governing an individual or group. The bottom line is this: ethics are those attitudes that influence the behavior of people toward each other.
- **Professionalism:** The conduct, aims, or qualities that characterize or mark a profession or a person within a profession. Professional individuals are good role models of judgment and behavior, which often are beyond reproach. Professionals observe, respect, and support the mission of their profession, as well as practice the concepts presented in the policy and procedure statements.

- **Professional Ethics:** Doing what is professionally (legally) right or befitting and/or conforming to professional standards of conduct. The concept of professional ethics involves the ability to make choices based on personal and legal knowledge. There are good and bad choices within the personal realm. The personal correct action may or may not be the legal/professional correct action.

Therefore, professional ethics is a system of moral principles, values, rules, and standards of conduct that govern the members of a profession. Although frequently used interchangeably, ethics is often a component of professionalism. Bear in mind that there are various types of ethical issues within the police profession.

Although we tend to think of morals as traits based on religious beliefs, we cannot ignore that morals play a significant role in how we come to establish our ethical parameters. In our work setting, the issue of morals may not seem appropriate, but it is important to briefly discuss the concept, which includes the roles and principles of ethical behavior that constitute the standards of behavior or personal beliefs adopted by an individual or group. These beliefs are held close to the heart and determine the right and wrong beliefs of individuals or groups. Ethical issues may involve personal conflict. An officer may question: Is this legal but immoral? A legal action that is not necessarily in the best interest of a person(s) may be overridden by a moral officer. For example, an officer sees an unattended toddler in the street but is already en route to a call. Will the officer stop and get the child to safety? Another area of concern asks whether an action is a violation of a law, policy, or procedure, albeit moral, for example, the use of work time to complete a personal project that may ultimately benefit the officer's job performance. Finally, an officer may challenge an action as illegal but moral. For example, how does one classify protesters who favor prayer in school?

The purpose of ethics in the workplace is to develop trust among officers, supervisors, and agencies. Trust is based on ethics, as well as competence, which is the ability to get the job done. Without ethics, there can be no professionalism. Incidences, which lacked ethical judgment, have become public scandals. Consider:

- The Rodney King beating in Los Angeles
- The California Savings and Loan scandal
- The White Water incident
- The Anita Hill/Clarence Thomas sexual harassment hearing
- The charges of ethical violations against Newt Gingrich
- The FBI investigation of the Oklahoma Bombing and the adherent improper investigation techniques
- The FBI invasion in Waco, Texas, and the subsequent fiasco

As a result of scandals such as these, the public has little confidence in authorities, officials, or government.

Virtues are moral goodness or excellence reflecting the basic character of a person. Virtues tend to be concerned with matters of the heart and are intangible. Values can be virtues, but typically are more concrete and usually represent the worth, excellence, usefulness, or importance given to an object or quality. Often it is difficult to discern the difference between morals, values, and virtues because, at times, these concepts seem interchangeable. It is important to understand that these concepts are used to measure what we call integrity. In the police profession, it is the administration that encourages or discourages the staff by modeling those concepts it believes will portray integrity.

All these values, virtues, morals, and integrity relate to ethical action while on the "job." Not only is it important to understand what is expected in terms of job duties, but it is also important to understand what is expected in terms of behavior on or off the job. The agency should clearly establish what is expected because the standards for professional, ethical behavior are usually set by the members of the organization. The importance of having information about ethics and professionalism is to give each member the tools to think wisely and do the right thing.

Ethical action may be taken to resolve or cope with dilemmas in which an individual takes personal responsibility for doing good or avoiding harm to others. In the criminal justice arena, through knowledge of laws, rules, regulations, policies, and procedures, decisions should be based on personal and professional ethics that support the goals, mission, and objectives of the system. Although not necessarily universal, criminal justice professionals tend to have strong values and ethics. Unfortunately, it would be impossible to anticipate and provide a patent solution to every situation that arises. Ethical issues arise in difficult situations when questionable/wrong choices are made. These can result in the loss of a job, demotion, penalty, punishment, career destruction, and so forth. It is important for administrators and fellow officers to model ethical behavior/professional standards for each other and the community. This ensures that the profession functions in a legal, orderly, safe, and humane environment.

Ethical considerations on the part of the agency head, as well as the entire staff, should be at the forefront of standard operating procedures. Policy and procedure should define ethical conduct that enhances the agency's reputation as perceived by the general public and other police agencies. A lack of ethics promotes a lack of confidence by the community.

Along with ethical considerations are those of professional courtesy. Professional courtesy needs to exist between agencies in order to establish cohesiveness. Officer-to-officer and agency-to-agency relations can only be positively impacted when all parties cooperate. Information sharing, honoring jurisdictional boundaries, and sharing resources are a few of the means by which professional courtesy is demonstrated. This cooperative measure strengthens the esprit de corps between agencies.

PUBLIC RELATIONS AND TRUST

Public relations and trust are vital to the survival of any police agency. The reputation of the agency is often gauged by how well and how often the media reports on the progress of crime issues. This reporting system, as well as the interaction with media representatives and public officials, is the window by which the public views the effectiveness of the agency. It is crucial that the information that reaches the public is factual and relevant to the issues at hand, while giving a clear understanding of the necessity of the actions taken by police. It is imperative that agency heads or those designees releasing information to the media do so in a professional manner, guarding against confrontations that can only lead to negative media coverage. It is a well-known cliché that you can't do battle with an organi-zation that buys ink by the barrel.

Open forums where the public can address concerns to the appropriate police agen-cies are instrumental in creating an atmosphere of confidence and trust. Likewise, pro-grams allowing the public to ride with police officers strengthen the community's confidence in its police agency's ability to ensure a consistent level of public safety. Community-Oriented Policing and Neighborhood Watch programs are just two examples of programs designed to enhance positive public opinion.

A major issue involving the public and trust is the handling of criminal situations that involve police officers. When this trust is abused, the entire police community suffers. For example, if an agency head fails to reprimand or discipline an officer who violates the law and/or allows special treatment that an average citizen would not receive, then this special treatment has a negative impact on the integrity of the police department and the criminal justice system as a whole.

RESOURCE INDEXING

Resource indexing is the method by which a systematic listing of all police-related re-sources available to each agency is orchestrated within a prescribed jurisdiction. This could be as simple as the confines of a county, a region of the state, a U.S. district, or an entire state. This listing can prove to be invaluable to agencies during normal operations or when a crisis exists. Often, resources within a local jurisdiction are limited due to manpower con-straints, monetary constraints, or lack of knowledge as to where resources can be obtained.

In an effort to establish such a system, it is necessary to locate an objective, outside entity that could coordinate the combined resources of each agency into an accessible database. This entity would be responsible for requiring the agencies within a prescribed area to submit a listing of the resources they are willing to share with other agencies in a cooperative spirit. This system only works if the resources identified will be given to the requesting agency in a timely manner. For example, the Criminal Justice Coordinating Council (CJCC) or the U.S. Attorney's Office in each state could facilitate such an initia-tive. In doing so, an exhaustive listing would be compiled from the many resources within federal, state, and local jurisdictions, thereby enhancing efficiency and performance of all agencies taking part in the program.

Some of the resources generally available in each state are listed below. This is not an exhaustive listing, merely a guide for identifying some universal resources that are commonly sought:

- Number of persons available for saturation investigations—sheer numbers of of-ficers for an immediate response to a crisis situation, such as disaster relief, mul-tiple homicide investigation, and so on
- Number of persons available for short-term undercover investigations
- Crime scene specialist
- Crime analysis specialist
- Computer forensics specialist

- Special response team (SRT)
- Foreign language capabilities
- Explosive ordinance disposal capabilities
- Polygraph specialist
- Drug enforcement capabilities
- Major crime capabilities—such as public corruption, interstate transportation of narcotics, and so on
- Qualified scuba divers
- Electronics specialist
- Money to assist in the purchase of evidence or information
- Crime lab services

Once this list is compiled, it will be necessary to keep it updated on a quarterly basis with all submitting agencies and, more importantly, to submit the list in its entirety to all participating agencies. The means for facilitating the dissemination of the list of resources can be done by the coordinating agency through e-mail, U.S. mail, and computer disk, whichever means is most convenient and/or efficient. This listing should be overseen by the command staff who has access not only to the list of resources but also a contact person to whom the request can be made. Again, it is imperative that when an agency submits its offer of resources they be made available in a timely manner.

Investigations are often thwarted and crime prevention techniques are not effectively utilized when resources have not been revealed that are available to assist an agency. Once the list of resources has been established and disseminated, it may be necessary and beneficial to the investigation to combine resources in a task force–type atmosphere. Working together, this resource of manpower creates one of the most effective and efficient uses of resources available to the police community. For this to work, each cooperating agency must subjugate all self-interest issues that can be counterproductive to the success of the mission.

The lead agencies would be responsible for controlling the direction of the mission and for the compilation of the investigative file and subsequent presentation to the appropriate prosecuting jurisdiction. A merger of policy and procedure, along with ethical considerations, will be determined by agency heads who have committed to the success of the mission. Combining resources is by far the most effective means for combating the criminal element. By working together, the criminal justice system is allowed to work freely and effectively.

CROSSING JURISDICTIONAL BOUNDARIES

Because crime occurs indiscriminately in and across jurisdictions, police agencies must be prepared to work with fellow agencies in investigating crimes and/or crime prevention initiatives. In some situations, one would make inquiries to surrounding cities, counties, and adjoining states in order to effectively determine the circumstances for which the inquiry is made. A Memorandum of Agreement between sister agencies allows for the exchange of information and other valuable resources that often cross jurisdictional boundaries. Databases from neighboring states may contain different and even enhanced information on suspects and crime trends that could easily solve crimes or solidify crime prevention initiatives. Only pride and inexperience would prevent an agency from utilizing the information/resources gleaned from employing cross-jurisdictional assistance.

In Georgia, an example of a cooperative effort in crossing jurisdictional boundaries was a program known as GRIP (Governor's Radar Interdiction Program) in the 1980s. This program was an effort in combining numerous state, local, and federal agencies, led by the Georgia Bureau of Investigation, in interdicting aircraft smuggling narcotics into Georgia, Florida, and other surrounding states. Those agencies involved were the Georgia Bureau of Investigation, the Georgia Air National Guard, the Drug Enforcement Administration, U.S. Customs, the Florida Department of Law Enforcement, Federal Aviation Administration, Georgia State Patrol Aviation Division, and numerous local police jurisdictions. Mobile radar sites were temporarily erected at three sites in Georgia and Florida in an effort to triangulate airplane activity entering the Atlantic Coast. Once a suspect aircraft was noted, police aircraft would be launched to help identify the cargo onboard. This program proved to be effective and was exemplary of the cooperative effort made during the influx of narcotics in the United States in the 1980s.

REVERSE 911

Outboard calling, or Reverse 911, is a means to communicate within the community by sending prerecorded messages to residents and/or businesses within a certain geographic location. This system has the ability to send hundreds of calls in a short amount of time, as well as track information and feedback from those calls. Residents and businesses are easily identifiable through the databases provided in both list and map formats. As an example, if inclement weather is expected in a certain sector of a community, then with the use of a computer-type screen, all residents within a prescribed area could receive notice of the impending situation via telephone.

This can be done on any number of crime prevention initiatives, as well as having the ability to notify citizens of current specific criminal activity. This system gives the community a greater sense of security because its members know that police can communicate directly with them in a proactive manner when the need arises. Some examples include:

- Help in finding a lost child or disoriented elderly person
- Information/witnesses to a specific crime
- Advising banks of recent robberies in the area
- Advising the community of recent burglaries in the area
- Warning merchants to be on the lookout for counterfeit currency
- Informing the community of school/road closings
- Warning the community of gas leaks/chemical spills
- Polling the community for its opinions on certain issues

This system also entails Guardian Calling, which allows police department members to contact individuals on prescribed days and times and to receive feedback on the individual's well-being. This allows residents of the community to have both a sense of safety and personal interaction with their police department without the use of additional manpower.

Reverse 911 also contains a Bulletin Board System (BBS) that supplies a means to offer public service information to the community. For example, a Christmas Day parade showing time and parade route. The BBS can provide a one-stop-shop where police agencies can post various types of information such as crime trends and suspects wanted in local crimes. It would also offer information regarding those who are involved in scams targeting members of the community. Other kinds of information that could be made available to the community include:

- Calendar of community events
- Directory of police department/city official phone numbers
- Instructional information (how to report an accident or where to pay a parking ticket
- Neighborhood crime statistics, by neighborhood
- Road conditions or road closing information
- Crime watch or safety tips
- Information about what the community has to offer (parks, museums, etc.)
- Information on how to report incidents of misconduct on the part of police officials

Reverse 911 is a powerful tool in disseminating community-oriented information in a timely manner without the use of excessive manpower or time.

CONCLUSION

The issues involving turf protection have to be recognized and often mediated by an independent agency. Pride can be the downfall of an agency's effectiveness if autonomy is the driving motivation. The use of outside resources more often than not lends itself to more success in problem solving. Intelligence information dissemination is the lifeblood of effective crime prevention and investigative efforts as it allows for communication officer-to-officer and agency-to-agency. Ethics and professional courtesy should allow agencies to cooperate in a manner indicative of the highest standards of professional service.

It is imperative that police officials and agencies conduct themselves in a manner that instills confidence by the public and other professionals. Resource indexing is a published listing of all resources available to police agencies to facilitate job performance. Combining resources is often necessary to be successful either inside or outside jurisdictional boundaries regarding crime prevention efforts or crime detection/solving initiatives. Crossing jurisdictional boundaries is a commonsense approach to crime solving, as crime is indiscriminant and not limited to one specified area. Reverse 911 offers a means to communicate with the public on community-oriented public safety issues in a proactive manner.

Crime prevention and crime detection/solving initiatives are paramount issues facing all levels of police in the United States today. Everything that can be done should be done in an effort to be effective. When pettiness, ineptness, and pride get a foothold within the ranks of participating agencies, the lack of effectiveness is easily identified. Criminal justice professionals need to be proactive problem solvers, hurdling every barrier possible in the interest of public safety and those being served.

3

Police versus Private Security

Whom Do We Trust?

Pamela Ann Sexton-Alyea

As the media reports daily about the increased number of violent personal and property crimes, it is no surprise that there has been an increased demand for both public and private security throughout the public and commercial sectors. Whether public or private security is needed, there are differing opinions as to which is more trustworthy and which is more desirable. Many people, when asked to think of a public security officer, would undoubtedly think of the ever-bumbling, one-bullet-totin' (in shirt pocket), inept Barney Fife, deputy sheriff, Mayberry, USA. Or, more recently, with all the turmoil in the New York City and the Los Angeles Police Departments, the vision of the men in blue has turned to one of extreme violence against the minority public, which is subsequently often hidden by the "code of silence" and the "blue curtain."

On the other hand, when asked to describe a private security officer, no doubt many picture an elderly gentleman asleep in his chair as the bank is being robbed. In an article titled "Thugs in Uniform," Richard Behar made the following statement: "Underscreened, underpaid and undertrained, private security guards are too often victimizing those they are hired to protect" (1992, p. 44). Although both of these symbols of security are unfavorable, they are often the stereotypes that public and private security officers must deal with and overcome. So, how do we decide who to hire to protect ourselves and our possessions?

There are numerous factors that must be considered when choosing between public or private security. A few of the factors to be discussed are (1) armed versus unarmed guards—many private security firms do not offer armed guards; (2) salary—in most circumstances, private security is more cost-effective than public security; (3) level of education—more than ever, municipal, county, and state security providers are requiring more training and education of their personnel, though in contrast, some states do not require private security officers to hold professional licenses; (4) number of guards needed—with more and more private security firms popping up every day, it seems the sheer number of private guards available would make it hard for public security to compete for large volume needs; and (5) union versus nonunion—many public security officers are members of their local Fraternal Order of Police (FOP), whereas many private security guards are without the union bargaining power.

These are just a few of the issues that must be considered when choosing between public and private security. However, they are not the only factors. As you will see, there are times when public and private security can work cohesively together. As noted by the United Way Strategic Institute (1989, p. 3), "There will be a blurring of the boundaries that have traditionally defined the roles of the public sector versus the private sector, as well as individual versus institutional responsibilities."

Security can be defined in many ways; however, we are primarily concerned with the basic concepts—safety, protection, and freedom from danger. Although this definition is very basic, we explore the history of security to better understand when and why people decided they were in need of security and how the definition has evolved through time.

HISTORICAL OVERVIEW OF SECURITY

Historical Definition of Public Security

Policing, whether public or private, has been accomplished under a variety of auspices. Historically, we have seen policing by national and/or local governments, revolutionary or nonrevolutionary parties, landowners, workers, peasants, neighborhoods, churches, or by businesses and professional associations. *Public policing* can be defined simply as any community or governmental agency that is given the responsibility for preventing and detecting crime, as well as the maintaining of public order. The basic police mission of preserving order by the enforcement of rules of conduct and laws is the same today as it was in ancient societies—"serve and protect."

History of Police Forces.   If we reflect back to when security was first recognized, we see in ancient Rome that the military body of the Praetorian Guards was being used as a protective and police organization—it was the guardian of peace. The ancient Romans achieved a high level of policing, which remained in effect until the decline of the empire and the onset of the Middle Ages. Beginning in the fifth century, policing became a function of the heads of fiefdoms and principalities. A fiefdom is defined as anything under a person's complete control or authority.

Early in recorded history, town dwellers often built walls and barricades and dug moats to provide themselves with a sense of security; however, without rules and systems to enforce the rules, many problems arose with the early security strategies. Even though walls and moats might intimidate, there still was a need for individuals to patrol those structures, hence, dilemmas arose.

During the Middle Ages, policing authority, particularly in England, was the responsibility of local nobles on their individual estates. Each noble generally appointed a constable to carry out the law. At that time in history, the constable was the highest-ranking official of a royal household or court. The constable's duties included keeping the peace, making arrests, and then guarding the criminals. For many decades, constables were unpaid citizens who took turns at the job, which became increasingly unpopular. By the mid-sixteenth century, towns required each resident to take turns in patrolling the town. Many of the wealthy citizens simply hired someone to take their place, whereas others simply refused and were banished from the town. The quality of the constables declined drastically as this practice became widespread.

Even when systems were in place, there arose additional problems. In early civilizations the military was often used to provide security; however, many of the military leaders abused the powers given them, which led to insurrection of the townspeople.

In France during the seventeenth century, King Louis XIV maintained a central police organization comprised of about forty officials who, with the help of paid informants, supplied the government with details about the conduct of private individuals. The king could then exercise a kind of arbitrary justice. This system continued during the reigns of Louis XV and Louis XVI. After the French Revolution, two separate police bodies were established: one handled ordinary duties and the other dealt with political crimes.

In 1663, the City of London began paying watchmen—generally elderly men who were unable to find other work—to guard the streets at night. Until the end of the eighteenth century, the watchmen, as inefficient as they were, as well as a few constables, remained the only form of policing in the city.

Sir Robert Peel.   The inability of watchmen and constables to curb lawlessness, particularly in London, led to a demand for a more effective force to deal with criminals and to protect the populace. After much deliberation in Parliament, British statesman Sir Robert Peel, in 1829, established the London Metropolitan Police—thereafter called "bobbies" after his first name—which became the world's first modern organized police force. The development of the British police system is especially significant because the pattern that emerged not only became a model for the American police system, but also had great influence on the style of policing in almost all industrial societies.

In the United States, the first full-time organized police departments were formed in New York City in 1845, and shortly thereafter in Boston. These departments were formed not only in response to crime, but also to control unrest. The British police have traditionally remained detached from partisan politics and have depended on loyalty to the law, rather than to elected officials, as the source of their authority and independence. The American police adopted many British methods, but at times they became involved in local partisan politics.

Historical Definition of Private Security

After examining the historical perspective of how security began, we can see how private security manifested from the human desire for more adequate protection both for the person and for property. The right to private security has long been recognized by governments and by the wide diversity of established policing mechanisms.

Allan Pinkerton (1819–1884).   From the beginning, efforts were made to cope with the problem of lawlessness on the U.S. frontier, and in time criminals were disciplined to a reasonable degree. Where official agents of the law (public security) were slow to arrive or were ineffective, frontiersmen sometimes banded together in vigilante committees to meet the threat themselves. A vigilante was originally defined as a watchman or someone who stayed alert to trouble or danger. However, the vigilantes soon took on the unauthorized responsibility of interpreting and acting upon matters of law and morality. The vigilantes, particularly in the mining camps, banished or executed some of the most blatant offenders.

Private policing eventually took on more permanent forms. Cattle ranchers often organized associations who hired men known as range detectives to apprehend rustlers. One such firm was the Pinkerton National Detective Agency, the first and currently the largest private security contract operation in the United States. When Allan Pinkerton immigrated to the United States from Glasgow, Scotland, he settled in Illinois. His capture of a counterfeiting ring in that state and several other feats led to his appointment as a deputy sheriff, first in Kane and later in Cook County. In 1843, Pinkerton was appointed Chicago's first detective. The slogan for the Pinkerton National Detective Agency was "We Never Sleep," and its logo was an open eye, probably the origin of the term "private eye."

Pinkerton quickly gained a reputation for chasing such well-known outlaws as Sam Bass, the James' and Younger Brothers' gangs, and Butch Cassidy's "wild bunch." Not only did the cattle ranchers hire Pinkerton's, banks, mining companies, railroads, and stage lines hired his guards and detectives to protect their property and customers. With virtually no national enforcement, Pinkerton's became famous.

As the West's inhabitants increased and its communities matured, local, state, and federal police agencies became increasingly organized and effective. Therefore, the problems that fueled the lawlessness, for example, isolation, a sparse population, and public indifference so common on the frontier, were overcome. In time, the Wild West frontier, which had once been known for its lawlessness, resembled much of the rest of the nation.

Even though the frontier had settled down, Pinkerton still found plenty of work for his detectives and guards. During the Civil War (1861–1865), Pinkerton was active in the

---

Box 1.

The Molly Maguires, a secret terrorist society, operated in the anthracite coal region of eastern Pennsylvania from the mid-1860s to the late 1870s. Named after a secret antilandlord group in Ireland, the largely Irish-American organization attempted to improve living and working conditions in the mining industry. To achieve this, the "Mollies" intimidated and murdered mineowners and superintendents, police officers, and judges, initiated several coal strikes, and formed a union. In 1874, Pinkerton detectives were hired to infiltrate the group, which was crushed by a series of murder convictions between 1875 and 1878 (Grolier, 1993).

Union cause, heading an organization engaged in spying on the Confederacy. When the war ended, Pinkerton resumed control of his agency and was instrumental in breaking strikes and in crushing the Molly Maguires (see Box 1).

In 1937, after a congressional inquiry into the labor-management relations, Robert A. Pinkerton, a descendant of Allan Pinkerton and then head of the agency, forbade any member of his agency to ever again accept undercover work involving the investigation of a labor union. Pinkerton's was also home to famous author Samuel Dashiell Hammett (see Box 2).

Currently, the Pinkerton Detective Agency employs between thirty-six and forty thousand people and concentrates in industry and institutions, security for sporting facilities, investigations of industrial thefts, and insurance investigations. Pinkerton's has offices in more than thirty countries worldwide, including the United States, Latin America, Canada, Europe, and Asia, with a network of trusted partners in other regions.

Wackenhut.   Another leader in private security is the Wackenhut Corporation (www.wackenhut.com), founded in 1954 by former FBI agent George Wackenhut. Wackenhut currently has operations throughout the United States and in over fifty other countries on six continents, and is a leader in the privatization of public services for municipal, state, and federal agencies. The Wackenhut Corporation's 1999 revenues were listed at $2.2 billion. Wackenhut is a prominent international provider of integrated business services to major corporations and a wide range of industrial and commercial customers. According to its Webpage, its principal business lines include security-related services, facility management, correctional services, and flexible staffing services.

Perhaps its most famous contract has been with the U.S. government. It is rumored that Wackenhut is providing perimeter security for Area 51. Area 51, also known as Groom Lake, is said to be a secret military facility north of Las Vegas. The Number refers to a six-by-ten-mile block of land, at the center of which is supposedly a large military base the U.S. government does not acknowledge. The area is widely associated with unidentified flying object (UFO) stories, U.S. government UFO coverups, and conspiracy theories. The claim that Wackenhut guards this alleged facility is a charge that has neither been proven nor denied by former employees.

In March 2000, The Wackenhut Corporation (NYSE: WAK and WAKB) scored higher than any other company in "overall satisfaction" in a survey of users of contract

---

Box 2.

Samuel Dashiell Hammett worked as a Pinkerton detective for 8 years before becoming an American crime novelist whose realistic style and settings created a new genre in mystery fiction. Hammett began publishing stories in Black Mask magazine after 1923. His first four novels—Red Harvest (1929), The Dain Curse (1929), The Maltese Falcon (1930, made into a film in 1941 with Humphrey Bogart), and The Glass Key (1931, made into films in 1935 and 1942), greatly influenced American thought and writing (Grolier, 1993).

Box 3.

As reported in 1985, John Walker, Jr., 47, worked for two years in the Norfolk branch of Wackenhut, a national firm providing industrial security services. While there he was sued for inflicting "emotional distress" by a wealthy Virginia Beach couple who claimed that Walker snooped around their home in varied disguises: as a birdwatcher wearing a green bag with eyeholes over his head and carrying a telescope; as a Boy Scout leader looking for a place to camp; as a Catholic priest. Walker was under criminal investigation for allegations that he was also a spy for the Soviet Union while he was a member of the U.S. Navy (Magnuson, Banta and Constable, 1985).

security services conducted by *Security Director's Report (SDR),* a monthly publication of the Institute of Management and Administration. However, Wackenhut, like all private security services, has not gone unscathed by less than perfect employees (See Box 3).

MAJOR ISSUES FACED BY PUBLIC & PRIVATE SECURITY

Public versus Private Security

According to Pinkerton's home page on the Internet (http://www.pinkertons.com), today's business enterprise is composed of many valuable assets—people, property, products, information, financial infrastructure, customers, partners, supplier relationships, reputation, and shareholders. Consistent, effective security of these assets is critical to the ongoing success, and basic viability, of the enterprise. How do we determine if we need private security or whether public security is enough? (see Box 4).

Similarities between Private and Public Officers

Private and public officers have many mutual traits, including the wearing of a recognizable uniform and badge, having the skill to compel obedience to their authority (whether actual or implied), and being liable for their actions. Both public and private security seek to prevent losses from criminal actions and, if such losses occur, to investigate and seize the person responsible. Additionally, both public and private officers may receive respect and cooperation from coworkers, or they may face hostility and aggression. Public and private officers may have a tremendous influence on the image of their employees; their every action has an impact on public relations.

Differences between Private and Public Officers

Four basic differences exist between private and public officers: (1) the financial orientation, (2) the employer, (3) the specific functions performed, and (4) the statutory power possessed (Hess & Wrobleski, 1992).

Private Security	Public Police/Policing
Profit-oriented enterprise	Nonprofit, governmental enterprise
Serving specific private clients	Serving the general public
To prevent crime, protect assets, and reduce losses	To combat crime, enforce laws, and apprehend offenders
To regulate noncriminal conduct not under the authority of public police	Statutory authority

Private security officers differ from public police officers in that private security officers operate in a profit-oriented venture, serving specific private clients to prevent crime, to protect assets, to reduce losses, and to regulate noncriminal conduct not under the authority of police. Private security officers are given their authority by their private clients. One specific area that the public police authorities seem willing to hand over to private security personnel is such economic crimes as shoplifting, employee theft and pilferage, and credit card and check fraud, which are usually low priority with the public police and high on the agenda of the private business entrepreneur. Public police officers, in contrast to private, operate in a nonprofit, governmental enterprise, serving the general public to act as a deterrent to crime, to combat crime when it occurs, and to enforce laws and apprehend offenders. Public police officers have statutory authority.

Box 4.

Marx (1987, p. 187) lists a series of questions to be asked in determining if policing is public or private:

- Where does the policing occur - in public, private, or mixed space?
- Whose interest is served by the policing - the general public, a private interest, or both?
- What is the function of the policing?
- Who pays for, or sponsors, the policing - public or private interests, or both?
- Who carries it out - regular sworn agents of the state with full police powers, special-purpose deputies with more limited powers, or citizens with no official powers?
- Who controls and directs the policing?
- Where the policing involves data collection and investigation, who has access to the results?
- What popular and self-definitions characterize those doing the policing?
- What organizational form does the policing take?
- To what extent are social control agents linked together in informal networks that transcend their nominal definition as public or private?

Other basic differences between private and public officers exist in the authority they have and the restrictions placed on them. If asked, most private citizens entering a building where private security officers are utilized would be of the opinion that the security officer actually has some legal authority that extends beyond them, the average citizen. However, private security officers usually have no more legal powers than the average citizen. As citizens, they ALL have the power to arrest, to investigate, to carry weapons, and to defend themselves, their property, or property entrusted to their care. In some instances, when management has given the private officer permission, the officer might also conduct inspections of personal items, for example, purses, briefcases, and lunch boxes. They can deny access to unauthorized individuals into their employers' business or company, and they can enforce all rules and regulations established by their employers.

Private security officers can also search employees and question them without giving the Miranda warning. In most states, private security officers, unlike public security officers, have the luxury of not giving the Miranda warning according to *Bowman v State* (1983). However, private security officers cannot invade another's privacy, electronically eavesdrop, trespass, or wear a uniform or badge that closely resembles that of a public police officer. In most instances, the private security officers' legal authority often does not surpass that of the private citizen, but because of their appearance in uniform (and some carry weapons), they often exude the appearance of authority.

The Complimentary Roles of Private and Public Officers

The advantages of private police using public police, according to Marx (1987), include the benefits of the power of state agents to arrest, search, interrogate, carry weapons, use force, electronic surveillance, and gain access to otherwise protected information. Their legal liability may also be reduced or eliminated. The training, experience, skill, and backup support the public police can offer are other factors (see Box 5).

Box 5.

The advantages of public police, says Marx (1987, p.183), include Information.

Sworn agents cannot be everywhere and they face restrictions on access to private places . . . But private agents, operating on private property and in contexts where persons appear voluntarily, are granted wide authority to carry out searches, to keep people under surveillance, and to collect and distribute extensive personnel information. In addition: Private police vastly extend surveillance and reduce demands on public police. In addition . . . they may offer public police a way to get things done that the former are prohibited from doing, such as interrogating without giving the Miranda warning and conducting searches and seizures without warrants. Private police are not bound by the Exclusionary Rule, which would make inadmissible any evidence obtained by means violating a person's constitutional rights.

Quality is measured through the client's eyes, whether the client is in the private or the public sector. Private and public security forces frequently engage in similar activities and have similar goals, including prevention of crime. Promoting cooperative interaction between private and public police officers is of the utmost importance. Public and private officers may work together, may hire or entrust authority to one another, or may move from one sector to the other. Regardless of which you choose, private or public security, the officers must have the right tools to perform their jobs effectively and to serve the clients. This requires alliances with companies that produce uniforms, radios, incident-tracking software, timekeeping systems, equipment, and so forth.

Restrictions on Private Security Officers

Laws governing the conduct of private security officers are derived from several sources: tort law, state statutes, criminal law, constitutional guarantees, and contract law. Because of actions they must perform in fulfilling their responsibilities, private security officers are more open to civil lawsuits than most other citizens (see Box 6).

Many of the restrictions on private security officers come from the tort law of each state. Tort law defines citizens' responsibilities to each other and provides for lawsuits to recover damages for injury caused by failing to carry out these responsibilities. State and federal criminal laws prohibit security officers from committing crimes such as assault. Assault is an intentional act causing reasonable apprehension of physical harm in the mind of another. An example is threatening someone, with or without a weapon, into obeying your demands. Other state and federal laws regulate wiretapping, surveillance, gathering information on individuals, impersonating public police officials, and purchasing and carrying firearms.

Box 6.

A track athlete from the University of Minnesota has sued the managers of the City Center mall, claiming racial discrimination and civil rights violations. Apasha A. Blocker, an award-winning track and field athlete who is black, said she went to the bathroom about noon May 23 (2000) on the third floor of City Center when a security guard said to her, "Can you freakin' read?" according to documents filed in US District Court on Monday. Brookfield Properties, which manages City Center and employs the security guards, denied any inappropriate behavior by the guards and said the company would review the reports of the guards, as well as surveillance videos that might have recorded the incident. Blocker told reporters Wednesday that the guard kicked her and she was later detained and taken to a basement holding cell, where several guards made racial slurs, continued to kick and strike her, then let her go with a warning not to come back to the mall for 90 days. Blocker is a graduate student at Minnesota who competed for the school from 1996–2000 in the pentathlon and heptathlon. The nine-count suit claims racial discrimination in a place of public accommodations, and violations of civil rights for not allowing Blocker equal rights to enjoy the shopping mall (Associated Press, 2000a).

When a public police officer works during off-hours in a private security position, he is considered to be a public police officer in many states. Therefore, many states do not allow their officers to work in the private capacity. Clearly, the distinction between public and private police is not always black and white, but various shades of gray. Other restrictions are placed on private security officers by local ordinances and state statutes that establish licensing regulations. These restrictions vary greatly from state to state.

Image Projected by Media

Private Policing.   In a 1992 article in *Time,* titled "Thugs in Uniform," Richard Behar addresses the issue that security guards are often underscreened, underpaid, and undertrained, and too often victimize those they are hired to protect (see Box 7).

For companies who rely on the $15 billion+ security industry, "problems" such as those discussed in Box 7 are all too common and raise the stakes of private security to new

---

Box 7.

- Still on probation for two separate weapon and cocaine possession convictions in 1990, John Padilla, 20, was hired last July by the HSC Security company as a guard at Carle Place High School on New York's Long Island. Now he is accused of firing 16 shots from a 9-mm gun, killing two young men and critically wounding three others as they sat in a parked Cadillac outside the school. HSC, which has since shut its operations, was required by law to submit Padilla's fingerprints to the state within 24 hours. Instead, the company waited more than seven weeks. According to Padilla's parents, their son is "mentally unstable."
- Members of his family say Michael Huston, 41, had been mentally disabled since the Vietnam War, which may explain why he blames "another person inside" him for setting a 1990 blaze that caused $25 million in damage to movie sets and property at Hollywood's Universal Studios. In January, Huston admitted in a Los Angeles courtroom that he had tossed a cigarette lighter into a trash can full of papers at Universal, then reported the fire to a superior, apparently hoping to earn praise. Wearing the ubiquitous uniform of Burns International Security Services, the nation's largest, Huston had been "guarding" the studio barely a month.
- Marita Juse, 48, of Burbank, Calif., will be sentenced later this month for embezzling more than $1 million from Pinkerton's, the oldest and second largest U.S. security firm. A fugitive on tax-fraud charges, Juse used an alias when Pinkerton's accounting division hired her. Obtaining computer codes, she made wire transfers of cash from the company's bank account. Juse faces up to 30 years in prison. Meanwhile, Pinkerton's, the company that once stalked Jesse James, Butch Cassidy and the Sundance Kid, is pitching a job-applicant screening service to its clients, which include half the Fortune 500.

levels. Although the majority of the estimated 1.1 million security guards in America do honest and capable work, Behar (1992, p. 44) argued the private security industry, which has grown dramatically in the past two decades, has become a "virtual dumping ground for the unstable, the dishonest and the violent." Behar further speculated that due to lax preemployment screenings, many private security officers who use drugs and/or have criminal records are not rejected from the applicant pool. It is standard operating procedure for private security officers to be hired directly off the street or through employment agencies; they are often given uniforms and assigned to posts the same day they are hired.

Many see the private security guard industry as "fragmented, intensely competitive and unwilling to police itself adequately, yet it is governed by weak laws that are often ignored" (Behar, 1992, p. 44). In addition to all the previously mentioned problems, the lack of strong management and inadequate pay may lead many guards to commit crimes while on-the-job. "Our industry needs leadership," says Robert McCrie, a professor at the John Jay College of Criminal Justice in New York City (Behar, 1992, p. 44).

Even though the private security industry's largest corporations all claim to screen and educate their applicants rigorously, crime continues to flourish in the industry. Burns, the private security industry's leader with reportedly more than $650 million in revenues, was founded in 1909 by Detective William J. Burns, later a director of the FBI. In recent years, Burns has employed several guards who had previous arrests for everything from arson, setting a fire to an abandoned building in Colorado which took forty-two firefighters to extinguish; to theft, vacuuming thousands of dollars in change from public bus boxes in San Francisco; to stealing $13,000 in computer equipment from a client in Syracuse. Other incidents that involved Burns' guards became the focus of a grand jury investigation and, after a five-month probe involving the New Jersey's Meadowlands Arena, the grand jury documented twenty cases in which the guards beat or otherwise abused patrons at the arena between 1987 and 1990. The Burns security contract was subsequently terminated. The grand jury further accused the arena's management of a "gross error in judgment" for renewing a contract with the security firm in 1989 (Behar, 1992, p. 45).

Although these troubles have surfaced and have cast a negative shadow on the Burns company, Burns does apparently provide high-quality service at roughly one-third of the nation's nuclear power plants. However, high-quality service is to be expected considering the extremely rigorous and thorough screening and training standards employed by the government.

Pinkerton's was involved in litigation in the 1980s that further acknowledged the need for industry standards. A Pinkerton's guard at Welsh Manufacturing, a former division of Textron in Rhode Island, acknowledged that he deliberately took the job in security so he could orchestrate the theft of the gold he was hired to protect. As a result, Welsh won punitive damages. The case, which led to an appellate decision in 1984, exposed Pinkerton's inadequate screening and supervision of its employees. Apparently, management never contacted any of the character references the guard provided. Although Pinkerton's did contact the guard's former employers, it received no information on his honesty and trustworthiness (Behar, 1992).

Problems such as the ones mentioned raise the question, "If you can't trust your security supplier, whom can you trust?" Simply stated, clients buy security services because they want to deter threats and reduce risk. They need a security provider in whom they have 100 percent trust and confidence. When you turn over the keys to the building to a security officer for the night, you need to know you can trust that person and the organization that person represents. How do you know your security guard isn't just another threat? According to Pinkerton's Webpage, it now takes numerous steps to assure the honesty of its security candidates which lead to a risk reduction for its company and its clients. Preemployment selection tools include the Stanton Survey, which tests qualities such as honesty and integrity. Other fail-safes utilized include Social Security traces, county criminal record checks, drug screening, employment and reference verification, military service verifications, Department of Motor Vehicles searches, and, where required, criminal history checks.

Public Policing.   Abuse at the hands of police officers in the United States is seen by some as one of the most serious and divisive human rights' violations in the country. Such violations are thought to persist nationwide, in rural, suburban, and urban areas of the country, and are being committed by various police officers ranging from city, county, and state to federal agents. We often see isolated images on "Real" television shows where the video camera has captured an officer in what appears to be an unjustified shooting, severe beatings being given to "noncombative" suspects, and general unnecessarily rough handling of handcuffed perpetrators.

In its July 1998 report "Shielded from Justice: Police Brutality and Accountability in the United States," Human Rights Watch documents police misconduct in fourteen cities: Atlanta, Boston, Chicago, Detroit, Indianapolis, Los Angeles, Minneapolis, New Orleans, New York, Philadelphia, Portland, Providence, San Francisco, and Washington, DC. Kenneth Roth, Executive Director of the Human Rights Watch, acknowledges that data on police abuse are very hard to obtain and accuses Internal Affairs units of operating under a cloak of secrecy. The group alleged cities pay tens of millions of taxpayers' dollars in civil lawsuits that allege police brutality rather than addressing the underlying issues. The offenses by officers are seen as "a betrayal of the public these officers are sworn to serve" (Roth, 1998). On April 15, 1999, in her first major speech on police brutality, Attorney General Janet Reno acknowledged "there is a problem," and that "effective policing does not mean abusive policing." The speech came on the heels of several high-profile incidents of alleged brutality (Roth, 1998).

Box 8.

New York: US Eastern District Court Judge Eugene Nickerson sentenced New York City police officer Charles Schwarz to 15 years and eight months in prison for his role in the 1997 assault of Haitian immigrant Abner Louima. Nickerson is also scheduled today to sentence Schwarz, 35, and officers Thomas Bruder, 34, and Thomas Wiese, 37, of up to five years each for conspiring to obstruct justice by concocting a story about Schwarz's involvement in the attack. They were convicted March 6. Schwarz, who could have been sentenced to up to 30 years in prison, was found guilty last June of restraining Louima while ex-officer Justin Volpe sodomized him with a broomstick in a Brooklyn police station. Volpe pleaded guilty and was sentenced to 30 years in prison (Bloomberg, 2000).

The public police officers are not without many of the same problems as the private security (see Box 8).

Public police officers are increasingly portrayed as the bad guys in such movies as *Gang in Blue, The Glass Shield,* and *Caught Up.* In these movies and many serial television dramas, officers are seen as thugs who administer their own brand of justice while the courts turn a deaf ear (Scoville, 2000). Many thought the federal government and federal officers were responsible for the deaths of eighty Branch Davidians during the cult's 1993 standoff with federal agents at Waco, Texas. However, a jury ruled the government does not bear responsibility for the deaths. The jury deliberated for just two and one-half hours in the $675 million wrongful-death lawsuit filed by surviving Branch Davidians and relatives of those who were killed in the standoff (Associated Press, 2000b).

Legal Considerations

Lawsuits Against Private Security Officers.   Private security officers are responsible for their actions. If such actions are unlawful, they may be sued. The unlawful action is technically called a tort. A tort is a civil wrong for which a person can be sued. Civil actions may be brought against any private security personnel who commit an unlawful action against another person. Often the officer's employer is sued as well as the officer. The most common civil suits brought against private security are for assault, battery, false imprisonment, defamation, intentional infliction of emotional distress, invasion of privacy, and negligence (see Box 9).

Box 9.

Assault is an intentional act causing reasonable apprehension of physical harm in the mind of another. An example is threatening someone, with or without a weapon, into obeying your demands.

Battery is the unconsented, offensive touching of another person, either directly or indirectly. An example is touching a person or his/her clothing in an angry or rude manner. Use of bodily force should be avoided whenever possible. At times, however, security officers may have to use force to defend themselves or others from serious bodily harm.

False imprisonment is unreasonably restraining another person using physical or psychological means to deny that person freedom of movement. An example is requiring someone to remain in a room while the police are being called. If a person is detained, there must be reasonable grounds to believe that a crime was committed and that the person being detained actually committed it. Mere suspicion is not enough.

Defamation is injuring a person's reputation, such as by falsely inferring, by either words or conduct, in front of a third disinterested party, that a person committed a crime. An example is to falsely accuse someone of shoplifting in front of friends or to falsely accuse an employee of pilferage in front of coworkers or visitors.

(Continued)

Intentional infliction of emotional distress refers to outrageous or grossly reckless conduct intended to and highly likely to cause a severe emotional reaction. An example is to threaten to have an employee fired because he/she is suspected of stealing.

Invasion of privacy refers to an unreasonable, unconsented intrusion into the personal affairs or property of a person. An example would be searching an employee's personal property outside of search guidelines established by the employer.

Negligence occurs when a person has a duty to act reasonably but fails to do so and, as a result, someone is injured. An example is failing to correct a dangerous situation on the premises or failing to give assistance to an employee in distress.

Hess, K. M. and Wrobleski, H. M. (Eds.). (1992). *Introduction to private security*. St. Paul MN: West Publishing Company.

Many will agree that civil liability could be reduced by hiring wisely, setting minimum standards for job performance, and establishing clear policies, as well as providing effective training and management (see Box 10).

Not only have lawsuits increased, but also judicial and legislative sanctions against the security industry have increased as well. Some of the reasons for this increase are:

- The exceptional growth of the industry
- The rising expectations of the public
- The quality of security services
- The increase in the number of new laws and lawyers

Lawsuits against Public Police Officers.   The case in New York City in which Haitian Abner Louima claimed officers sodomized him with a broomstick and then beat him, needless to say, shocked the world. The officers who had knowledge of the incident were unwilling to report the incident immediately or to come forward with information later. The alleged perpetrators apparently believed they would get away with this crime even though it took place in a busy police station. Many American cities, and even foreign countries, look to New York when it comes to styling their own police forces. After all, the first full-time organized police department was formed in New York City in 1845.

It is argued by the Human Rights Watch that civil lawsuits actually allow police departments to ignore abuse committed by officers. They further state that damages paid to victims do not come from the budget of the police department or officer personally. In almost all cases, the city pays any settlement or jury award. In most cities, no investigation is triggered by the filing, the settlement, or the judgment relating to a lawsuit against an officer, no matter how severe the allegation. The officer's performance evaluations are usually unaffected (Roth, 1998).

Box 10.

A concert violinist Tuesday sued the upscale department store that wrongly accused her of shoplifting, alleging that rough treatment by security guards left her unable to play her instrument. Sando Shia, 49, a member of the Chicago Symphony Orchestra since 1990, said she was accused of trying to steal the shirt she was wearing and was taken to an interrogation room at a Marshall Field's store in Chicago three weeks ago. Shia says she was pushed against a wall and handcuffed to a table by three security guards. Shia is undergoing physical therapy on her injured left wrist and elbow but is unable to practice the violin, her attorney, Robert Clifford, said. She missed three concert dates. "It was humiliating," he said. "We hope she'll be able to play again." Clifford said Shia was released from the store without explanation, and later received a letter of apology. A statement by Marshall Field's, a subsidiary of Minneapolis-based Target Corp., called it an "unfortunate situation (that) appeared to be retail theft and turned out to be otherwise." It said the investigator involved was no longer with the company. Shia's lawsuit in Cook County Circuit Court did not specify damages, but alleged false imprisonment, battery and intentional infliction of emotional distress (Reuters, 2000).

Although civil lawsuits against police officers are becoming more common, criminal prosecution of police officers is rare. Many believe local prosecutors are reluctant to pursue cases against officers accused of criminal actions, especially human rights violations, because they typically work closely with police to prosecute criminals.

ISSUES TO CONSIDER WHEN CHOOSING SECURITY

With everything we have discussed, the following five areas should be considered when trying to decide between private and public security, keeping in mind the question "Whom do we trust?"

Armed versus Unarmed

Twenty years ago, according to Behar (1992), a Rand report stated that half the nation's private guards bore arms on the job. Today, 10 percent or fewer do so, but that still leaves 100,000 gun-toting guards, which is reportedly more than the combined police forces of the country's thirty largest cities. Yet, weapons training for this army is generally inadequate. A recent survey found that eight hours was about average, and a large part of the training consists of the mechanics of shooting rather than preparation for the real-life situations guards are likely to encounter. The survey also found that 40 percent of armed guards claim to be self-taught in the use of their weapons.

Although most national security guard firms maintain they provide about eight hours of general training (mostly showing films) for unarmed guards, Wackenhut, the third largest guard employer, boasts that its minimum has been sixteen hours since the 1970s. Yet, according to Behar (1992), two former executives who have left the firm insist the real figure was far lower. "'Four hours was pretty much it,' says Frank Bisogno, who ran Wackenhut's New York City office until he left in 1989. 'If you were required by the customer, you would do more, but if the manager could avoid expending a nonbillable cost such as that, he would avoid it'" (p. 46).

Unfortunately, weak and piecemeal legislation enables many questionable security practices to prosper. As of 1992, only seventeen states require guard companies to carry general liability insurance, and only fourteen require any training for unarmed guards. Eighteen states have absolutely no training requirements, even for those who carry guns, and an astonishing eighteen states allow convicted felons to be hired. Even though many states are attempting to update and/or create legislation that covers private security, many find it is an area still developing and must look to other states for role models.

In Florida, the state statute governing the regulation of professions and occupations, which includes private investigative, private security, and repossession services, is statute 493. This statute covers everything from the number of patches required on the uniform to the type of badge allowed to be displayed, as well as the training required to be licensed. In Florida, for example, security guards are allowed to begin work as soon as they have applied to the state for licensure. This practice leaves the state and security guard firms open for lawsuits, because the guards are working prior to their background checks being completed.

Salary

The disturbing aspect of the uneven regulation and management of the industry is the rate at which private firms are taking over responsibilities once reserved for police forces, such as ambulance services, parking regulations, neighborhood patrols, and even background investigations for federal job applicants. According to Behar (1992), Kansas City's Chief of Police stated he would like to contract with private firms to perform twenty-two tasks that were assigned to the public police officers, in order to save an estimated 37 percent in cost. The tasks he was looking to privatize included the transporting of prisoners, assisting stranded motorists, and guarding crime scenes. Similarly, to save money, armed Wackenhut guards, at one point in time, replaced sheriff's deputies on commuter trains in Miami and Palm Beach, Florida (Behar, 1992, p. 47).

In 1971, a Rand Corporation report described the average security guard as an "aging white male who was underscreened, undertrained, undersupervised, underpaid and underregulated" (Behar, 1992, p. 44). According to Hallcrest Systems of McLean, VA, which closely monitors the security industry, the only significant change in that profile is that today's private guard is more likely to be much younger and black or Hispanic (Behar, 1992).

Few industries have expanded as rapidly as the private security industry. The number of security guards has grown since 1980 to nearly twice the size of the U.S. public police community. Today, there are ten thousand security companies in America, the vast majority operating on a shoestring budget and paying their guards $5 to $7 an hour. "The little mom-and-pops are often undercapitalized, cutting corners all over the place, opening and closing regularly under new names, even providing payoffs in exchange for work," says Richard Rockwell, who runs Professional Security Bureau (Behar, 1992, p. 44). Industry consultants agree that clients refuse to pay for training, and the average security guard firm cannot afford to provide additional training. Others have acknowledged that contracts have been lost for something as little as 5 cents per man-hour. Unless the cost for additional training can be incorporated into the cost to the client, the security firms maintain it is something they simply cannot afford to provide. Management asserts every penny bid on a contract counts toward whether they win the bidding war.

Level of Education

One common trait that both public and private security have in common is the desire to be seen as "professionals." Many states are requiring continuing education classes for their public officers and professional training and licensure for private security officers. In addition, many public police agencies are attempting to become accredited by the Commission on Accreditation for Police Agencies.

Some states restrict the access of guard companies to official criminal records, whereas others require fingerprint checks. In California, nearly 20 percent of the applications for guard licenses are rejected each year because background checks disclose prior criminal convictions. Yet, even that kind of screening helps only to a degree. A 1989 study by the New York State Senate Committee on Crime and Correction found that 16 percent of guards were still hired despite such criminal backgrounds (Behar, 1992, p. 46).

One key reason for the abundance of uniformed "thugs" is the inexcusable length of time it takes most states to check the fingerprints and report back to the security firms. Arizona and Arkansas, for example, can tell a company in less than two weeks whether it has just hired a Hillside Strangler (who, incidentally, worked for several private security firms after he had been rejected by some police departments). In contrast, in Alaska and Oklahoma, it can take six months for the same information. In states that do not scan the FBI's national data bank, such as New York, it is impossible to know whether a guard applicant committed a crime elsewhere (Behar, 1992).

In New York, where even beauticians and real estate brokers are licensed, more than a dozen bills have been brought before the state legislature since 1976 to license or regulate security guards. Industry lobbyists helped kill them all. Some would argue that no matter how much licensing and education is required of both public and private security officers, there will always be those who simply give the rest a bad reputation (see Box 11).

Although many argue that private security officers do not receive enough training and education in their trade, many would also acknowledge the public officers seem to be

---

Box 11.

Huntsville, TX (AP)—a former security guard who raped and strangled a 61-year-old woman while high on drugs and alcohol was executed by injection. Paul Nuncio, 31, was condemned for killing Pauline Farris at her Plainview home on December 3, 1993. The prosecutor called the crime "animalistic" and said it was the worst capital murder case he had ever seen. (Associated Press, 2000c).

receiving more training than ever. At a typical police academy, an officer is subjected to approximately one thousand hours of intensive schooling. That person is subjected to thorough background and psychological evaluations that often include a polygraph test. Police officers, unlike private security officers, must pass a physician's physical exam and demonstrate a level of physical agility. While at the academy, officers are also instructed in the use of firearms and tactical weapons. It can be argued that a trained police officer can more readily recognize a potentially dangerous situation and react in the most appropriate manner, often diffusing the situation before it progresses to a more violent stage. Therefore, the argument is that an off-duty police officer is more desirable as a "private security guard" due to the officer's experience and judgment as a public police officer. Many hire off-duty police officers in lieu of private security officers in hopes of reducing their potential liability; however, their costs also increase due to the increase of wages for the public officer.

Number of Guards Needed

Citizen fear of crime and the awareness that criminal justice resources alone are unable to effectively control crime problems have led to a growing use of private security services (see Box 12).

Union versus Nonunion

Today's police departments' goals are to prevent crime, investigate crime, apprehend offenders, control traffic, maintain order, and deal with emergencies and disasters. In the United States today, important and controversial issues have arisen regarding the administration and operations of police forces, especially in urban centers.

In recent years, police unions, including groups associated with national labor organizations, have grown rapidly. Most unions operate as nonprofit organizations consisting of both sworn and nonsworn members. Their general purpose is the promotion of harmonious relations between the municipality, county, or state employer and the employ-

---

Box 12.

According to Bocklet (1990, p. 54): "Today private security plays a major role in the national scene, employing an estimated two million people, and is growing. By contrast, there's about 600,000 police officers, experiencing zero growth over the last two decades and apparently stabilizing at that level. In 1986, private protection services spent $22 billion, while the police budgets came in at $13 billion." There are now almost twice as many people employed in private security as there are public police. Their roles are complementary. They may work together, may hire or delegate authority to each other, or may move from one sector to the other.

ees, as well as a grievance process for the resolution of problems. The union also is instrumental in bargaining for rates of pay, hours of work, and other conditions of employment.

The Fraternal Order of Police (FOP) is the world's largest organization of sworn police officers, with more than 290,000 members. The FOP has a long tradition of serving the professional police officers. Founded in 1915 in Pittsburgh, PA, the FOP has evolved into over 2,200 local lodges, as well as lodges overseas, comprising the FOP International (Fraternal Order of Police, 2000a). The FOP exists to strive for betterment of the police profession for the individual officer and the collective membership. By improving working conditions, wages, benefits, and by monitoring and proposing effective legislation, the FOP provides a service and benefit to the police profession and the public. FOP members across the nation believe in the nation's motto *Jus Fidus Libertatum—Law is the Safeguard of Freedom* (Fraternal Order of Police, 2000b).

Critics of this trend argue that unionized police forces are less likely to be neutral in controlling disorders that occur during labor strikes. Some people also believe union affiliation will weaken official authority in maintaining discipline. Others argue management deficiencies often prompt the need for unions and unionization will lead to greater job satisfaction, higher morale, and increased tenure. Because police are public employees, laws restrict their right to strike or to participate in other job actions. The trend seems to be for police unions to engage in compulsory or binding arbitration when labor disputes arise.

Although many public police agencies are associated with either a union and/or FOP, many private security guard operations are without that benefit. Most private security guard firms are small in employee numbers and can't afford to operate if they have to meet the demand for higher salaries union members expect. Therefore, the majority of security guard firms are nonunion and lack the basic assistance that might be afforded to them (see Box 13).

Box 13.

Through a local union, you could have some or all of the following:

- Democratically determine negotiation priorities such as wages, benefits and work rules.
- Follow a predetermined grievance process which will guarantee that your contract is upheld and your rights protected.
- Run for union office and elect leaders from among your peers to negotiate your contracts, represent your concerns with management.
- Communicate with other office, technical and professional employees about the issues of common concern.

(Office & Professional Employees International Union, 2000).

SOLUTIONS

Bridging the Gap and Interfacing

The similarities in goals and objectives of private and public policing and the differences in their legal authority suggest that, in many ways, public and private policing efforts are complimentary. An example of where we will be seeing both public and private security working side by side is at the upcoming Olympic games in Athens, Greece (see Box 14).

An exchange of personnel occurs frequently. Some individuals use security jobs as stepping-stones into police/policing, whereas other police/policing officers are moonlighting as private security officers. Still other public officers retire and then go into private security; some become security directors for corporations.

One way public and private security organizations can help strengthen their mutual ties to the community (client) is to have a quick response by their management teams when problems arise. A proactive management must be responsiveness to clients' needs and have the built-in flexibility to meet the daily needs of clients and any emergency situations that arise. Some techniques commonly utilized include, but are not limited to, the following:

- Create an open dialogue with the clients and prepare mutually agreeable plans. Partner with clients to address issues before they become problems.
- Have specific training programs focused on satisfying clients' needs. Address how to identify client needs, then how to provide resolution and how to be proactive toward problem solving.
- Management personnel need to be out in the field to work with clients and employees for twenty-four-hour coverage.
- Make sure personnel are available in times of emergency—have contingency staffing plans.
- Be certain that management can be reached twenty-four hours a day, seven days a week.
- Understand the importance of open communication with clients to address service performance.

Box 14.

The head of the police admits Greece does not yet have the expertise to protect the athletes, officials, and visitors at the 2004 Olympics. Public order Minister Michalis Chrisohoides said an estimated 50,000 police officers—nearly the current strength of the department—will be used during the games. He said about 1,000 special guards will be hired to protect people thought to be at risk and an international security consultant may be hired. Greece expects to pay at least $416 million for security (Associated Press, 2000d).

- Measure performance through client surveys, employee surveys, account planning, client action plans, site performance assessments, quarterly reviews, process improvement suggestions, and exit interviews (http://pinkertons.com/home/main.html).

CONCLUSION

Although security can be defined in many ways, we have primarily concentrated on the basic concepts of safety, protection, and freedom from danger. Whether public or private security is needed, there will continue to be differing opinions as to which is more trustworthy and which is more desirable. There are times when public security is a must, but also there are times when private security can substitute just as well. There will also be times when public and private security can work cohesively together, such as the security to be used at the Olympics. As noted by the United Way Strategic Institute (1989, p. 3), "There will be a blurring of the boundaries that have traditionally defined the roles of the public sector versus the private sector, as well as individual versus institutional responsibilities."

Security services, whether public or private, need to devote extensive time and resources to hiring the right people, developing them, and striving to ensure they are the right person for the client's needs. We have seen by numerous examples that even wealthy clients may find themselves the victims of those they have hired to protect them unless there are built-in measures to ensure employee honesty, integrity, and respect between the employer, employee, and the client. This theory held true in the beginning when town dwellers lost faith in the constables and still rings true today as the public becomes more and more concerned with its own safety, and struggles with the confusion over whom it can trust to protect it.

Even though there is no silver bullet to fix the situation, the public and private security industries should take note that with the media more readily available today than in any time in history, the public is watching and the demand for better service has been voiced. So, whom do we trust? In theory, we trust both public and private security everyday in places of business, the public sectors, and, in many situations, we trust them both and don't know the difference. Therefore, we need to realize that with so many security personnel in the public eye, there will always (unfortunately) be those who give the industry the "black eyes" we have seen. Most of the people working in both public and private security are persons who are there to do their job, not to take advantage of the employer or the public. Ask any officer and he or she will gladly tell you his/her job is a thankless one. Yet we, as the public, continue to demand the services of police officers. Whether in the public or private sector, those officers will continue to provide their services.

REFERENCES

Associated Press (a). (No date). Track star sues, claiming racial bias at mall. Retrieved June 15, 2000 from the World Wide Web: http://www.aol.com.news.

Associated Press (b). (No date). Waco, Texas. Retrieved July 14, 2000 from the World Wide Web: http:// www.aol.com.news.

ASSOCIATED PRESS (c). (No date). Texas executes killer by injection. Retrieved June 15, 2000 from the World Wide Web: http://www.aol.com.news.

ASSOCIATED PRESS (d). (No date). Greeks admit Olympic security needs work. Retrieved June 26, 2000 from the World Wide Web: http://www.aol.com.news.

BEHAR, R. (1992, March). Thugs in Uniform. *TIME*, 44–47.

BOCKLET, RICHARD. (1990, December). Police-private security cooperation. *Law and Order*, 54–59.

BLOOMBERG. (No date). New York business. Retrieved June 27, 2000 from the World Wide Web: http://www.aol.com.news.

FRATERNAL ORDER OF POLICE. (a) (No date). Retrieved June 27, 2000 from the World Wide Web: http://www.grandlodgefop.org

FRATERNAL ORDER OF POLICE. (b) (No date). Retrieved June 27, 2000 from the World Wide Web: http://www.austin360.com

THE NEW GROLIER MULTIMEDIA ENCYCLOPEDIA, 1993

Bibliography: Horan, James D., The Pinkertons (1967); Morn, Frank, The eye that never sleeps: A history of the Pinkerton National Detective Agency (1982); Pinkerton, Allan, Criminal reminiscences and detective sketches (1879) and Thirty years a detective (1884); Rowan, Richard W., The Pinkertons: A Detective Dynasty (1931).

Bibliography: Johnson, Diane, Dashiell Hammett (1987); Layman, Richard, The shadow man: A documentary life of Dashiell Hammett (1981; repr. 1984); Nolan, William F., Dashiell Hammett: A casebook (1969); and Hammett: A life at the edge (1983); Parker, Dorothy, The constant reader (1970).

Bibliography: Broehl, W. Jr., The Molly Maguires (1964; repr. 1968).

Bibliography: Wolff, Leon, Lockout: Homestead Strike of 1892 (1965).

HESS, K. M. AND WROBLESKI, H. M. (Eds.). (1992). *Introduction to private security.* St. Paul MN: West Publishing Company.

HUMAN RIGHTS WATCH. (1998, July 7). Retrieved July 9, 2000 from the World Wide Web: http://www.org/about/initiatives/police.htm

MAGNUSON, E., BANTA, K. W. AND CONSTABLE, A. (1985, June). Very serious losses. [CD-Rom] Time Almanac 1995.

MARX, G. T. (1987). The interweaving of public and private police in undercover work. In C. D. Shearing and P. C. Stenning (Eds.), *Private Policing* (pp. 172–193). Beverly Hills, CA: Sage Publications.

OFFICE & PROFESSIONAL EMPLOYEES INTERNATIONAL UNION. (No date). Retrieved June 28, 2000 from the World Wide Web: http://www.opeiu.org

REUTERS. (No date). Chicago violinist sues department store. Retrieved June 20, 2000 from the World Wide Web: http://www.aol.com.news

ROTH, K. (1998). Report charges police abuse in U.S. goes undetected. Retrieved July 7, 2000 from the World Wide Web: http://www.hrw.org/hrw/press98/july/polic707.htm.

SCOVILLE, D. (2000). How are cops reflected in the world of film and television? *American Police Beat.* Retrieved June 29, 2000 from the World Wide Web: http://www.apbweb.com/articles.htm.

STRATEGIC INSTITUTE. (1989). Nine forces reshaping America. Bethesda, MD: World Future Society.

4

Crime Prevention Through Environmental Design (CPTED) in Elementary and Secondary Schools

Matthew B. Robinson

There is a perception, which is measured by increased fear of crime at school, increased media coverage of school crime, and the recent mass murder at Columbine High School in Colorado, that crime at school is increasing. Stated simply, this perception is false. Crimes at school are no more prevalent in the twenty-first century than they were at any time in the twentieth century. In fact, schools were safer in the year of the mass murder at Columbine High School than they were at any other time in the 1990s. Some statistics (Brener, Simon, Krug, and Lowry, 1999) bear this out:

- Between 1991 and 1997, the percentage of students involved in physical fights decreased 14 percent (from 42.5 percent to 36.6 percent).
- The percentage of students injured in physical fights decreased 20 percent (from 4.4 percent to 3.5 percent).
- The percentage of students who carried weapons to school decreased 30 percent (from 26.1 percent to 18.3 percent).

FIGURE 4–1   Recent school violence incidents
Source: Adapted from CNN.com.

THE PROBLEM

Figure 4–1 shows some of the highly publicized cases of school violence in the United States. These types of cases are no doubt evidence of the serious nature of juvenile violence in America (Barrett, 1992; Bastian & Taylor, 1991; Brooks, 1993; Freed, 1992). Because of the intensive media coverage of these cases, particularly the mass murder at Columbine, students report being more afraid of school violence (see Figure 4–2) and are more likely to avoid certain places at school (see Figure 4–3). In addition, schools have begun forcing children to walk through metal detectors and carry see-through book bags (Firestone, 1999).

Figures prove the image of school violence is much worse than the reality of it (Hanke, 1996; National Council on Crime and Delinquency, 1994; Schwartz, 1992). As stated in the *Annual Report on School Safety* (U.S. Department of Education [USDOE] & U.S. Department of Justice [USDOJ], 1999, p. iv): "The vast majority of America's schools are safe places. In fact, notwithstanding the disturbing reports of violence in our schools, they are becoming even safer."

Fortunately, schools are relatively safe places (USDOE & USDOJ, 1999; Billinsley, 1991; Ewing, 1992; Miller, 1992; Muir, 1992), even with the large numbers of guns brought to school each day (Callahan & Rivara, 1992; Center for the Prevention of Handgun Violence, 1992; Webster, Gainer, and Champion, 1993). Figure 4–4 illustrates that the rate of violent acts at schools and away from schools per 1,000 people has slightly declined over time. According to Savoye (2000), the total number of school crimes declined

Fear of Attack or Harm at School

Percentage of students ages 12 through 19 who reported fearing being attacked
or harmed at school, by race-ethnicity: 1989 and 1995

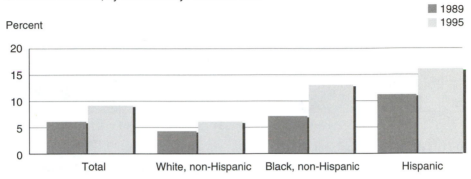

FIGURE 4–2   Fear of crime at school

Note: Includes students who reported that they sometimes or most of the time feared
being victimized in this way. "At school" means in the school building, on the school
grounds, or on a school bus.

Source: U.S. Department of Justice, Bureau of Justice Statistics, School Crime Supplement to the National Crime Victimization Survey, 1989 and 1995.

Avoidance of Places at School

Percentage of students ages 12 through 19 who reported that they avoided one or more
places in school, by race-ethnicity: 1989 and 1995

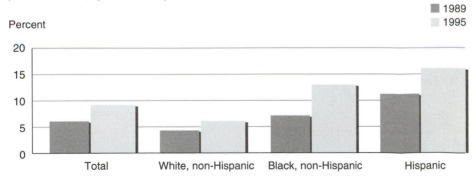

FIGURE 4–3   Perception of risk at school

Note: Places include the entrance into the school, any hallways or stairs in the school,
parts of the school cafeteria, any school restrooms, and other places inside the school
building.

Source: U.S. Department of Justice, Bureau of Justice Statistics, School Crime Supplement to the National Crime Victimization Survey, 1989 and 1995.

Serious Violent Crime Against Students At and Away from School

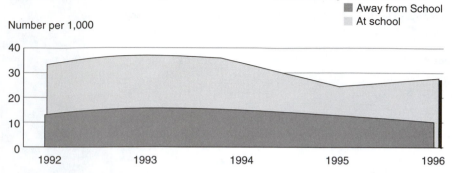

FIGURE 4–4   School violence trends

Note: Serious violent crimes include murder, rape, other types of sexual battery, suicide, physical attack or fighting with a weapon, and robbery.

Source: U.S. Department of Justice, Bureau of Justice Statistics, National Crime Victimization Survey, 1992 to 1996.

from 3.8 million to 2.7 million between 1993 and 1997. Figure 4–5 depicts the number of school shootings each year from 1992 to the present. As you can see, there has been no dramatic increase.

The perception about violent crime at schools was stated nicely in a report titled *Early Warning, Timely Response: A Guide to Safe Schools*. The report states, "Violence can happen at any time, anywhere." This statement is not very reassuring for parents, to say the least, particularly because it comes from the USDOE and USDOJ report based on the work of an independent panel of experts in the fields of education, policing, and mental health.

According to the USDOE and USDOJ (1998a), the realities of school crime in America include:

- The most common type of school crime is a physical attack or fight without a weapon (see Figure 4–6).
- The least common type of school crime is a murder.
- One's chance of dying at school is roughly 1 in a million.
- Less that 1 percent of killings of juveniles occur at schools (see Figure 4–7).

In a recent survey of American schools, only 10 percent reported they had at least one serious violent crime. Almost half of the schools in America (43 percent) reported they experienced no incidents of serious crimes (see Figure 4–8). Even most violent crimes committed at schools *do not* result in any actual injury to anyone (Hanke, 1996).

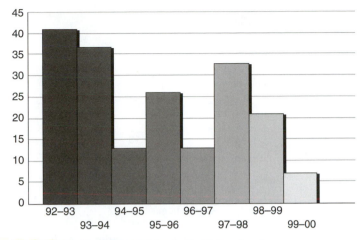

FIGURE 4–5 Shooting deaths in U.S. schools

Number of various crimes occurring
in public schools: 1996–97

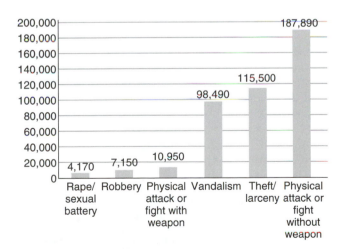

FIGURE 4–6 Crime at school

Source: U.S. Department of Education, National Center for
Education Statistics, Fast Response Survey System, "Prin-
cipal/ School Disciplinarian Survey on School Violence,"
FRSS 63, 1977.

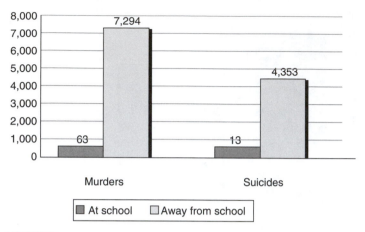

FIGURE 4–7   Number of murders and suicides of students at school and away from school (1992–1993)

Percent of public schools indicating the seriousness of reported crimes occurring at the school: 1996–97

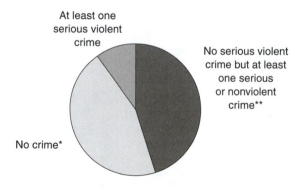

*Schools reported no crimes to police during the school year
**Serious violent crimes include: murder, rape, sexual battery, suicide, fight, or attack with a weapon or robbery. Less serious and nonviolent crimes include attacks without a weapon, theft and vandalism.

FIGURE 4–8   Prevalence of serious crimes at school

Source: U.S. Department of Education, National Center for Education Statistics, Fast Response Survey System, "Principal/ School Disciplinarian Survey on School Violence," FRSS 63, 1977.

Despite this good news, a recent survey of schools (Agron and Anderson, 2000) found that:

- Concern for security is among the top concerns of school administrators.
- Administrators are much more concerned with everyday problems such as fights and vandalism rather than random acts of violence.
- Media attention to school violence has prompted school administrators to review their security plans, despite the small likelihood of a major violent crime occurring on any given campus.
- Public schools alone will spend about $795 million on school security in 2000.

Some statistics suggest a more alarming problem. Consider these statistics from the American Counseling Association (1999) as an example:

- Nine hundred teachers are threatened per hour in the United States.
- Twenty percent of high school seniors report being threatened with violence every year.
- Two thousand students are actually attacked per hour.
- Forty teachers are attacked per hour.
- One hundred thousand guns are brought to school every day (*USA Today*, 1999).
- The ratio of students to counselors in elementary and secondary schools is 513:1.

When one considers how many students and teachers are in American schools, it is easier to get a proper perspective on the problem. Table 4–1 illustrates there are more than 51 million students and approximately 3 million teachers in American schools. There were approximately 380,000 violent victimizations at school in 1996 against these roughly 54 million people. This means the rate of violent victimization at American schools is about 704 per 100,000 people. Stated differently, about 0.7 percent of people can expect to become victims of serious violent crimes at schools.

TABLE 4–1   Serious Victimization at School

	Total Number of Students and Teachers	
	Total	Violent Victimizations
Students	51,500,000	255,000 (ages 12–18, 1996)
Teachers	3,000,000	123,000 (avg. 1992–1996)

Sources: Digest of Education Statistics, 1997 (December 1997, NCES-98–015); Overview of Public Elementary and Secondary Schools and Districts, School Year 1996–1997 (October 1998, NCES 98–204).

Note: Number of students (public and private) are projected data from 1996–1997. Number of public schools are from 1996–1997; number of private schools are from 1995–1996.

I conclude the statement of the problem by saying that violence at school is less common than portrayed in the media, but it is still a real problem that will continue to plague our nation's schools. And it can, after all, happen anywhere. Luckily for us, evidence suggests prevention and early intervention efforts can reduce violence in schools (USDOE & USDOJ, 1998b).

WHAT CAN BE DONE?

Crime Control, Crime Prevention, and CPTED

As with most crime problems in America, we have mostly resorted to *crime control* efforts as opposed to *crime prevention* efforts to deal with crimes committed at school. What is the difference? Crime control essentially amounts to maintaining a certain level of crime but also attempting to reduce it (after it already exists through reactive approaches); crime prevention is stopping crime (before it happens through proactive approaches).

In the United States, crime control is primarily achieved through police who are responsible for apprehending alleged criminals, courts who are responsible for determining the guilt or innocence of alleged criminals and sentencing those found legally guilty of crimes, and corrections facilities responsible for punishing convicted offenders. Crime control is reactive rather than proactive, and addresses the symptoms of problems rather than the actual problems that produce the symptoms.

American crime control efforts aimed at reducing crime are generally not successful. As explained by Lab (1997, p. 5), "The level of crime exceeds the limits of what the criminal justice system can hope to handle. The system is already overburdened and often simply processes people through the maze of legal requirements without having an impact on the crime rate." Amazingly, the criminal justice system does not even know about *most* crimes. It is estimated that only 30 to 50 percent of street crimes are even known to the police (Robinson, 1999). Plus, we do not make much effort to reduce intentionally committed harmful acts that are either legal or in violation of the criminal law but not the major focus of local police (Robinson, 2000). From these facts, I would go as far as to suggest the United States is a *miserable failure* at controlling crime.

Given this, crime prevention is a sensible alternative. As noted earlier, crime prevention is aimed at stopping crime before it occurs. Most criminologists and criminal justice scholars agree that crime prevention activities can be divided into three main types. These include (Lab, 1997, pp. 21–23):

- Primary—efforts aimed at avoiding the development of initial problems in society that may lead to crime
- Secondary—efforts aimed at avoiding the development of problems in individuals and specific places where it is most likely to happen
- Tertiary—efforts aimed at avoiding the recurrence of problems in individuals and specific places where it has already happened

To clarify, primary crime prevention would eliminate the problems that produce crime (e.g., poverty, inequality, unemployment, etc.) in society generally. Secondary crime prevention would eliminate these problems in particular areas and/or at particular times where and when crime is most likely to result from these problems. Tertiary crime prevention would eliminate these problems only after they have already produced crime. In many ways criminal justice activity in America can be considered tertiary crime prevention in that it is largely reactive.

As I mentioned, the most common type of crime reduction in schools can be classified as tertiary or reactive crime control efforts. Some of these efforts can be classified as Crime Prevention Through Environmental Design or CPTED. One of the earliest definitions of CPTED was "identifying conditions of the physical and social environment that provide opportunities for or precipitate criminal acts . . . and the alteration of those conditions so that no crimes occur" (Brantingham & Faust, 1976, p. 289). A number of variations and refinements of the basic CPTED concept have been offered. Generally, CPTED "focuses on the settings in which crimes occur and on techniques for reducing vulnerability of the settings" (Taylor & Harrell, 1996, p. 1), because its central premise is that crime can be facilitated or inhibited by features of the physical environment. Although CPTED generally involves changing the environment to reduce the opportunity for crime, it is aimed at other outcomes as well. These include reducing fear of crime and perceptions of crime risks, increasing the aesthetic quality of an environment, and increasing the quality of life for law-abiding citizens, especially by reducing the propensity of the physical environment to support criminal behavior (Crowe, 1991; Robinson, 1999).

Recently, Robinson (1999) suggested that the original, specific concept of CPTED posited by Jeffery (1971, 1977) has evolved into a more general notion of CPTED, as found in his subsequent works (1990). As explained by Robinson (1999, p. 429), "Jeffery's work has evolved into a more general notion of crime prevention, which includes both the *external* physical environment and the *internal* physical organism, as well as interactions between the two." In other words, CPTED can now be understood as a much more comprehensive term used to denote crime prevention, generally, because all crime prevention initiatives involve modifications to some environment. Robinson (1999) suggested other writers of CPTED literature ignore its theoretical development beyond changes to the external, physical environment.

For purposes of this chapter, I follow the lead of Jeffery and use the term CPTED to mean changing factors in *any* environment, aimed at preventing or reducing crime, reducing fear of crime and perceptions of crime risks, increasing the aesthetic quality of an environment, and increasing the quality of life for law-abiding citizens, especially by reducing the propensity of the physical environment to support criminal behavior. The rest of the chapter now turns to how CPTED has been used and is being used in American elementary and secondary schools to meet these intended objectives. Following a systems approach to studying problems, such as school crime (e.g., see Jeffery, 1990), I organize these efforts around the following levels of analysis:

- Individual Level—efforts aimed at changing factors unique to individuals that produce school crime, fear of crime, perceptions of risk, and increasing the aesthetic quality of life of the school environment
- Group Level—efforts aimed at changing factors within groups that produce school crime, fear of crime, perceptions of risk, and increasing the aesthetic quality of life of the school environment

- School Level—efforts aimed at changing factors within schools that promote school crime, fear of crime, perceptions of risk, and increasing the aesthetic quality of the school environment
- Community Level—efforts aimed at changing factors within communities that promote crime at school, fear of crime, perceptions of risk, and increasing the aesthetic quality of the school environment
- Society Level—efforts aimed at changing factors within the larger American society that are related to school crime, fear of crime, perceptions of risk, and increasing the aesthetic quality of life of the school environment.

Put together, these types of approaches are likely to be more effective than when CPTED efforts are made at only one or two levels of analysis.

Individual Level Approaches.   Perhaps most controversial are the efforts of schools and governments to identify those individuals who are most likely to be offenders in incidents of school violence. Much like any exercise in profiling, statistics can be used to gain an accurate image of the typical victim and the typical offender in acts of school violence (Dryfoos, 1990).

Research shows the most likely victims are students in the upper grades (9–12), especially for serious violent crimes. They also come from racial and ethnic minority groups (the highest rate is for African Americans). Victims of violent crime tend to be standouts from large, public, city schools. Violence is more common in high/middle schools (with bullying being the highest in sixth grade). As for teachers, the most likely victims of violence are male teachers in urban middle schools (USDOE & USDOJ, 1998b). The *American Teacher* (1993) claims strict teachers with high standards are also more likely to be victimized.

The most likely perpetrators, according to statistics, are students in the middle to upper grades (6–10), especially for serious violent crimes. They tend to be Caucasian males in large, public, city schools (USDOE & USDOJ, 1998b; American Teacher, 1993). The most likely locations of serious violent crimes at schools are common areas such as hallways, cafeterias, libraries, unattended classrooms, and gyms and locker areas (American Teacher, 1993). Serious violent crimes are more reported at schools where there are street gangs and higher levels of drug use (USDOE & USDOJ, 1998b).

Although the federal government, particularly the USDOE and the USDOJ, have specifically warned about using such profiles to stereotype and harm children, reports from news organizations such as CNN indicate the U.S. Secret Service has been conducting a study in order to complete a training manual for police and schools to assist them in recognizing and dealing with potentially troubling students. This practice qualifies as CPTED because it is aimed at identifying potentially dangerous individuals in the environment before they commit harmful acts at schools. Presumably, students will be identified and referred to necessary treatment and/or counseling services in order to prevent crimes at schools. The academic literature is literally filled with examples of how to assess potential troublemakers (e.g., see Agron, 1999).

Common warning signs, according to the USDOE and USDOJ (1998a), include signs of inattention, hyperactivity, difficulty following directions, truancy, acting out, talking back, and running away. Other early warning signs, which are indicators a student may need help, include social withdrawal, excessive feelings of isolation and loneliness, excessive feelings of rejection, victimization by violent crime, feelings of persecution by others, low school interest and poor academic performance, expressions of violence, uncontrolled anger, impulsiveness, chronic bullying, a history of discipline problems, a history of violence and aggression, intolerance for differences and prejudicial attitudes, drug use (including alcohol), affiliation with gangs, and access to firearms. Another significant early warning sign is serious threats of violence, which are sequential, overt, hostile behaviors or threats directed at self or others.

Although one may witness such warning signs in his or her students and children and become concerned that they will commit a serious violent crime at school, experts suggest it is when individual factors occur together that one should take action. After all, many of these factors seem somewhat normal if they present themselves in isolation. Patterns of warning signs require us to act to prevent an escalation of the problem. The federal government clearly states we should avoid labeling children and keep the warning signs in their proper context. They also advocate a "no harm" policy, meaning that such warning signs must not be used to identify and label children to their detriment.

At the same time, the USDOE and the USDOJ hold that everyone must learn the warning signs. They suggest school board policies should support training and consultation about the warning signs and expect schools will encourage others to report them to school officials. A referral system to community specialists must be in place when reports are made.

Almost nothing is being done to counter the troubling risk factors for violence that develop from conception to about age six years in children. These include neonatal difficulties such as low birth weight and drug use by pregnant mothers, as well as oxygen deprivation, physical trauma to infants, physical abnormalities, and brain damage (Hawkins, Farrington, and Catalano, 1998). The fact that such factors are being ignored as important for understanding and preventing school violence is not surprising, given most people are not aware of their importance, and the prevention of such factors would require additional governmental interventions into the lives of Americans.

Group Level Approaches.   Several popular theories of crime indicate groups are particularly important for understanding and preventing all types of crime, including school crimes. Behavior really starts before birth, at the first exposure of any child to his or her family. Although the development of the brain and thus behavior starts in the womb, virtually nothing is being done to prevent violent tendencies before birth, mostly because of the troubling ethical considerations. Nevertheless, some programs (e.g., Head Start/Healthy Start) do seem to be quite effective in eliminating disadvantages commonly linked to later violent behavior. A major crime prevention study by Sherman et al. (1997) indicates that home visits by nurses reduce illnesses, injury, abuse, and delinquency in children.

Criminological theories that implicate groups in crime include social learning, social control, and strain theories (Bohm, 1997). Social learning theories posit that crime is learned in close, intimate groups. Social control theories hold that crime is normal, especially when kids are not adequately bonded to society—for example, crime is more likely when children are not attached to their loved ones, are not committed to and involved in legitimate means of success, and do not believe in the norms of society. Strain theories suggest that as children become frustrated with being unable to achieve their goals legitimately, they turn to crime to achieve them illegitimately. Logical crime prevention policies based on these theories thus would include:

- Reducing exposure to bad influences (e.g., deviant peers)
- Increasing attachment to families, commitment to education, and involvement in legal activities
- Instilling prosocial values in children
- Reducing frustration by equipping students to succeed legitimately

Hawkins et al. (1998) point out similar risk factors for violent behavior which arise in families. They include parents' failure to set clear expectations for their children, failure to supervise and monitor their children's behavior, excessively harsh or inconsistent discipline, and abusive and neglectful parenting.

The comprehensive review of federally funded crime prevention programs by Sherman et al. (1997) found that effective programs within families include home visits by nurses and other trained professionals, classes for preschoolers with weekly home visits, family therapy, and parent training classes about risk factors of juvenile delinquency. Families can also protect their children from becoming offenders by fostering resiliency to adverse conditions in their children (Benard, 1991).

School Level Approaches.   The most common forms of school CPTED efforts are tertiary in nature because they are not intended to prevent crimes at schools but are instead aimed at reducing the amount of harms associated with school crimes (after they occur). Many schools across the country have begun practicing special drills aimed at getting children out of buildings as quickly as possible after an attack on a school occurs. These drills, part of school crisis management plans, are efforts to respond most appropriately to school crimes, *after* they occur. Hull (2000), a superintendent of schools in Kansas, discusses his experiences with monthly meetings to review crisis plans. Because of this, they can be considered tertiary crime prevention.

The largest share of the literature on preventing school violence suggests that officials should make alterations to the physical school environment (Gonzalez, 1994; Johnson & Johnson, 1995; Petersen & Petersen, 1993; Stephens, 1995; Watson, 1995). Literally, dozens of lists of CPTED strategies have been developed. One such list, developed by the Center for the Study and Prevention of Violence, is included as Appendix A.

Many wonder whether investments in alarm systems, security cameras, and so on are actually worth the money (Kaufer, 1997). Additionally, schools in large cities, such as New York City, have begun installing metal detectors at school entrances and allowing police to patrol schools considered "tough" and/or "dangerous." New York City schools also have mandated that anyone who brings any weapon to school will be expelled if he/she is over seventeen years of age. Other school jurisdictions will now expel students who are caught in possession of any weapon, including knives packed in their school lunches by their parents.

Schools all across America have resorted to target hardening mechanisms to reduce the likelihood of school violence at their campuses. Target hardening devices, such as locks on doors and bars on windows, reduce opportunities for crime by simply making it harder to get to potential targets (Crowe, 1990). Kelly (1999) outlines America's growing reliance on technology to help harden school targets. The survey of schools by Agron and Anderson (2000) found the most common security features in schools were locks in elementary, middle, and high schools. The second most common form of technology varied: at elementary schools, it was call boxes; at middle schools, it was ID card systems; and at high schools, it was CCTV (closed-circuit television).

The most common programs in American schools are intervention programs for troubled children, zero tolerance policies for fighting and weapons violations, and increased searches of students and their lockers. Table 4–2 illustrates the most common forms of school security equipment in America's schools. Also note that other schools have added police officers to their campuses to do routine patrols (Chapeau & White, 1993).

Gaustad (1999), author of the report titled "The Fundamentals of School Security," suggests schools across the country should conduct periodic, routine security assessments of their campuses. Her report also advocates conducting surveys of parents, students, police, community representatives, and school staffers. Gaustad outlines many of the target hardening practices of schools, including handheld metal detectors, security cameras, and space allocation modifications. In fact, entire articles have been written about each security mechanism available (e.g., see Fickes, 1998; Flanary, 1997; Hylton, 1998; Kotlarczyk, 1998; Lebowitz, 1997; Maranzano, 1998; Moore, 1999; Trump, 1998). Easterbrook (1999) specifically discusses the installation of spiked fences and metal detectors, as well as the use of student searches and teacher training to diffuse violent situations. Other schools require visitors to sign in, have purchased two-way radios for all staff, and have installed panic buttons in common areas. Still others have set up anonymous telephone and Internet tipping sites to call in potential trouble before it happens (Clayton, 1998).

Green's (1999) report, *The Appropriate and Effective Use of Security Technologies in U.S. Schools: A Guide for Schools and Law Enforcement Agencies*, outlines methods to keep outsiders off campus, to prevent fights on campus, to fight vandalism, to prevent theft, to reduce drug use, to keep weapons off campus, to prevent malicious acts, to reduce parking lot problems, to prevent false fire alarms, to prevent bomb threats, to avoid bus problems, and to ensure teacher safety. These methods are described in Appendix B.

TABLE 4–2   Percentage of Schools Planning to or Having Already Installed Types of Security Equipment

Locks / door hardware	96.8 percent
CCTV (closed circuit television)	47.9 percent
ID card systems	40.1 percent
Call boxes	27.4 percent
Handheld metal detectors	23.4 percent
Access control card systems	17.3 percent
Stationary metal detectors	4.6 percent

Source: Agron and Anderson (2000).

Most people writing about how schools themselves can prevent violence rely on the traditional CPTED strategies of access control (reducing accessibility to outsiders), natural surveillance (increasing visibility to passersby), formal surveillance (using security to watch students), defensible space (making space users feel more responsible for watching their own spaces), and target hardening (making it harder to offend against a space) (See, for example, Safe Schools Facilities Planner, 1998). Such alterations to the physical environment are based around the premise that crime can be effectively prevented simply by changing the conditions conducive to it. Schneider (1998) suggests a well-designed office at schools could and should be the focal point of such CPTED strategies, with high levels of surveillance of both the outside and inside of schools, of entryways, as well as hallways and other common areas, particularly as these areas are those perceived to be where violent acts are most likely to occur (Crowe, 1990).

According to the USDOE and USDOJ (1998a, 1998b), designing "crime free" campuses will likely involve alterations to the physical environment, including:

- Controlling access to outsiders
- Reducing class and school size
- Diverting traffic flows away from risky areas
- Scheduling routine activities such as lunch
- Closing schools during lunch
- Adopting policies on school uniforms
- Rearranging supervision
- Prohibiting students from congregating in common areas
- Creating a constant adult presence in common areas
- Staggering dismissal times, lunch periods, gym periods
- Monitoring school grounds
- Eliminating "incivilities"
- Creating an effective communication system

Other popular efforts involve various forms of school discipline codes (Curwin & Mendler, 1993; Futrell, 1985; Hollinsworth, Lufler, and Clune, 1984; Leonard & Purvis, 1985; McBee, 1995; Menacker, Hurwitz, and Weldon, 1988; Menacker, Weldon, and Hurwitz, 1990b; Sauer & Chamberlain, 1985); mentoring at school (Ferguson & Snipes, 1994); mandating school uniforms (USDOE, 1996); school clubs (Office of Juvenile Justice and Delinquency Prevention, 1992); training teachers for potential violence (Glenn, 1990; Hughes, 1994); intervening in gang activity (Goldstein & Huff, 1993; Kodluboy & Evenrud, 1993); and reducing drug use by students (Garner, Green, and Marcus, 1994; Gaustad, 1991; Gibbs & Bennett, 1990; USDOE, 1987; Van Kammin & Loeber, 1992). Refreshing alternatives to target hardening and increased security mechanisms (which leave schools looking more like fortresses than schools) are available. Consider, for example, the numerous approaches called by names such as "invitational education" (Purkey, 1999), "teaching responsibility" (Kerr, 1985), "critical thinking" (Paul, Binker, Jensen, and Kreklau, 1990), and "moral education" (Wynne & Ryan, 1993). These efforts are geared toward making school more exciting, satisfying, and enriching to students and instilling values in students in the hopes that these students will be more engaged and connected to their schools, teachers, and classmates. These approaches involve altering the curriculum in order to prevent crime. Another approach aims to make schools "gentler" (Dill & Haberman, 1995).

Other efforts, such as after-school programs, are also aimed at reducing school crimes. Chaiken (1998) provides some details about these programs aimed at giving students something productive to do after school. According to Chaiken, violent juvenile crimes are typically committed during after-school hours between 2:30 and 8:30 P.M. More than five hundred organizations currently receive federal funds to prevent youth violence, including Boys and Girls Clubs of America, Boy Scouts of America, Girls Incorporated, Girl Scouts of the U.S.A., National Association of Police Athletic Leagues, National 4-H Council, and YMCA of the U.S.A. These organizations provide recreational opportunities for children not available elsewhere. Chaiken explains that effective after-school initiatives include high standards for children and assistance in meeting these standards, clearly stated rules and explicitly defined consequences, and activities that are varied, challenging, goal-directed, and humorous. Such research shows viable programs minimally need an adequate and safe meeting space, funding, well-trained leaders who understand children's needs, and community support.

Schools seem to be moving forward based on the premise that preventing school violence takes a team approach, including, at a minimum, students, teachers, and staff (Dean & Leaming, 1997). Many programs are problem-oriented in nature. Kenney (1998) discusses the results on one successful program. The School Safety Program, implemented in one school in North Carolina, was designed to bring together students, teachers, administrators, and the police to focus on and identify the school's problems and to develop effective responses to them. Its main components included regular meetings among faculty, administrators, and the police, problem-solving classes for the students, and regular reviews by the police and teachers to identify problem students. The program developed a required curriculum based on the SARA (scanning, analysis, response, and assessment) problem-solving model and was student driven (students identified and prioritized problems through open class discussions, then analyzed the problems and formulated responses and solutions).

Results showed less fear of crime at school, fewer acts of violence at school, fewer class disruptions, and fewer calls for police service. One notable example was that more than one thousand students were allowed to leave for lunch at the same time, increasing the likelihood of violence during lunch because there were only two serving lines in the lunchroom. Students identified this as a significant problem and proposed several solutions, one of which was actually adopted by the school, leading to a decrease in fighting behaviors during lunch time.

Conflict resolution programs are some of the most written about in school CPTED approaches (Bettmann & Moore, 1994; Bodine, Crawford, and Schrumpf, 1994; Brendtro & Long, 1995; DeJong, 1994a; Girard & Koch, 1996; Hocker & Wilmot, 1991; Inger, 1991; Kreidler, 1984; Meeks & Heit, 1995; National Association for Mediation in Education, 1994; National Institute for Dispute Resolution, 1994; Stephens, 1993; Townley & Lee, 1993). These programs will ideally prevent minor problems from escalating into serious violent behaviors.

Despite the success of some programs, our society must be careful not to invest in quick, short-term fixes. For example, Cox (1999) reviewed an alternative education program for at-risk delinquent youth and found the program only produced short-lived increases in student GPAs, school attendance, and self-esteem, as the effects were not observed in a follow-up period. Other crime prevention programs, such as DARE (Drug Abuse Resistance Education) have also been proven ineffective (Rosenbaum & Hanson, 1998), yet funding for this program continues in the millions of dollars.

Sherman et al. (1997) conclude effective crime prevention programs within schools include programs that communicate and reinforce clear, consistent norms (e.g., antibullying campaigns), classes for preschoolers with weekly home visits, and teaching of social competency and thinking skills (e.g., stress management, problem solving). Promising programs include schools within schools that offer more support and individual attention, behavior modification programs, classroom management training for teachers, conflict management, and skills and job placement programs. Programs that do not work include individual counseling and peer counseling, DARE, drug prevention classes focusing on fear and emotion, and leisure-time enrichment programs (e.g., supervised homework, self-esteem exercises).

Community Level Approaches.   Many successful crime prevention programs are conducted with the assistance of local communities, based on the premise that violence in neighborhoods and schools stem from the same factors (DeJong, 1994b; Linquanti, 1992; Menacker, Weldon, and Hurwitz, 1990a; Price, Cioci, Penner, and Trautlein, 1990). These programs have been aimed at preventing violence at school, as well as during travel to and from school (Casement, St. George, Tallent, and Bonnett, 1994). For example, the STARS program (Students Traveling and Arriving Safely) in California involves parent patrols, increased student awareness of potential dangers, as well as participation of city employees, citizen patrols, school district personnel, and police officers. The founders of the program assert the effectiveness of the program is based on the deterrent message sent to society that harming children in the community will not be tolerated (Bridges, 1999).

At least one study has found that characteristics of the surrounding neighborhood are not important for understanding in-school crime victimizations (Clark & Lab, 2000). Although this might imply school violence can happen in any neighborhood or community, we might also gain from such findings an understanding of how important it is for citizens in all communities to get involved in school crime prevention activities.

Indeed, the *Annual Report on School Safety* (1999, p. 11) reports "[s]chools cannot effectively deal with (serious crime and violence) problems without significant community support. Many communities are successfully reducing school crime and violence by adopting comprehensive, integrated community-wide plans that promote healthy childhood development and address the problems of school violence and alcohol and other drug abuse." To effectively reduce the likelihood of violence in schools in the community, community members and organizations must establish school-community partnerships and be intimately involved in the steps of program development, implementation, and evaluation.

Society Level Approaches.   In addition to the studies being conducted by agencies of government, such as the Secret Service, the U.S. Justice Department has, for two consecutive years, offered as much as $15 million in grants to help local police agencies deal with school violence in local communities. The grants, intended to be used for problem-oriented policing and crime analysis, are aimed at establishing meaningful partnerships between the police and schools in order to identify problems before they result in school violence and to respond most appropriately to crisis conditions (Bridges, 1999).

There is good reason for government to get involved in the problems of school crime and violence. Acts of violence committed at school do not occur in a vacuum; they are instead affected by factors in the larger society (Lindquist & Molnar, 1995; Nisbett, 1993). For example, there is an undeniable link between substance abuse and violence at the street level (Blaser, 1994; Center for Substance Abuse Prevention, 1995; Cleffman, 1992; Edwards, 1994; Elliott, Huizinga, and Menard, 1989; Martin, 1992; Spunt, Goldstein, Bellucci, and Miller, 1992; Wittman, 1990). Other important factors implicated as important for understanding violent behavior at the street level include low-economic status, high-population turnover, race and ethnicity, high-housing density, single-parent families, and ineffective child rearing (Laub & Lauritsen, 1998). And, according to the *Annual Report on School Safety* (1999), the prevalence of guns in society is a major source of school violence; thus, it advises parents to ensure that guns and other weapons are not available to unsupervised children. The Report also advises businesses and governments to get involved in school crime prevention. Specifically, the Report suggests businesses adopt local schools, provide training in basic job skills, provide internships and employment opportunities, provide scholarships, and offer resources to schools. Governments should provide leadership for school violence prevention through legislation and sponsoring of community forums, support empirical research into the problem, provide necessary funding to carry out school safety plans, and encourage collaboration by all parties. The bottom line is that school violence can only be prevented with the assistance of all concerned parties in society.

SYNTHESIS

Based on the research, it is quite apparent the most effective approach to preventing school crimes would be a comprehensive prevention program which incorporates all levels of analysis, from individual to society. That is, it would contain general primary and more specific secondary CPTED strategies aimed at making modifications to all types of environments. The government, in its *Annual Report on School Safety* (1999, p. 31), agrees by writing "safe schools are the product of careful planning and attention to physical, social, and cultural environments." It would also be one that involves cooperation of all interested parties (Axelrod, 1984; Beane, 1991; Bruner, 1991; Stephens, 1994). Given that families and schools have the most contact with children (and thus students), families and schools should be the focal point of school violence prevention programs. These institutions shape the children's brains and behavior. Logically, families and schools are best suited to identify problems before they "graduate" into criminal behavior and can best identify problem children before they commit crimes at schools (Seydlitz & Jenkins, 1998).

According to *A Guide for Safe Schools* (USDOE & USDOJ, 1998a), to prevent crime, schools should:

- Place a solid focus on academic achievement
- Involve families in meaningful ways

- Develop other meaningful links to the community
- Emphasize positive relationships among students and staff
- Discuss safety issues openly
- Treat all students with respect and promote good citizenship
- Encourage students to express concerns and find ways for them to share feelings
- Create referral systems for abused and neglected children
- Offer extended day care programs for children
- Conduct an environment assessment of each campus for correlates of criminal victimization
- Attempt to eliminate student mental and emotional problems
- Establish procedures for early identification of warning signs with clear procedures for communicating them to people who can use them effectively
- Conduct environmental assessments of campus
- Support students in making a transition to adulthood
- Provide service opportunities, work study programs, and career counseling
- Prepare a reactive, crisis preparation plan in case acts of serious violence do occur

Virtually every source out there on the problem of school violence advocates a team approach. Each suggests following *every single recommendation* to reduce the probability of school violence, even though "school communities could do everything recommended and still experience violence" (USDOE & USDOJ, 1998a). Another way to understand the problem of school violence is that the likelihood it will happen can be reduced by following certain recommendations, but it can still happen anywhere.

CONCLUSION

Crime Prevention Through Environmental Design (CPTED) strategies are aimed at changing factors in various environments to reduce the opportunity for those environments to support crime. CPTED is also geared to reduce fear of crime and perceptions of crime risks, increase the aesthetic quality of an environment, and increase the quality of life for law-abiding citizens, especially by reducing the propensity of the physical environment to support criminal behavior. Although there is no doubt that school violence has *not increased* in the last decade, many CPTED strategies can be used to reduce school violence even further.

In this chapter, I outlined numerous CPTED programs, including those at the individual level, group level, school level, community level, and society level. Because factors at each of these levels influence the amount and nature of school violence, each of these levels must be taken into account when designing, implementing, and evaluating school violence prevention programs. The effectiveness of prevention programs will likely be directly related to the number of factors within each of the levels of analysis that are taken into account. That being said, the most successful programs are likely to not only be comprehensive, but also flexible and responsive to the needs within each school and community in which it is housed.

Although we can be confident that CPTED efforts will work in most situations, particularly primary and secondary approaches, we can learn a valuable lesson about school crime prevention from the discipline of criminology. Evidence suggests about 5 percent of offenders commit more than 50 percent of street crimes. Similarly, "5 to 10 percent of students will need more intensive interventions to decrease their high-risk behaviors" (USDOE & USDOJ, 1998a). These truly needy children will need referrals to specialists. It will be impossible to prevent serious school violence without first admitting to the undeniable link between individual factors and criminality.

Finally, many model programs have already been developed and demonstrated as effective. These model programs ought to be copied by communities and schools seeking to start from scratch to address school problems. They include programs aimed at reducing aggression/fighting, bullying, family problems, gangs, racial bias and conflict, sexual harassment and violence, substance abuse, truancy and dropouts, vandalism, and weapons possession.

REFERENCES

AGRON, J. (1999). Safe havens: Preventing violence and crime in schools. *American School & University, 71*(6): 18–20, 22, 24.

AGRON, J., & ANDERSON, L. (2000). School security by the numbers. *American School & University, 72*(9): 6–11.

AMERICAN COUNSELING ASSOCIATION. (1999). *Professional counselors respond to school violence* [Online textfile]. Retrieved April 18, 2000 from the World Wide Web: http://www.counseling.org/schoolviolence

AMERICAN TEACHER. (1993). *Violence in America's public schools: The Metropolitan Life survey.* New York: Louis Harris and Associates, Inc.

AXELROD, R. M. (1984). *The evolution of cooperation.* New York: Basic Books.

BARRETT, P. M. (1992). Youth violence is a serious problem. In M. D. Biskup & C. P. Cozic (Eds.), *Youth violence* (pp. 17–22). San Diego, CA: Greenhaven Press.

BASTIAN, L., & TAYLOR, B. (1991). *School crime: A national crime victimization survey report.* Washington, DC: U.S. Department of Justice, Bureau of Justice Statistics.

BEANE, J. (1991). The middle school: The natural home of the integrated curriculum. *Educational Leadership, 49*(2), 9–13.

BENARD, B. (1991). *Fostering resiliency in kids: Protective factors in the family, school, and community.* Portland, OR: Northwest Regional Educational Laboratory.

BETTMANN, E. H., & MOORE, P. (1994). Conflict resolution programs and social justice. *Education and Urban Society, 27*(1), 11–21.

BILLINSLEY, K. (1991). School safety index. *School Safety, Spring,* 26.

BLASER, J. (1994). Violence and substance abuse in rural America: Foreword. Retrieved April 20, 2000 from the World Wide Web: http://www.ncrel.org/sdrs/areas/issues/envrnmnt/drugfree/v1blaser.htm

BODINE, R., CRAWFORD, D., & SCHRUMPF, F. (1994). *Creating the peaceable school: A comprehensive program for teaching conflict resolution.* Champaign, IL: Research Press.

BOHM, R. (1997). *A Primer on Crime and Delinquency.* Belmont, CA: Wadsworth.

BRANTINGHAM, P. J. & FAUST, F. L. (1976). A conceptual model of crime prevention. *Crime and Delinquency, 7,* 284–95.

BRENDTRO, L., & LONG, N. (1995). Breaking the cycle of conflict. *Educational Leadership, 52*(5), 52–56.

BRENER N., SIMON, T., KRUG, E., & LOWRY, R. (1999). Recent trends in violence-related behaviors among high school students in the United States. *Journal of the American Medical Association, 282*(5), 440–446.

BRIDGES, D. (1999). The STARS program: Students traveling and arriving safely. FBI Law Enforcement Bulletin, 68(8): 16–19.

BROOKS, B. D. (1993). Signs of the times. *School Safety, Winter*, 4–7.

BRUNER, C. (1991). *Thinking collaboratively: Ten questions and answers to help policy makers improve children's services.* Washington, DC: Education and Human Services Consortium.

CALLAHAN, C. M., & Rivara, S. P. (1992). Urban high school youth and handguns: A school-based survey. *Journal of the American Medical Association, 267,* 3038–3042.

CASEMENT, M. R., ST. GEORGE, D. M., TALLENT, K. A., & BONNETT, D. M. (1994). *OAD-related violence prevention tools for planning in your community.* Rockville, MD: Center for Substance Abuse Prevention (CSAP) Training System, New and Emerging Issues Project.

CENTER FOR SUBSTANCE ABUSE PREVENTION. (1995). *Making the link: Violence and crime & alcohol and other drugs (Prevention Works publication ML002).* Rockville, MD: Author.

CENTER FOR THE PREVENTION OF HANDGUN VIOLENCE. (1992). *Kids and handguns.* Washington, DC: Author.

CHAIKEN, M. R. (1998). Tailoring established after-school programs to meet urban realities. In D. S. Elliott, Hamburg, B. & Williams, K. R. (Eds.) *Violence in American Schools: A New Perspective* (pp. 348–375). New York: Cambridge University Press.

CHAPEAU, A. & WHITE, L. (1993). School resource officer creates positive image. *School Safety, Fall*, 16–17.

CLARK, R. D., & LAB, S. V. (2000). Community characteristics and in-school criminal victimization. *Journal of Criminal Justice, 28*(1): 33–42.

CLAYTON, M. (1998). Campus crime's new watchdog: The web. *Christian Science Monitor, 91*(23): 20.

CLEFFMAN, V. G. (1992). Drug use and discipline: A disturbing connection. *School Safety, Spring,* 20–23.

COX, S. M. (1999). An assessment of an alternative education program for at-risk delinquent youth. *Journal of Research in Crime and Delinquency, 36*(3): 323–336.

CROWE, T. D. (1990). Designing safer schools. *School Safety, Fall,* 9–13.

CROWE, T. D. (1991). *Crime prevention through environmental design: Applications of architectural design and space management concepts.* Boston: Butterworth-Heinemann.

CURWIN, R. L., & MENDLER, A. N. (1993). Classroom discipline without cultural bias. *School Safety, Fall*, 24–26.

DEAN, A. W. & LEAMING, M. P. (1997). A team effort. *American School & University 70*(1), 36, 38.

DEJONG, W. (1994a). *Building the peace: The resolving conflict creatively program.* Washington, DC: U.S. Dept. of Justice, National Institute of Justice.

DEJONG, W. (1994b). School-based violence prevention: From the peaceable school to the peaceable neighborhood. *NIDR Forum, 25,* 8–18.

DILL, V. S., & HABERMAN, M. (1995). Building a gentler school. *Educational Leadership, 52*(5), 69–71.

DRYFOOS, J. G. (1990). *Adolescents at risk.* New York: Oxford University Press.

EASTERBROOK, M. (1999). Taking aim at violence. *Psychology Today, 32*(4): 52–56.

EDWARDS, R. (1994). *Links among violence, drug use, and gang involvement.* Retrieved April 2, 2000 from the World Wide Web:http://www.ncrel.org/sdrs/ areas/issues/envrnmnt/ drugfree/ v1note.htm

ELLIOTT, D. L., HUIZINGA, D., & MENARD, S. (1989). *Multiple problem youth: Delinquency, substance use, and mental health problems.* New York: Springer-Verlag.

EWING, C. P. (1992). Violent youth crimes are not a serious problem. In M. D. Biskup & C. P. Cozic (Eds.), *Youth violence* (pp. 55–59). San Diego, CA: Greenhaven Press.

FERGUSON, R. F., & SNIPES, J. (1994). Outcomes of mentoring: Healthy identities for youth. *Journal of Emotional and Behavioral Disturbance Problems, 3*(2), 19–22.

FICKES, M. (1998). Guns, knives, and schools. *School Planning and Management, 37*(5), 20–22, 24–27.

FIRESTONE, D. (1999). After shootings, nation's schools add to security. *New York Times,* 148(51613), A1.

FLANARY, R. A. (1997). Making your school a safe place for learning. *Schools in the Middle, 7*(2), 43–45, 64.

FREED, D. (1992). The number of victims of teenage violence is increasing. In M. D. Biskup & C. P. Cozic (Eds.), *Youth violence* (pp. 23–30). San Diego, CA: Greenhaven Press.

FUTRELL, M. H. (1985). Cultivating the value of self-discipline. *School Safety, Fall, 6.*

GARNER, S. E., GREEN, P. F., & MARCUS, C. (Eds.). (1994). *Signs of effectiveness II: Preventing alcohol, tobacco, and other drug use: A risk factor/resiliency-based approach. (DHHS Publication No. SAM 94-2098).* Washington, DC: U.S. Government Printing Office.

GAUSTAD, J. (1991). *Schools respond to gangs and violence.* Oak Brook, IL: Midwest Regional Center for Drug-Free Schools and Communities.

GAUSTAD, J. (1999). The fundamentals of schools security. [Digest]. *ERIC Digest.* Retrieved from the World Wide Web: http://eric.uoregon.edu.

GIBBS, J., & BENNETT, S. (1990). *Together we can reduce the risks of alcohol and drug abuse among youth.* Seattle, WA: Comprehensive Health Education Foundation.

GIRARD, K., & KOCH, S. (1996). *Conflict resolution in the schools: A manual for educators.* San Francisco: Josey-Bass, Inc.

GLENN, J. (1990). Training teachers for troubled times. *School Safety, Fall, 20.*

GOLDSTEIN, A. P., & HUFF, C. R. (1993). *The gang intervention handbook.* Champaign, IL: Research Press.

GONZALEZ, L. D. (1994). *Preventing violence: Creating a safe schools infrastructure.* Minneapolis, MN: Center for Safe Schools and Communities.

GREEN, M. (1999). *The appropriate and effective use of security technologies in U.S. schools: A guide for schools and law enforcement agencies.* Albuquerque, NM: Sandia National Labs.

HANKE, P. J. (1996). Putting school crime into perspective: Self-reported school victimizations of high school seniors. *Journal of Criminal Justice, 24*(3), 207–226.

HAWKINS, J. D., FARRINGTON, D. P., & CATALANO, R. F. (1998). Reducing school violence through the schools. In Elliott, D. S., Hamburg, B., & Williams, K. R. (Eds.) *Violence in American Schools: A New Perspective* (pp. 127–155). New York: Cambridge University Press.

HOCKER, J., & WILMOT, W. (1991). *Interpersonal conflict (3rd ed).* Dubuque, IA: W. C. Brown.

HOLLINSWORTH, E. J., LUFLER, H. S., & CLUNE III, W. H. (1984). *School discipline: Order and autonomy.* New York: Praeger.

HUGHES, H. W. (1994, February). *From fistfights to gunfights: Preparing teachers and administrators to cope with violence in school.* Paper presented at the annual meeting of the American Association of Colleges for Teacher Education, Chicago, IL. ED 366 584.

HULL, B. (2000). The question is not if, but when . . . *American School & University, 72*(9), 68–69.

HYLTON, J. B. (1998). Security in motion. *American School & University, 70*(8), 21–22, 24.

INGER, M. (1991). Conflict resolution programs in schools. *ERIC digest no.74.* New York: ERIC Clearinghouse on Urban Education. ED 338 791.

JEFFERY, C. R. (1971). *Crime prevention through environmental design.* Beverly Hills, CA: Sage.

JEFFERY, C. R. (1977). *Crime prevention through environmental design.* Beverly Hills, CA: Sage.

JEFFERY, C. R. (1990). *Criminology: An interdisciplinary approach.* Englewood Cliffs, NJ: Prentice-Hall.

JOHNSON, D., & JOHNSON, R. (1995). Why violence prevention programs don't work and what does. *Educational Leadership, 52*(5), 63–67.

KAUFER, S. (1997). Is your security budget used effectively? *School Planning and Management, 26*(8), 28–30.

KELLY, A. (1999). Security gap. *EducationFM, 2*(1),16–19.

KENNEY, D. (1998). Crime in the schools: A problem-solving approach [Online service textfile]. Washington, DC: U.S. Department of Justice. Retrieved from the World Wide Web: http://www.ncjrs.org/txtfiles/fs000224.txt.

KERR, D. M. (1985). Class management teaches social responsibility. *School Safety, Fall,* 14.

KODLUBOY, D.W. & EVENRUD, L. A. (1993). School-based interventions: Best practices and critical issues. In A. P. Goldstein & R.C. Huff (Eds.) *The gang intervention handbook* (pp. 257–299). Champaign, IL: Research Press.

KOTLARCZYK, C. (1998). Playing it safe. *EducationFM 1*(1). Retrieved from the World Wide Web: http://www.facilitiesnet.com/NS/NS3e8bb.html.

KREIDLER, W. J. (1984). *Creative conflict resolution: More than 200 activities for keeping peace in the classroom-K-6.* Glenview, IL: Scott, Foresman.

LAB, S. L. (1997). *Crime prevention: approaches, practices, and evaluations* (3rd ed.). Cincinnati, OH : Anderson Publishing.

LAUB, J. H., & LAURITSEN, J. L. (1998). The interdependence of school violence with neighborhood and family conditions. In Elliott, D.S., Hamburg, B., & Williams, K. R. (Eds.) *Violence in American Schools: A New Perspective* (pp. 127–155). New York: Cambridge University Press.

LEBOWITZ, M. (1997). Smile, vandals—You're on candid camera. *School Planning and Management, 36*(12), 28–29.

LEONARD, R. L., & PURVIS, J. R. (1985). A lesson plan for effective student discipline. *School Safety, Fall,* 10.

LINDQUIST, B., & MOLNAR, A. (1995). Children learn what they live. *Educational Leadership, 52*(5), 50–51.

LINQUANTI, R. (1992). *Using community-wide collaboration to foster resiliency in kids: A conceptual framework.* San Francisco, CA: Western Regional Center for Drug-Free Schools and Communities, Far West Laboratory for Educational Research and Development.

MARANZANO, C. (1998). Are video cameras the key to school safety? *High School Magazine, 5*(5), 42–43.

MARTIN, S. E. (1992). The epidemiology of alcohol-related interpersonal violence. *Alcohol Health and Research World, 16,* 230–237.

MCBEE, R. H. (1995). Law-related education and violence prevention. *School Safety, Spring,* 24–28.

MEEKS, L. P., & HEIT, P. (1995). Conflict resolution and peer mediation. In M. Baker (Ed.), *Violence prevention: Totally awesome teaching strategies for safe and drug-free schools* (pp. 56–64). Columbus, OH: Meeks Heit Publishing.

MENACKER, J., HURWITZ, E., & WELDON, W. (1988). Legislating school discipline: The application of a systemwide discipline code to schools in a large urban district. *Urban Education, 23*(1), 12–23.

MENACKER, J., WELDON, W., & HURWITZ, E. (1990a) Community influences on school crime and violence. *Urban Education, 25*(1), 68–80.

MENACKER, J., WELDON, W., & HURWITZ, E. (1990b). Schools lay down the law. *School Safety, Winter,* 27–30.

MILLER, J. G. (1992). No, youth violence is not a serious problem. In M. D. Biskup & C. P. Cozic (Eds.), *Youth violence* (pp. 44–49). San Diego, CA: Greenhaven Press.

MOORE, D.P. (1999). Designing safer schools. *School Planning & Management, 38*(8), 12.

MUIR, E. (1992). School staff victimization: Monitoring the trends. *School Safety, Fall,* 4–6.

NATIONAL ASSOCIATION FOR MEDIATION IN EDUCATION [NAME]. (1994). *Initiating conflict resolution in schools: Teaching skills for effective, non-violent problem solving.* Amherst, MA: Author.

NATIONAL COUNCIL ON CRIME AND DELINQUENCY. (1994). *Images and reality: Juvenile crime, youth, violence and public policy.* San Francisco: Author.

NATIONAL INSTITUTE FOR DISPUTE RESOLUTION [NIDR]. (1994). Survey of schools dispute resolution programs across the country. *NIDR News, 1*(7), 6–9.

NISBETT, R. E. (1993). Violence in U.S. regional culture. *American Psychologist, 48*(4), 441–449.

OFFICE OF JUVENILE JUSTICE AND DELINQUENCY PREVENTION. (1992). Youth clubs will prevent youth violence. In M.D. Biskup & C.P. Cozic (Eds.), *Youth Violence* (pp. 151–158). San Diego, CA: Greenhaven Press.

PAUL, R., BINKER., A., JENSEN, K., & KREKLAU, H. (1990). *Critical thinking handbook: A guide for remodeling lesson plans in language arts, social studies and science.* Rohnert Park, CA: Foundation for Critical Thinking.

PETERSEN, O., & PETERSEN, E. (1993). Creating safe and caring elementary schools. *School Safety, Fall,* 11–15.

PRICE, R. H., CIOCI, M., PENNER, W., & TRAUTLEIN, B. (1990). *School and community support programs that enhance adolescent health and education.* Washington, DC: Carnegie Council on Adolescent Development.

ROBINSON, M. (2000). The construction and reinforcement of myths of race and crime. *Journal of Contemporary Criminal Justice 16*(2), 133–156.

ROBINSON, M. (1999). The theoretical development of crime prevention through environmental design (CPTED). *Advances in Criminological Theory, 8,* 427–462.

ROSENBAUM, D. P. & HANSON, G. S. (1998). Assessing the effects of school-based drug education: A six year multilevel analysis of project DARE. J*ournal of Research in Crime and Delinquency, 35*(4), 318–412.

SAFE SCHOOLS FACILITIES PLANNER. (1998*). Improving schools climate and order through facilities design* [Online textfile]. Retrieved from the World Wide Web: http://www.schoolclearinghouse.org/Availability.

SAUER, R., & CHAMBERLAIN, D. (1985). Discipline code improves climate. *School Safety, Fall,* 22.

SAVOYE, C. (2000). Violence dips in nation's schools. *Christian Science Monitor, 92*(141), 1.

SCHNEIDER, T. (1998). *Crime prevention through environmental design: School CPTED basics.* Retrieved from the World Wide Web: http://www.arch.vt.edu/crimeprev/pages.

SCHWARTZ, I. M. (1992). The problem of youth violence is exaggerated. In M. D. Biskup & C. P. Cozic (Eds.), *Youth violence* (pp. 49–54). San Diego, CA: Greenhaven Press.

SEYDLITZ, R., & JENKINS, P. (1998). The influence of families, friends, schools, and community on delinquent behavior. In Gullotta, T., Adams, G. R, & Montemayor, R. (Eds) *Delinquent Violent Youth: Theory and Interventions.* Advances in Adolescent Development: An Annual Book Series, 9 (pp. 53–97). Thousand Oaks, CA, Sage.

SHERMAN, L.W., GOTTFREDSON, D., MACKENZIE, D., ECK, J., REUTER, P. & BUSHWAY. S. (1997). *Preventing crime: What works, what doesn't, what's promising.* A report to the United States Congress. Prepared for the National Institute of Justice.

SPUNT, B. J., GOLDSTEIN, P. J., BELLUCCI, P. A., & MILLER, T. (1992). Race/ethnicity and gender differences in the drugs-violence relationship. *Journal of Psychoactive Drugs,22,* 293–303.

STEPHENS, J. B. (1993). A better way to resolve disputes. *School Safety, Winter,* 12–14.

STEPHENS, R. D. (1994). Developing and meeting objectives for school/community collaboration. In R.D. Stephens (Ed.), *Developing strategies for a safe school climate* (pp. 15–16). Westlake Village, CA: National School Safety Center.

STEPHENS, R. D. (1995). *Safe schools: A handbook for violence prevention.* Bloomington, IN: National Educational Service.

TAYLOR, R. B. & HARRELL, A. V. (1996). *Physical Environment and Crime.* National Institute of Justice Research Report. Washington, D.C.: U.S. Department of Justice.

TOWNLEY, A., & LEE, M. (1993). *Training for trainers: Staff development in conflict resolution skills.* Amherst, MA: National Association for Mediation in Education.

TRUMP, K. (1998). *Practical school security: Basic guidelines for safe and secure schools.* Thousand Oaks, CA: Corwin Press.

USA TODAY (1999). *Tragedy in Colorado.* Retrieved from the World Wide Web: http://www.usatoday.com/news/index/colo/colo000.htm.

U.S. DEPARTMENT OF EDUCATION. (1987). *What works: Schools without drugs.* Washington, DC: U.S. Government Printing Office.

U.S. DEPARTMENT OF EDUCATION. (1996). School uniforms: Where they are and why they work. [On-line]. Available: *www.ed.gov/updates/uniforms.html.*

U.S. DEPARTMENT OF EDUCATION (USDOE) AND U.S. DEPARTMENT OF JUSTICE (USDOJ). (1998a). *A Guide to Safe Schools* [Online service textfile]. Washington, DC: Author. Retrieved May 2, 2000 from the World Wide Web: http://www.ed.gov/offices/OSERS/OSEP/earlywrn.html

U.S. DEPARTMENT OF EDUCATION (USDOE) AND U.S. DEPARTMENT OF JUSTICE (USDOJ). (1998b). *Annual Report on School Safety* [Online service textfile]. Washington, DC: Author. Retrieved April 16, 2000 from the World Wide Web: http://www.ed.gov/pubs/edpubs.html

U.S. DEPARTMENT OF EDUCATION (USDOE) AND U.S. DEPARTMENT OF JUSTICE (USDOJ). (1999). *Annual Report on School Safety* [Online service textfile]. Washington, DC: Author. Retrieved April 16, 2000 from the World Wide Web: http://www.ed.gov/pubs/edpubs.html

VAN KAMMIN, W., & LOEBER, R. (1992). Drugs, delinquency and discipline. *School Safety, Spring,* 7–10.

WATSON, R. (1995). A guide to violence prevention. *Educational Leadership, 52*(5), 57–59.

WEBSTER, D. W., GAINER, P. S., & CHAMPION, H. R. (1993). Weapons carrying among inner-city junior high school students: Defensive behavior versus aggressive delinquency. *American Journal of Public Health, 63,* 1604–1608.

WITTMAN, F. D. (1990). Environmental design to prevent problems of alcohol availability: Concepts and prospects. In *Research, action, and the community: Experiences in the prevention of alcohol and other drug problems (OSAP Prevention Monograph-4).* Rockville, MD: U.S. Department of Health and Human Services.

WYNNE, E.A., & RYAN, K. (1993). Curriculum as moral educator. *American Educator, Spring,* 20–24, 44.

APPENDIX A   CENTER FOR THE STUDY AND PREVENTION OF VIOLENCE, RECOMMENDATIONS FOR SAFE SCHOOL PLANS

Campus Access and Control:

- Control campus access
- Define campus perimeters with appropriate landscaping and fencing
- Remove posters and student decorations from all window glass
- Establish uniform visitor screening procedures

- Post appropriate directional signs on the campus
- Require picture identification cards for each student and staff member
- Carefully manage and monitor hall passes
- Clearly separate and segregate mixed vehicular and pedestrian functions

Administrative Leadership:

- Mandate crime reporting and tracking
- Place school safety on the educational agenda
- Include school safety in the mission statement
- Develop a comprehensive, systemwide safe school plan
- Disseminate a summary of laws pertaining to school disorder
- Establish a state-of-the-art "Emergency Operation Communications Center"
- Develop a clear job description of duties and responsibilities for school peace officers
- Establish a crisis response plan
- Identify specifically assigned roles and responsibilities concerning security
- Work with administration to expand the network of alternative placement for troubled youth
- Establish a restitution and community service program at district schools
- Recognize the politics of safe schools
- Establish good management practices
- Conduct an annual review
- Promote crime prevention through environmental design
- Establish two-way communication between the front office and each classroom
- Identify and track repeat offenders
- Provide close supervision, remedial training, and restitution for serious habitual offenders
- Carefully screen and select new employees
- Conduct periodic joint meetings of all school staff and faculty
- Utilize existing technologies that promote crime prevention

School Climate:

- Make the campus safe and welcoming, beginning early in the morning
- Develop a nuisance abatement plan
- Develop a graffiti abatement and community cleanup program
- Create a climate of ownership and school pride
- Establish a parent center on each campus
- Enhance multicultural understanding
- Establish a vibrant system of extracurricular programs

Student Behavior and Management:

- Review the student handbook
- Articulate a clearly defined locker policy
- Develop and enforce a school dress code
- Review discipline and weapon possession policies
- Place students and parents on notice
- Provide adequate adult supervision
- Limit opportunities for the transport and storing of contraband
- Automobile and parking polices should state that campus parking is a privilege, not a right
- Add "hard looks" and "stare downs" as actionable offenses to the student code of conduct
- Train students to take responsibility for their own safety
- Conduct emergency drills

Staff Training:

- Conduct annual school safety training programs
- Establish an active school peace officer training program
- Provide teacher training in behavior management
- Establish professional development programs for campus supervisors and student personnel workers
- Establish a physical restraint policy

Student Involvement:

- Create an active student component
- Implement a peer counseling and peer mediation program at every school site
- Incorporate life skills curricula
- Create a student advisory council
- Develop a student crime prevention program
- Consider teen court as an option

Building Community Partnerships:

- Identify community resources
- Enhance interagency cooperation by creating a partnership among youth serving professionals
- Seek intensive community support and involvement in making the journey to and from school safe

- Establish a close police partnership
- Closely supervise troublemakers across agencies
- Capitalize on the school's ability as an organizational vehicle to provide comprehensive student services
- Consistently enforce the information sharing agreements
- Consider placing a probation officer on campus for students on probation

Source: Stephens (1998).

APPENDIX B: APPROPRIATE USE OF TECHNOLOGIES ON SCHOOLS' CAMPUSES

How to Keep Outsiders Off Campus

- Posted signs regarding penalties for trespassing
- Enclosed campus (fencing)
- Guard at main entry gate to campus
- Greeters in strategic locations
- Student IDs or badges
- Vehicle parking stickers
- Uniforms or dress codes
- Exterior doors locked from the outside
- A challenge procedure for anyone out of class
- Cameras in remote locations
- School laid out so all visitors must pass through front office
- Temporary "fading" badges issued to all visitors

How to Prevent Fights

- Cameras
- Duress alarms
- Whistles

How to Fight Vandalism

- Graffiti-resistant sealers
- Glass-break sensors
- Aesthetically pleasing wall murals (these usually are not hit by graffiti)
- Police officers living on campus

- Eight-foot fencing
- Well-lit campus at night

How to Prevent Theft

- Interior intrusion detection sensors
- Property marking (including microdots) to deter theft
- Bars on windows
- Reinforced doors
- Elimination of access points up to rooftops
- Cameras
- Doors with hingepins on secure side
- Bolting down computers and TVs
- Locating high-value assets in interior rooms
- Key control
- Biometric entry into rooms with high-value assets
- Police officer living on campus

How to Stop Drug Use (Including Alcohol)

- Drug detection swipes
- Hair analysis kits for drug use detection (intended for parental application)
- Drug dogs
- Removal of lockers
- Random searches
- Vapor detection of drugs
- No open campus at lunch
- Breathalyzer test equipment
- No access to vehicles
- No lockers
- Clear or open mesh backpacks
- Saliva test kits

How to Keep Weapons Off Campus

- Walk-through metal detectors
- Handheld metal detectors
- Vapor detection of gunpowder
- Crimestopper hotline with rewards for information
- Gunpowder detection swipes
- Random locker, backpack, and vehicle searches

- X-ray inspection of book bags and purses

How to Prevent Malicious Acts

- Setback of all school buildings from vehicle areas
- Inaccessibility of air intake and water source
- All adults on campus required to have a badge
- Vehicle barriers near main entries and student gathering areas

How to Prevent Parking Lot Problems

- Cameras
- Parking decals
- Fencing
- Card ID systems for parking lot entry
- Parking lots sectioned off for different student schedules
- Sensors in parking areas that should have no access during schooldays
- Roving guards
- Bike patrol

How to Prevent False Fire Alarms

- Sophisticated alarm systems that allow assessment of alarms (and cancellation if false) before they become audible
- Boxes installed over alarm pulls that alarm locally (screamer boxes)

How to Prevent Bomb Threats

- Caller ID on phone system
- Crimestopper program with big rewards for information
- Recording all phone calls, with a message regarding this at the beginning of each incoming call
- All incoming calls routed through a district office
- Phone company support
- No pay phones on campus
- Policy to extend the school year when plagued with bomb threats and subsequent evacuations

How to Avoid Bus Problems

- Video cameras and recorders within enclosures on buses
- IDs required to get on school buses

- Security aides on buses
- Smaller buses
- Duress alarm system or radios for bus drivers

How to Ensure Teacher Safety

- Duress alarms
- Roving patrols
- Classroom doors left open during class
- Cameras in black boxes in classrooms
- Controlled access to classroom areas

Source: Green (1999).

5

The Bibb County Model for Community Policing in Schools

Michael Dorn

❖

As the Chief of Police for the Bibb County Board of Education Campus Police Department in Macon, Georgia, for ten years, I was able to witness and be a part of a growing, dynamic, and unique police force, which has since become widely featured as a model school police unit. As I began to organize my thoughts for this chapter, my mind was flooded with memories of the exceptional work of the outstanding men and women who served with me in protecting the children of Bibb County. Just a few of the events that come to mind include:

- Sergeant Leroy Morgan was called to investigate an allegation that a middle school student had made threatening remarks to several students. The student was arrested after a partially constructed explosive device was recovered during a search of his bedroom. The investigation revealed that a planned school bombing had been prevented.

- Officer Earl Evans became frustrated when funding was unavailable for T-shirts for students graduating from the charter class of the Gang Resistance, Education, and Training Program (G.R.E.A.T.®). Officer Evans purchased $1,200 worth of T-shirts for these students with his own funds. He was instrumental in expanding this program to include seven certified officers. Currently, the program receives more than $300,000 in grant funding, with more than four thousand Bibb County students in attendance each year.

- Sergeant Stephanie Prater, working with her partner, a school social worker, was successful in getting a student back into school after this student missed more than 150 school days in the previous year. She served as a driving force in developing the department's Return to School Program, which significantly reduced truancy in the district.
- Officer Levi Rozier noticed a satanic symbol on a student's key chain during a random metal detector check of students. He worked closely with school administrators and school mental health specialists to investigate the situation. The team learned the student and his girlfriend had prepared a suicide pact and were about to take their own lives. Both students are alive today as a result of his alertness.
- Sergeant Steve Meadows of the Special Operations Unit observed two groups of gang members gathered under an overpass located near two different schools. As he is riding his mountain bike toward the area to intervene, several gang members open fire with handguns. Sergeant Meadows rides into the gunfire to break up the gunfight. Officer Kenneth Bronson of the same unit rode more than four miles on his mountain bike and arrived before any of the patrol cars from three responding agencies. Together, Officers Meadows and Bronson arrested two gang members and recovered three handguns. Another member of the department, former Deputy Chief Jeff Whitfield, apprehended a third suspect after a one-mile foot chase.
- The Georgia Women in Law Enforcement recognized Officer Lavonia Shropshire as the female police officer of the year. Among her accomplishments are two thwarted gang shooting attempts with six guns seized and seven suspects arrested, and her arrest of more than twenty individuals for stealing copper gutters from several area schools (causing more than $50,000 in damage).

Although these are only a few of the instances that come to mind, they serve to illustrate a level of dedication where Bibb County Board of Education Campus Police Officers frequently went above and beyond the call of duty. These examples show a desire to serve; they are the result of an effective partnership between the department and the community it serves. It was truly an honor and a privilege for me to serve with these men and women.

THE BIBB COUNTY MODEL

How did the department achieve such excellence? What forces brought the department and the community together? What motivated these individuals to work so stridently to live up to their motto "Let None Learn in Fear"? It will be helpful to go back in time to answer these questions.

The outlook for the Bibb County Board of Education Campus Police Department in August 1989 was bleak. The previous agency head had just been indicted and acquitted on criminal charges. He had been accused of obstructing a Macon Police Department investigation. One of his police officers had been convicted of charges relating to sexual acts involving a fourteen-year-old girl who was in his lawful custody for criminal charges. The scandal had been widely covered by the local and national media and had raised serious doubts about the integrity of a department that also lacked a reputation for efficiency and professionalism. I had been appointed as the new chief of police and given the task of guiding the department through a reorganization effort.

The reputation of the department was so poor that police officers from other area agencies would not even return a friendly wave when a Bibb Campus Police cruiser passed them on the roadway. The regional police training center would not accept recruits from the department for basic training as recognized police officers, and the Georgia Public Safety Training Center would not allow the department's officers to attend classes.

Within a decade, however, the men and women of the Bibb County Board of Education Campus Police Department would earn the right to wear their shields with pride. They would achieve remarkable results in reducing student weapons violations by an estimated 90 percent. They would see all criminal incidents on school property drop by an estimated 80 percent. Officers from the department would foil six planned school shooting attempts without a shot being fired, they would thwart a planned middle school bombing, and prevent a planned double suicide by two high school students. The men and women of the department would develop techniques that would be used by school districts and police agencies across the nation.

Bibb County Board of Education Campus Police Officers would become instructors in high demand. The department would build a strong working relationship with the Middle Georgia Law Enforcement Training Center and the Georgia Public Safety Training Center. Both institutions have frequently requested that officers from the department serve as guest instructors. District police officers would become popular presenters at seminars around the nation. In fact, officers from the department trained more than five thousand educators and public safety officials from all fifty states and six countries in 1999.

The department has since been widely highlighted as an international model for community policing in the school setting. With a strategy that is far more comprehensive than the standard School Resource Officer Triad approach, the Bibb County Model would draw increasing interest from many corners. A yearlong study commissioned by U.S. Attorney Janet Reno selected the Bibb County Model as one of the top sixty gun violence reduction programs in the United States. The U.S. Department of Education also selected the Bibb County program as one of the nation's top strategies following another intensive research effort conducted by the Hamilton Fish Institute for School and Community Violence. More than one hundred police agencies, school districts, and government organizations have sent personnel to Bibb County for on-site visits to learn more about the department's methods.

The Bibb County Model would be featured in numerous national news stories and in training videos produced by Georgia, Utah, and South Carolina state agencies. More than ten thousand copies of the video *Weapons in Schools* would be distributed worldwide in only one year. More than seven thousand five hundred copies of the video *Safe Schools: Prevention, Planning, and Response* that is produced by the Georgia Emergency Management Agency, Office of the Governor, the Bibb County Board of Education Campus Police Department, and Garrett Metal Detector would be distributed in the first year of production.

Most importantly, the men and women of the Bibb County Board of Education Campus Police Department would win the trust, respect, and gratitude of the community they served. When mass shooting incidents in schools grabbed the headlines, students and parents would stop officers on patrol to thank them for their efforts. Cards, letters, faxes, and e-mails of gratitude would arrive to show support for the department's efforts.

How did so much positive change take place in a community that is plagued with political divisions, funding problems, and significant youth gang activity? How can other communities benefit from the lessons learned in Bibb County? The answers lie in the forthright community-based approach utilized to develop practical solutions to pressing school violence problems. By involving the community in an open and honest way, incredible improvement has been attained.

In 1989, the Bibb County School Board decided that it needed to restructure and significantly upgrade the district police department. Created in 1972 as the Bibb County Board of Education Security Department, it had not kept pace with the changes in the school system. It was clear that a new image for the department was needed, and, more importantly, that meaningful change in the way the department and the school district addressed crime problems needed to take place. Over the next ten years, a comprehensive strategy was developed and implemented.

The Model can serve as a framework to develop a truly effective community policing strategy in any community. By focusing on the following components, any police agency can develop a strategy that is tailored to fit the unique requirements of its community. The key components in the Bibb County Model are:

1. The use of standardized reporting of all school criminal incidents and analysis of the resulting data to develop focused prevention and response measures.
2. Significant and meaningful involvement of a wide range of segments of the community within and external to the school system in the problem solving process. Utilizing the rich and vast resources available in the community to develop a comprehensive approach that addresses, as a whole, the wide range of challenges posed by our violent and complex society.
3. Careful selection of department personnel to recruit and retain quality personnel dedicated to the mission of providing a safe and productive environment for the education and healthy development of young people.
4. Intensive and continual employee development with an emphasis on a high degree of formal training and advanced education of personnel.
5. Empowering the department's personnel to do what it takes to get the job done—being correct in what is done rather than focusing on what is "politically correct."
6. Keeping the department in touch with the pulse of the community—remaining current on what those who are to be protected want and expect from the protectors. Keeping the public informed as to the dangers so it can understand, participate in, and support efforts that might otherwise be controversial.
7. Providing police personnel with the best available equipment to get the job done. Spending available funds on the most important tools for personnel rather than on expensive office trappings and administrative positions.
8. Developing a comprehensive salary and benefits package that allows the organization to attract and retain high-caliber personnel.
9. Utilizing a leadership style that views human resources as the organization's most valuable asset. Treating employees with genuine care, concern, fairness, and dignity and then demanding that they treat the public in the same manner.

10. Being open minded as an organization. Refusing to accept the "status quo" and thinking out of the box to develop effective solutions. Developing and fostering a mind-set among the department's members that the vast majority of school crime is preventable. Instilling the ideal that when a crime occurs on campus, the department has failed in its primary mission. Thinking beyond the traditional boundaries of the school and including the neighborhood surrounding the school in all safety efforts.

The Bibb County Model is very ambitious; it is also very pragmatic. The Model was far from simple or easy to put into place, but it has been remarkably effective. The dramatic improvement in the level of safety in and around the community's public schools is nothing short of a miracle. For a district that had traditionally experienced edged weapons assaults every year to achieve a level of safety that has caught the attention of major government research projects, the national and international media, and countless other organizations, it is nothing short of incredible. The Model required the support of a community that was unwilling to allow its children to be subjected to a level of violence in school that has been unfortunately accepted in many locales.

I would not suggest that the Bibb County Model is perfect. I would not even begin to recommend other communities try to replicate the system that has been designed and put into place to fit the needs of this community. What I would argue is that the key concepts used to develop the program that has worked so well in Bibb County will work in any community. A successful school safety strategy must be developed to fit the particular hazards, resources, and needs of the individual community. Although there are a number of concerns shared by every community, each is unique to a certain extent. Only a custom-tailored approach designed to fit the particular community will be truly effective.

There is a great demand for a simple approach or product to make schools safer. It would be wonderful if we could pass a law, buy something, or simply copy a single program and make our schools safer. However, life is not that simple. There is no single solution that will have a significant and lasting effect. Only a comprehensive approach can make a meaningful difference. One of the most critical components of a comprehensive approach is the development of an effective school/police partnership. No school safety program can work without this valuable and necessary component.

When I present seminars regarding the Model, I urge participants not to get too focused on the particular techniques used in Bibb County. Instead, I suggest they focus on the process that was used to develop the community's approach and on the key components of the Model. The specific techniques that have worked so well in Bibb County may or may not work as well in other specific settings. They are provided more as menu item ideas for consideration. The most important aspect of many of these techniques is that they demonstrate how we need to think outside of our traditional boundaries when we address school safety issues.

Many people get distracted by the idea of school district police departments and school resource officer programs. In working with more than one thousand school districts and police agencies from around the country, I have seen a great variety of both approaches. I have seen excellent examples of both types of operations, and I believe that either type can function well. Each scenario has its benefits and shortcomings. What is most important is that there is a quality operation with either situation.

This chapter includes an examination of the chain of events that took place in one community with the idea of providing useful "lessons learned" for the reader. I try to provide information that is useful no matter where your agency is in the process of assigning police personnel to the school setting.

THE KEY COMPONENTS

The following is a discussion of the specific key components of the Bibb County Model. The components are not ranked by order of importance; however, each concept has been critical in the development of the Model.

Standardized Reporting and Analysis of School Crime

The first step in addressing the district's crime problems involved the development of uniform reporting of incidents and analysis of data so that effective strategies could be developed. School districts in the United States and in many other countries are well known for trying to downplay, and even conceal, criminal incidents that occur on campus. Incidents that involve firearms seized from students, drugs on campus, sexual assaults, and other acts of violence have been and are still infrequently reported to police agencies in many areas. One Georgia alternative school administrator did not even notify the police when he found a bomb in a student's book bag. The Bibb County Public School System was no exception to this common problem in 1989.

Underreporting of school crime makes it difficult, if not impossible, to solve school safety problems. It is often amazing how far some public and private schools will go to maintain the image that their schools are safe. In the highly publicized mass school shootings in recent years, we have seen astounding examples of this. In one mass shooting incident, the principal began cleaning up the blood at the crime scene before the police arrived. Following another mass shooting incident, the school initially tried to submit its mandatory federal gun free schools report indicating that no weapons had been recovered from students even though a number of students had been shot by a student on campus. In another case, the city police chief had to advise a local principal that he would be arrested if he continued to fail to report criminal acts occurring on campus. The administrator was routinely flushing marijuana down a toilet and not reporting incidents to the police—this after a mass shooting had taken place in the district.

Underreporting can be sporadic or it can be institutionalized. In one large public school district, the school board attorney recently instructed school administrators, at a training session, to search students for firearms themselves and not to report gun violence to the police. These instructions are reckless from a safety standpoint, and the reporting instructions are in direct violation of state law.

The problem is also common in the private school setting. One private school did not notify the police after a student held his teacher and classmates at gunpoint for some time before being persuaded to give the gun to his teacher. Nowhere in the criminal code does the law maintain that a hostage situation is not a crime if it takes place on private school property. Years later, the board of directors of the same institution voted to instruct the headmaster to violate state law and not report criminal acts to the police because of the bad publicity that could ensue.

The failure of school officials to recognize and report school crimes is probably the single most difficult hurdle for police agencies to breach when it comes to improving the level of safety for students. Unless school officials are willing to work to discover and report all criminal acts in the school setting, effective strategies to increase the level of safety will be seriously compromised.

In many cases, school officials simply do not recognize school crime for what it is because they have not been properly trained. It is not uncommon for school officials to miss weapons, drugs, or other contraband when they attempt to search students, or their lockers, book bags, and vehicles. Many school districts unreasonably restrict their employees in searching students and their belongings, causing many items of contraband to be missed. School officials are rarely skilled at contraband recovery. In one of the recent mass school shooting incidents, school officials searched the suspect for a handgun prior to the shooting and failed to recover it.

Many school officials will state they have not recovered a gun from a student in several years as proof that they have a safe school. When we look at the available data, we find that only a tiny percentage of weapons brought to school are recovered. The School Safety Project of the Georgia Emergency Management Agency—Office of the Governor has developed estimates that indicate that for every gun recovered from a student, four thousand five hundred gun violations are missed. Self-surveys of students conducted annually by the Centers for Disease Control indicate that public and private school students carry weapons, drugs, and alcohol to school and use them at school far more often than most schools recover or report them.

Dr. Thomas Hagler was the Superintendent of Schools for the Bibb County Public School System in 1989. He provided a clear message "from the top" that administrators must begin reporting all serious criminal incidents to the campus police department. Some years later, Bibb County School Superintendent Dr. Gene Buinger further improved this approach with a written policy requiring school administrators to report any misdemeanor or felony violation to campus police. Very few school districts in the United States follow this practice, even today.

Accurate reporting requires not only that police officers be notified, but also that agency guidelines ensure reports are actually filed and can be tracked when incidents are reported to the police. Such reporting and tracking is required to properly and efficiently utilize available resources. Frequently, school district police units have resources that are not being used to address existing problems because the resources have not been properly matched to the problem areas.

Incomplete data will also greatly limit the ability of the community to compete for the numerous funding opportunities available through grant programs. A number of communities have been surprised when they could not obtain grant funding for school safety initiatives when they faced significant school safety challenges. Upon further examination, it is typically found that these communities were unable to adequately demonstrate need due to lack of statistical data.

Another important aspect of proper documentation is liability reduction. School systems that fail to comply with state and federal reporting requirements may find their violations of the law haunt them if they are sued following an incident. Plaintiffs' attorneys may find it quite easy to paint them as dishonest in a court of law following a major act of violence when it can be shown that incidents have not been reported as required by law.

Reporting is only one critical aspect. Another aspect just as important is the implementation of a system to make it easier to efficiently use the information gathered. For many communities like Bibb County, this can best be accomplished with computer software.

There are a number of quality computer software programs to record and track incidents that take place on and near school property. The Bibb County Campus Police Department initially used a computer program written by one of the department's officers. Later, grant funding was used to purchase a much more sophisticated software system, which also allowed for incident mapping. This system allowed the department's crime analyst to track and map incidents on campus and in the school safety zones surrounding each campus.

In Bibb County, the effort went as far as to obtain a grant-funded position for a full-time crime analyst. Deputy Chief Russell Bentley was able to successfully compete for this funding to purchase software systems, the crime mapping system, a number of computer terminals, and the crime analyst position because he could demonstrate that the resources were needed and would be wisely utilized. Through proper documentation and tracking of incidents, he was not only able to obtain nearly one million dollars in federal grants to address school crime problems, but he was also able to set up an improved information system to see that those resources were used in the most efficient manner. As a bonus, the detailed information generated by the improved tracking and analysis make it easier for the department to compete for future grant programs.

In the case of larger school districts, it is highly recommended that a computer tracking system be utilized. In some cases, it will be practical to utilize existing software used by a municipal or county police agency providing school resource officers. It is often surprising to see how computer tracking of incidents can highlight problems not identified in the past.

Involvement of the Community in the Problem Solving Process

Another issue of considerable importance is that of public confidence. Time after time, we see school systems lose the confidence of their communities when it becomes clear they have been hiding their problems. Over time, the public is slowly becoming better informed about school crime. Once public confidence is lost, it is difficult to restore it without a change in leadership. In some communities, this has occurred when school superintendents have been replaced following a major incident.

Dr. Thomas Hagler, who was the Bibb County School Superintendent when the reorganization process began, was stunned when he became aware of the volume and types of weapons being seized on his campuses. After he viewed a table covered with guns and knives confiscated from students and given hard numbers involving criminal incidents on school property, he decided that significant action was required: he brought the community into the problem solving process.

Dr. Hagler created a community task force to help the district develop more effective ways to improve the level of safety in local schools. Efforts were made to include every segment of the community in the process. Public meetings were scheduled at each of the district's high schools. Representatives from the Macon Police Department, the Bibb County Sheriff's Department, the local faith community, the Juvenile Court of Bibb County, the Macon Judicial Circuit District Attorney's Office, the media, the general public, and, most importantly, educators and students were invited.

Although a number of school safety centers now advocate this type of approach, it was rather unique to see such efforts more than a decade ago. At the time, Dr. Ronald Stephens of the National School Safety Center was a lone voice in the forest with his advocacy of such intensive community involvement in school safety. Such a move in the early 1990s was bold and innovative.

The meetings held by Dr. Hagler were not simply public relations dog and pony shows which only serve to further alienate the public from school systems. Too often, we see efforts that turn out to be lip service to the public. This was not the case with these meetings. The public could see that Dr. Hagler was genuine in his desire to involve them in the process of making the children safer.

I am often asked by participants in my seminars how the Bibb County Public School System was so far ahead of many similar school systems in its safety program. I point out that these meetings were held long before school safety became such a hot topic. In fact, they began almost a decade before the general public became alarmed by the series of highly publicized major school violence incidents of the late 1990s. The major difference in the Bibb County Model is the school system accepted that a risk of a shooting was present and openly communicated this fact with the public. This rather unique approach resulted in an unprecedented level of community support and involvement in changing the situation.

It should also be remembered that the Bibb County Public School System has had sworn police officers assigned to its schools since 1972. In 1989, there were only twelve school districts in the State of Georgia that had sworn police personnel assigned to their schools. Although most Georgia school districts have followed Bibb County's lead and developed a police partnership, the school district had already addressed many issues by the early 1990s that are still new to other communities. This previous history of police involvement in the school system allowed the Bibb program to develop at an accelerated rate.

Our school district's key personnel realized at the time that any school district could be impacted by a major act of violence. Even though the first meetings drew less than fifty people each, they did serve to bring the most critical players to the table. We began to make significant progress immediately as each group represented began to input. Some of the usual problems of turf and politics surfaced, but by and large, people came together in a positive manner.

One aspect of these meetings that helped to create a positive environment was the direct approach to problem identification and problem solving. People who attended the meetings were very appreciative about receiving accurate and meaningful information regarding problems in the district relating to weapons, drugs, and acts of violence. They also were pleased to see the school system's willingness to work with other agencies to address school system concerns as part of a larger picture of community problems.

Using the concepts developed in part by the National School Safety Center, the community-based approach began to show immediate results. The community task force quickly accepted responsibility for problem solving with the school district. This is a critical point that should not be underestimated. By allowing the community, through its representatives, to buy into the problems, a base of powerful support began to grow. In addition, innovative and creative suggestions came from the new partners.

One of the first and most significant developments involved the staffing level of the campus police department. Once the group was made aware of how many sworn personnel were on staff in the department and how they were deployed, a consensus was formed that additional personnel were needed. Over the next ten years, the department added three civilian personnel and thirteen sworn officers. This expansion of the department could not have occurred without the strong support of the task force. In one instance, more than four hundred parents signed a petition to the school board requesting that an extra police officer be funded for the Southeast High School District. This information was used to help demonstrate need for a Community Oriented Policing Grant that was awarded to the campus police department.

Another important achievement came from a suggestion made by a student who attended one of the task force meetings. When informed of the number and types of weapons being seized from students, the group felt a program to reduce weapons violations must be developed. When a study concerning entry point metal detection was made, it was determined that it would require millions of dollars each year to maintain. There were also significant concerns that such a program would be ineffective due to the configuration of many of the district's facilities and the way class changes were structured.

During this discussion, a student asked what at first seemed like a stupid question. He asked why every student had to be checked by a metal detector each day. He suggested that district police officers conduct random surprise metal detector checks on a regular basis to deter potential violators. At first, the idea was dismissed because of concerns that it would not be legal to conduct such checks. But after discussing the idea with Dr. Gary Avery, who is a nationally recognized expert in school search and seizure, we learned that such searches were legal if done properly. The random weapons screening system that was developed from the student's suggestion is now used by many districts across the nation as a result of the successful use of the concept in Bibb County.

Over the next decade, a variety of formal and informal meetings were held with different groups in the community. This continual dialogue has led to significant progress, as the department has been able to adapt to the changing needs of the community. There have also been numerous new ideas to come from those implemented as part of a broad strategy, creating a much safer school environment. This continual dialogue with the community has led to a strong support system that has allowed the campus police department to successfully address a wide range of problems.

Careful Selection of Department Personnel

One of my management professors had a saying: "If you hire bums and train them, all you have are trained bums." This caution has particular relevance for police officers. Police personnel must be exceptional individuals to properly apply the skills they learn in the academy. Unfortunately, some police agencies are preoccupied with filling slots rather than taking the time to locate and hire individuals who can truly succeed and who will provide a lasting contribution to the agency. Police chief positions are filled with new personnel every twenty-four to thirty-six months nationally, and turnover rates for many departments run in the 20 to 30 percent range annually. In many cases, high turnover is beyond the control of the chief police officer, but in other situations it is not.

The field of K–12 policing is a very specialized one. The assignment is much more complex than the typical patrol or traffic division position. Any school police unit with moderate to high turnover of personnel will not be as effective as it could be. One of the best ways to reduce turnover in the unit is through proper screening of personnel. Fortunately, there has been a shift toward proper screening of police personnel during the past two decades. But the field of campus policing requires a modified screening approach compared with what is used for other types of assignments.

Police personnel assigned to protect our schools must first be screened for integrity and moral fortitude just as with other policing assignments. Standard screening procedures should be utilized including:

- Criminal history check
- Driver history check
- Credit history check
- Drug screen
- Polygraph
- Reference checks
- Psychological testing
- Integrity testing
- Assessment panel

For the purposes of this chapter, it shall be presumed that a thorough background investigation has been conducted on all sworn personnel prior to their assignment. We now examine the unique screening considerations that help match the right personnel to the school community they will serve.

It is first important to understand that many excellent street officers are not well suited for assignment to the K–12 environment. It is a great disservice to police personnel and to the school community to assign officers who will only have to be replaced at a later time because they do not match the assignment. A key consideration is to ensure the school assignment is one considered desirable in the eyes of sworn staff. In some departments, the School Resource Officer (SRO) assignment is utilized as a "goof up squad" for officers who cannot qualify on the firearms range, cannot handle street duties, or receive poor performance evaluations. Of course, such practices are prone to result in a unit that is limited in effectiveness.

Some school police agencies ensure that top-flight personnel will be attracted to their organizations by offering a premium salary and benefits package. In some areas of the country, it is not unusual to see a school district police force that offers a salary and benefits package considerably more attractive than what is available from area police agencies. Some school district police departments also allow their officers to have the same work schedule as teachers to enhance their recruiting efforts. Compensation is only one factor; it is difficult to compete for top personnel without offering a competitive package.

Many county and municipal police agencies have also found ways to ensure that assignment to the School Resource Officer unit is seen as desirable. Some agencies have used a salary supplement to ensure that officers assigned to the school setting are paid a higher salary. Others have created a work schedule that allows officers who work in schools to be off from work during the summer months, similar to those used by some school district police agencies. Regardless of the particular incentives offered, these agencies have made the assignment a choice one.

Attractive positions alone do not ensure quality. The author is familiar with two school district police departments that offer compensation packages that are nothing short of extraordinary. Both are widely considered to be agencies of poor quality. In each case, the agencies are considered by many to be a facade of police service rather than focused on providing quality protection. Any competent police executive understands that police personnel are motivated by a variety of factors. Pride is one of the most important of these factors.

Once quality personnel have been attracted to the unit, they must be developed to fit the role for which they are selected. The program should also be designed to minimize turnover to be efficient. To meet these objectives, leadership styles and practices need to be appropriate for the unique situations presented by the school/police partnership.

Intensive and Continual Employee Development

Georgia requires that all sworn personnel complete a ten-week basic training program prior to certification. Officers must also complete twenty hours of classroom training each year. Although this provides a solid basic foundation, individual departments are tasked to provide advanced training appropriate to their agency after officers complete the basic training program. Georgia police agencies are blessed with easy access to a wide range of high-quality police training for their personnel. The philosophy of the Bibb County Model is that all school-based officers require a high degree of advanced training.

In 1990, an intensive training effort began for all sworn campus personnel. Over the next ten years, campus police officers would receive between three and six weeks of advanced training per officer per year. Officers would regularly attend classes at the Middle Georgia Law Enforcement Training Center, the Georgia Public Safety Training Center, the Macon Police Academy, the Federal Law Enforcement Training Center, the Regional Counter-Drug Training Academy in Mississippi, and other locations throughout the region.

Officers received training in basic policing skill areas, such as advanced firearms and driver training, and in specialty areas, such as statement analysis or child abuse investigation. A standardized training program was developed that would require each officer to attend the thirteen advanced level courses required for Georgia intermediate and advanced peace officer certifications. A concerted effort was made to have all sworn personnel complete these courses in as short a time frame as possible.

Particular emphasis was placed on use of force training. Officers received training in verbal skills, open hand control and restraint, pepper spray, baton, and firearm techniques annually. The annual use of force refresher course was set at forty hours to ensure that officers remain current on critical perishable skills. When scheduling permitted, officers fired on a different combat pistol practice course each month.

At the same time, individual officers received advanced training in specific topical areas. Officers were groomed with high levels of advanced training in areas where they demonstrated a willingness to learn and an aptitude to grasp the concepts covered in the training programs. If an officer was interested in youth gangs and demonstrated a commitment to working with youth gang problems, the officer would be sent to attend courses pertinent to that topic. Within a few years, the department had the luxury of having a number of officers who were extremely skilled and well trained in a number of specialty areas. Within a decade, the average level of training in the department was ten months of academy training per officer.

As a result of this intensive training, the level of effectiveness of the department began to increase. As officers became more skilled, they also became more confident in their ability to perform their duties. Officers were able to apply their skills to resolve problems, not just handle calls for service. As the capabilities of the officers increased, so did the amount of respect the public had for them.

It is interesting to note that no civil actions were filed against the school district, the department, or any officers for any reason from 1989 to the present. Considering the large number of enforcement actions taken by officers in the department, this is an excellent track record. There is little doubt the extensive training of officers played a part in keeping the department out of litigation, while making use of assertive enforcement tactics.

As demonstrated by the total absence of civil suits, such a high level of training is cost-effective. But cost-effectiveness was seen in other ways as well. In one incident involving a school bus accident, the department's traffic accident reconstructionist was able to charge and convict a motorist who was driving under the influence of cocaine, at twice the posted speed limit, with a suspended driver license. The accident was originally being worked by an outside agency as it occurred off school property. The officer who originally investigated the accident missed all of the contributing factors except for speed and had cited the bus driver for the accident! As the school bus was totaled and more than ten students were injured, the accident could have been a costly one for the district. Our officer was able to prove the other driver to be at fault in court, and thus shift the civil liability where it belonged. A school board attorney estimated this one reconstruction saved the district insurance carrier in excess of $750,000.

By continually demonstrating the money saved through extensive training, others in the school system could see the importance of training efforts. Over time, the central office administration not only allowed officers to receive regular high quality training, but they also came to expect officers to get it. As an extra benefit, this high level of training made employment with the department even more desirable.

Employee Empowerment

As the capabilities of the officers in the department improved, they were given increased latitude to perform their duties. The chief and deputy chief focused on resisting the temptation to structure every aspect of an officer's work environment. They believed many police departments become too focused on paramilitary discipline to gain compliance from their personnel at the sacrifice of performance.

Officers were continually told to focus on solving problems rather than simply responding to calls for service. They were also continually drilled with the idea that they should strive to bring lasting resolutions to situations that interfere with a peaceful learning environment.

The school setting is an environment where small disputes between individuals can turn into major incidents of violence if proper intervention does not occur. A seemingly routine complaint of a verbal altercation between two students in today's world can end up in a school homicide. Such a severe case is statistically uncommon, but investigating officers may not initially know which of the many thousands of such cases has this potential. Only by handling each case thoroughly can we hope to intervene in those with the potential for tragedy.

Police officers can be loaded with policies and concerns to the point of being disciplined and very efficient at following rules, yet be ineffective at providing meaningful solutions to the citizens they serve. Because of the unique nature of the school assignment, this can be even more of an issue for officers assigned to this setting. A typical example of this would be the many police departments who fail to or refuse to properly research the area of school search and seizure. By requiring their officers to follow the department's standard search and seizure guidelines, weapons are not recovered, and weapons assaults occur that could have been prevented.

The approach utilized in the Bibb County Model involved intensive research into the legal authority of schools to protect the children under its care. In particular, guidance was sought from legal experts who specialize in the field of policing in the school setting. The Law Advisory Group is a firm specializing in school/policing matters. Attorney instructors from the group help ensure school districts make full use of the enhanced authority granted to schools by the courts to provide a safe learning environment. The department began sending officers to training sessions given by this group. Using information provided in the seminars, the department began using its enhanced authority to provide an increased level of protection for Bibb County students.

As a result of the legal research, officers were empowered to search students and their belongings much more readily than had been common practice in Georgia schools. The number of weapons and contraband recovered increased dramatically as guns, knives, drugs, and other items were seized that would not have been recovered in the past. It became clear that those who believed the majority of weapons carried to school were already being recovered were overly optimistic.

Due to the compensation package and working conditions, most officers hired were seasoned officers in good standing from other agencies. New officers came to the department from a variety of agencies from Georgia and other states. The officers in the department have expressed a freedom to operate—an ability not present in their previous agencies—as one of their primary reasons for coming to this department. The Model created an environment that allowed our personnel to excel with the freedom to perform their duties.

This unique operating environment is very different than the typical police operation. It does allow for some minor inefficiency to exist (or what some could see as inefficiency). It is important to remember the amazing performance of the unit when this aspect is considered. The departmental philosophy became one of quality service with a great deal more empowerment for line employees than what is the norm in the field of policing. Accordingly, there was an explosion of creativity in the agency.

Alignment with Community Expectations

One problem in many school districts is that students and parents are not provided the level of protection they expect and, in fact, deserve. By involving every aspect of the community and by listening to what the public really wants, the department can be in tune with what is desired. One of the biggest barriers in many communities is the lack of trust that results when the public begins to realize they are not being provided with accurate information relating to incidents that take place in the school setting. When schools cover up criminal incidents, word still gets around. When people find out that one incident has been covered up, they typically assume many other incidents are also being concealed.

My experience in Bibb County and in working with schools around the nation is that when students and parents are informed of incidents which occur, they can accept the fact that their community is faced with the same challenges as other communities around the country. More importantly, they begin to trust school and police officials and lend their support in solving the problems faced by schools. This trust and support is essential for the creation of meaningful solutions.

The Bibb County community was prone to the same concerns as many communities. By being open and honest with the community, the department demonstrated it was open to the idea that improvement could be attained. When the public began to view the school system as willing to admit it faced problems and wanted public input, many people became willing to take a seat at the table. When this took place, people were quick to identify what was expected of the school system. Once this situation existed, the department could begin the process of aligning itself with what was expected from it.

The community provided a clear message that it wanted a larger and more active school system police department than what had been in place in past years. It is also important to note this process is not a one-time proposition. The concept of alignment with the community is continual. School crime trends are not static. As the concerns posed by our changing society evolve, so must the police agency.

For example, when the public became frightened by the series of highly publicized mass school shootings, they began to expect an increased level of protection from officers assigned to the school setting. The Bibb County Board of Education Campus Police Department responded by increasing the capabilities of the department to prevent such situations and by extensive work with the media to make the public aware of these efforts.

The process of maintaining alignment with the public is not a one-time event. Continual efforts to solicit feedback are necessary as community expectations change over time. New concerns arise as our society changes and as communities develop. By continually providing opportunities to communicate with the public, school police personnel can ensure that their efforts reflect what the community expects.

Providing Personnel with Quality Equipment

Like any other service provider, a police officer must have the tools of the trade to get the job done. A high priority in the department was to provide each officer with high-quality equipment for the job. Like most police agencies, the Bibb County Board of Education

Campus Police Department did not have an adequate budget. It became a priority to acquire quality equipment for the department.

In 1989, the campus police department had only a $5,000 budget per year to purchase uniforms and equipment. At the time, the department was staffed by only fifteen officers and five dispatchers, but the meager budget was not adequate for the department's needs. Officers had to provide their own service weapons, and were provided with only the most meager compliment of uniforms and basic equipment.

A complete assessment of the department's equipment was begun. Officers were asked what types of equipment they needed, and a general concept of what was needed was formed. Considerable efforts were made to convince the school board to dramatically increase the department's equipment budget. A series of presentations were made to key school district administrative personnel and to the school board.

Over time, the district began to increase funding levels for the department's equipment needs. A midyear budget transfer funded a new dedicated radio system so the department would no longer be forced to operate on the school system maintenance radio frequency. Over the next few years, four radio repeater stations were added to improve radio communications. The first new police package police vehicles in the department's history were purchased and fully equipped. More importantly, the annual budget allotment was raised to $45,000 for the purchase of uniforms and equipment.

The department was the first in the region to adopt a standardized semiautomatic service pistol. All officers were issued boom microphones to enable them to communicate more reliably during athletic events, pep rallies, and other environments where background noise can be a problem. Officers were also issued a variety of specialized uniforms for different work assignments.

By 1999, more than half of the officers in the department had been issued laptop computers. The department had acquired two LCD projectors for use in teaching programs to students, school system personnel, and community groups. Eighteen police vehicles had been purchased, including two sport utility vehicles. Eleven police bicycles had been purchased through the use of asset forfeiture funds. Every officer had been issued heavy tactical body armor and a kevlar helmet. In short, officers were very well equipped for a department of its size.

Through proper training and equipment, Bibb County Board of Education Campus Police Officers were able to reach their full potential in reducing crime in local schools and to considerably clean up the neighborhoods around the schools. These areas were made safer and policing more efficient by providing the officers with the "tools of the trade."

A Competitive Salary and Benefits Package

One common problem faced by many police agencies is the difficulty in attracting and retaining quality personnel. Many factors other than salary and benefits are important to departments in recruiting and keeping top-quality officers. However, any department not competitive with area agencies will have difficulty in this regard. The pay structure in the campus police department was not structured like the pay scales used by other agencies in the area. The department's pay scale was competitive in some ways and not inadequate in others.

The department's pay scale was below the area average when hiring a new officer who did not have many years of police experience. The scale did allow officers to be credited with up to fifteen years of policing experience, making the salary attractive to veteran officers. Unfortunately, the system did not provide any credit for advanced training or college education.

The department increased its qualifications to include a minimum of two years of college coursework, or two years of police experience, or a combination of the two equaling two years. This raised the minimum standard well above that of most agencies in the region. The City of Perry Police Department was and still is the only other middle Georgia police agency with a college requirement.

The ideal candidate for employment with the department would have a four-year degree, advanced training, and more than two years of policing experience. However, to attract quality individuals with these credentials, a pay scale that reflects the value of these qualities had to be developed. In 1998, the department finally had the opportunity to do so.

The school district had tried to supplement the sworn staff of the department by contracting with a private security company to hire a number of security officers. The experiment was a dismal failure. The company sometimes provided individuals who had previous arrests for serious crimes and who were otherwise unfit for duty. When the service was discontinued, the decision was made to utilize a significant portion of the contract funds to improve the compensation package offered by the department.

A series of meetings was organized to provide all personnel with the opportunity to help develop the new pay structure. Due to the limited amount of available funds, Deputy Chief Russell Bentley and I made the decision to take care of the needs of line personnel and to not make any adjustments to our salary levels. The meetings were well attended and quite productive.

As a result of the meetings, it was decided that the most efficient way to use the available funds (about $75,000 for that year's budget) would be to upgrade the salary level of communications personnel by three full pay grades and to develop a credential-based incentive pay plan. Through much discussion, a consensus was reached as to what credentials we wanted to reward with bonus pay. The idea was to make the department more attractive to the types of applicants the department needed, while adequately compensating those members of the existing staff who either had those credentials or the motivation to acquire them.

The process identified the following to be of value to the department:

- Police experience (counted at twice the rate for experience with the department)
- Advanced police training with additional credit for major training programs such as the FBI National Academy
- Advanced police certifications or completion of specifically beneficial advanced training programs (such as the School Resource Officer Program, Instructor Training Certification, or certification to teach the Gang Resistance, Education, and Training Program)
- College coursework with additional credit for earned degrees
- Prior military service

A separate incentive pay scale was designed for the position of police sergeant. This pay schedule was geared to those desirable assets for a supervisor, such as supervision experience and advanced leadership training and certifications.

When the group had reached a consensus, it was decided that Deputy Chief Bentley and I would design a point scale using feedback from the group. The point scale was painstakingly developed which would make maximum use of available funding to attract and retain officers with the experience, training, and education needed by the department. When the proposal was completed, it allowed officers to be compensated with an incentive pay amount ranging from $1,000 to 4,200 per year. Officers could also move up into the next supplement range at any point during the year if they earned enough points to qualify for the next level.

Any police executive knows it can be extremely difficult to obtain significant pay increases for officers. It is interesting to note that the only two questions raised by school board members prior to voting had related to concerns that the raise was not large enough. The school board voted quickly to approve the pay increase which made the high end starting salary of a Bibb County Board of Education Campus Police Officer approximately $8,000 per year more than any other local agency in Middle Georgia (about 25 percent higher).

We received numerous inquiries from other agencies about our incentive pay plan. One question always asked was "How did you get approval for the plan by a school district that was so financially strapped?" One reason the school board members were so quick to support their police officers is that they were regularly made aware of the excellent work of their officers. When a planned shooting was prevented, board members typically received a copy of the incident report and a briefing by the superintendent. Our school board was typically much more aware of the dangers present and the manner in which they were addressed than most school boards. They were also fully informed regarding the qualifications of their police personnel. Through a detailed presentation, board members were well briefed on the high level of training, experience, and education of our personnel, along with information relating to the department's performance. The board members were also made aware that every member in the department had been given the opportunity to participate in creating the incentive pay plan.

To say the incentive pay plan was helpful would be a major understatement. Everyone involved benefited from the program. Obviously, the officers came out ahead with increased pay, more opportunity for advancement, and direct evidence that their efforts were appreciated. The school system has seen the cost savings that occur when turnover is reduced. As a chief of police, I was in a much better position to recruit and retain the caliber of officer I needed. Most importantly, the people we were sworn to protect received an even higher level of quality service than in the past.

I regularly advise school superintendents, school board members, mayors, city council members, and other key officials that such a compensation package is less costly and much more efficient in the long run. How much is it worth to prevent just one major act of school violence? One school district has spent more than $20 million in building renovations and increased security measures following a major school shooting. With civil actions commonly costing school districts millions of dollars, what is actually more cost-effective—prevention or cleaning up the mess? Of course, the emotional costs of such acts are impossible to measure in dollars.

If we put things in perspective, we can quickly realize what a daunting task we ask our police officers to perform. We also realize how stringent our "rules" are for these individuals. Who else is asked to urinate into a cup, undergo a polygraph test, submit to a credit history check, allow us to ask their neighbors what they think of them, and are examined for emotional stability just to be hired? And once hired, how many employees can be fired and lose their ability to ever work in their field for a single lapse in judgment? How many employees would see the same catastrophic consequences for being arrested for driving under the influence while not at work? And when we add to this the fact that we are asking them to seek out extremely dangerous individuals with weapons and to capture them, it is time to ask what we do for them in return.

When we talk about police officers who must face all these issues in the school setting, we should give pause to consider what we expect to get and what we should expect to pay for it in return. But, as has already been mentioned, money is not the only important factor when we consider how to attract and retain quality personnel.

Like other police operations, school police personnel often must work long and irregular hours. A compensatory time system was developed to keep costs down and to reduce the chances of burning out personnel. This system allows for the department to maximize coverage while meeting budget limitations. By allowing officers to build a comp time bank, they are able to take much needed recovery time during periods when school is out of session. This system results in an excellent work situation for employees while maximizing the use of personnel available through the annual budget.

Of just as much importance as the compensation package is the way police officers are treated. Through a focus on leadership, job enrichment, and quality service principles, a positive work environment was created.

Leadership of Personnel Rather Than Management of Human Resources

One important aspect of the Bibb County Model is the philosophy of leadership of personnel rather than the use of more traditional management techniques. Utilizing the concepts of quality service management, the department was organized to put an emphasis on people. Students, school system employees, other criminal justice organizations, and the general public are viewed as customers. By continually stressing the need to provide quality service, the department institutionalized the same practices proven to be successful in the private sector.

One basic tenant of quality service management is that the organization's human resources will achieve more if they are led rather than managed. Particularly in a service field such as policing, it is critical that employees have the ability and the desire to act in the interest of the customers they are to serve. The concept of quality service management allows the employee to achieve that end. For this environment to exist, police officers need leadership rather than management.

To some, the difference may seem insignificant. To police officers in the field, the difference in approach is obvious. Policing is traditionally a discipline-intense field. The challenge in applying the concepts of quality service management is to provide the freedom to perform while maintaining acceptable standards of discipline. When the proper balance can be attained, officers can provide an unparalleled level of service to those they are sworn to protect.

The school setting provides an excellent opportunity for the principles of quality service management by police officers. The nature of the problems faced in our schools lends itself to the strengths of an approach that focuses on people as a valuable resource rather than treating them like so many widgets. Police officers are in a position to improve many situations in the school setting, but they must be empowered to maximize their efficiency.

Through the use of progressive leadership styles, departmental personnel developed the confidence to become fully involved in determining how the organization was operated. Extensive efforts were made to ensure that all personnel had a voice in the manner in which objectives were met. As one example, all department personnel were asked to evaluate the chief and deputy chief annually. To encourage personnel to be direct and honest in their comments, they were asked to type the evaluation forms, seal them in an envelope, and to deposit the envelopes in a locked drop box during a period of several days. This system was designed to make employees feel comfortable as their comments could be made without fear of retribution.

The feedback received from these evaluations was quite revealing. There were times it seemed negative comments were made without foundation and intended as personal attacks. But, by and large, the majority of comments made seemed to be the legitimate views of employees. Each year, a dispatcher was selected to open the comment box and tally and post the results of the evaluations in the squad room. Although many would question why police executives would allow their "subordinates" to say virtually anything they want about them and post the comments for all to see, the truth of the matter is, employees will make these comments whether or not we provide them a legitimate forum to do so. With this approach, the departmental leadership has an accurate idea of what employees really think. More importantly, employees believe they have a chance to voice their honest opinions.

From the chief executive's perspective, this approach provides job security. As odd as this may seem to some, it is true. This leadership technique provides the opportunity to deal with organizational problems before they develop into major issues. A leader who has the confidence to truly listen to departmental employees has the benefit of learning if a problem needs to be corrected before it is pointed out to him/her by the media or by his/her community.

Another quality service management principle is that our employees are afforded the same opportunity to learn how those they serve view them. Survey instruments were developed for different groups of internal and external service recipients. Students, teachers, administrators, school bus drivers, court personnel, and other individuals who had contact with the school district were allowed to express their opinions on the police department and its officers. This allowed for an open exchange of information, ideas, and concerns regarding the officers and their effectiveness.

Being Open Minded as an Organization

One unique aspect of the Bibb County Model is the numerous initiatives that originated due to a philosophy of "thinking out of the box." All staff members were urged to focus on solving problems rather than concentrating on what was considered to be "traditional." The more conventional approaches have failed to improve the level of school safety. In Bibb County, new approaches were either adapted from other environments or created. For this type of creativity to flourish, a departmental philosophy that encourages new ideas must exist.

By routinely involving personnel in the problem-solving process and actively listening to their suggestions, line involvement in decision making was the norm in the department, and it paid big dividends. The open and creative environment resulted in a wide variety of practical, effective, and innovative solutions to problems faced in the district.

Another practice that helped mold the environment into a creative one was sending departmental personnel to visit police agencies in other regions. Officers and dispatch personnel visited dozens of school system police agencies, university police departments, military police operations, and local police agencies. Officers were asked to provide formal and informal evaluations during these visits. In many cases, officers would return from departmental visits with useful ideas for implementation in Bibb County.

Another important environmental practice involved a specific effort to ensure that personnel received training in other states. A wide range of excellent training programs is available at the Georgia Public Safety Training Center, which is only twenty miles from the department. It would have been very easy for the department to send officers for training exclusively at the center, but this would have limited the interaction of our personnel to other officers and support personnel from Georgia.

It is very easy for a police agency to become cloistered through its training program. By sending personnel to a variety of training sites in other states, Bibb County officers were provided the opportunity to interact with police personnel from around the nation and other countries. On a fairly routine basis, our personnel were able to learn of successful strategies from other regions. These individual concepts could then be brought back to Bibb County for implementation.

A similar concept involved the common practice of loaning personnel out to teach in other states. When Bibb County Campus Police personnel traveled to other states to serve as guest instructors, they were not only able to share the successful concepts developed in Georgia, but also were able to obtain new ideas from those communities. When combined with ideas obtained when officers from other states and nations came to Bibb County for on-site training visits, the amount of information exchange was significant.

There is no doubt the creativity and innovative nature of the department assisted in it becoming a cutting edge leader in school safety. Without successful responses to challenging problems, the department would not have gained the incredible amount of public support that it did, and without a philosophy of being open to new ideas, problem-solving efforts would have been far less effective.

CONCLUSION

Where Will the Department Go from Here?

Due to the incredible success of the department, Deputy Chief Russell Bentley and I began to receive inquiries and even direct job offers from school systems and government agencies. I was astounded to receive job offers at twice my salary and benefits package as chief of police. Neither of us ever dreamed we would receive phone calls where we would be asked to apply for desirable police chief positions. Due to the unfortunate incidents of mass school violence around the nation, our proven background in addressing school violence issues was in great demand.

During my last two years with the department, I worked extensively with the Georgia Emergency Management Agency—Office of the Governor (GEMA) in developing a new school safety program. Director Gary McConnell saw a critical unmet need in Georgia for school safety assistance at the state level. When Governor Roy E. Barnes signed Georgia Senate Bill 74 into law in 1999, GEMA became the lead state agency for school safety matters. Director McConnell offered me a position as his School Safety Specialist, and I accepted. In this capacity, I report to Director McConnell and also provide technical expertise to support the twelve-person School Safety Project. GEMA's School Safety Project has quickly become the most comprehensive school safety center in the United States.

As difficult as it was to leave the department I loved so much, I could not resist the chance to have an even broader impact on school safety. Complete freedom from the rigorous demands of leading a police agency offered me the chance to focus on research and development of new school safety initiatives, teaching opportunities, and the chance to provide technical assistance to others around the nation. Deputy Chief Bentley and I had frequently gone for months at a time without a single day off while trying to run a very active police agency and providing assistance to school districts, police agencies, and government agencies around the globe.

A new leader has been selected for the Bibb County Board of Education Campus Police Department and is now at the helm. He is a very well trained, educated, career police officer. The new chief has more traditional philosophies and is moving the department away from some of its community policing concepts. Three officer positions have been eliminated, the school system has made it optional for schools to prosecute misdemeanor and even felony criminal acts, and the department no longer engages in school safety zone enforcement efforts.

Changes in philosophy when police executives are replaced are common. Each executive must follow the direction provided by his/her supervisor and must utilize the techniques that made him/her successful. Such is the case in Bibb County. Hopefully, the department will continue to provide the high level of protection it has been known for around the world.

Regardless of what course the department takes now, it is clear men and women who have given their best for the children of Bibb County have proven something to the rest of the nation. It is possible to create a reasonably safe school environment even in a community where youth violence is a major problem. Their efforts worked in spite of a significant youth gang problem, poorly funded schools, and sometimes politically divisive government entities.

Community policing efforts like those in Bibb County are needed in schools across the nation. We have a legal obligation to protect those who we compel by force of law to attend school. More importantly, we have a moral obligation to provide a safe and peaceful learning environment. It is the right thing to do. We can no longer accept school violence as the way it must be. We can no longer sacrifice our children at the altar of "what is politically correct." We must protect the children and those who educate them. It is not an easy task. The challenges are great and require much creativity and considerable effort, but our children deserve no less than the best we can give them.

6

Creating That Invisible Shield

James W. Rowe Sr.

Deborah Mitchell Robinson

The present-day chief of police who chooses to apply his/her knowledge and expertise on a college or university campus is going to be challenged with how the delivery of safety services is rendered. It is not necessarily what services are delivered, for example, routine or informal approaches to patrol, answering calls for service, or the investigation of incidents, it is the manner in which these services are delivered.

There are expectations of the students, parents and guardians, the faculty and staff, and, most importantly, those special expectations the administrators of the institution expect, if not demand. High school graduates are attracted to a particular institution of higher education for a wide variety of reasons. Parents, however, influence their sons' and daughters' decisions based upon a whole different set of facts. The safety and well-being of sons and daughters are of paramount concern.

Important to the delivery of police services on a university or college campus are the issues brought forth by the federally enacted Jeane Cleary Act, formerly the Campus Security Act. The Clearys encouraged their now deceased daughter to choose Lehigh University based upon their conclusion that her safety was guaranteed by the institution. This conclusion was based upon information supplied them by the University administration.

The loss of their daughter brought about wide-ranging changes in crime reporting laws. College and university heads face the loss of federal financial aid if they are found to be in violation of the reporting laws as required by the Cleary Act. As a result, the manner in which crimes, arrests, and related factors are reported to the general public has been unified across the country so statistics can be compared, regardless of whether the institution is privately funded or part of a statewide system. These considerations require the college or university police chief to tailor how public safety services are presented to those who live, learn, and visit college and university campuses.

This chapter was titled with the notion that an "invisible shield" has to be offered by the campus police chief when the individual program of service is created. It was done so with the complete assurance that most, if not all, college and university presidents, chancellors, and top administrators want and expect a well-organized, disciplined, competently trained, responsive police force. Administrators also want to be able to call upon this group of professionals whenever the need arises. They do not, however, want that force to be recognized as an armed camp of hired hands, so visible that their presence scares away would-be freshmen and their parents.

Administrators want a latent image that is there, on call if necessary, yet toned down in appearance and approach. They want to provide the impression that the primary function of their police force is service-related, providing protection as opposed to arrests, detention, and prosecution. They expect the police force to function with an immediate, legal response with as little force as possible. When this force does function, it is to be on a situational basis only.

Based upon the premise that this "invisible shield" approach is what high-ranking college and university administrators truly want, there are several approaches the campus police chief can implement and still satisfy the president, chancellor, and board of trustees. These approaches also allow the campus police chief to feel comfortable that the delivery of services is in line with traditional approaches employed by police agencies across the country.

These approaches might not be new, but they will work, provided they are tailored to suit the demographic and geographic considerations individual to each campus. No two campuses are alike. What might work in an urban setting might not work on a campus surrounded by walls or fences, or one situated in a rural location.

TRADITIONAL APPROACHES

Given that college and university administrators would want to employ the "invisible shield" approach, it is important to recognize and examine more traditional approaches to how the delivery of police services might be accomplished. The average young man or woman of college age and his/her parents are used to seeing uniformed police officers in their daily lives. In fact, some might look for such a uniformed presence when they visit a college or university campus for the first time. As such, there should be no hesitation on using uniformed police officers in a campus setting to answer service calls, enforce the rules of the campus, or assist with enforcement of local or community ordinances.

How campus police officers are uniformed might send another message to the campus visitor. The campus police chief has many avenues available when it comes to how campus police officers look in uniform. The options range from the use of blazers and slacks to varied combinations of uniform colors. Options also allow for the distinction between sworn and armed police officers to service officers who merely provide service calls and render assistance, information, directions, and the like. Equally important is how these uniformed police officers travel about the campus, for example, on foot, on bicycles, in golf carts, or in police cars.

Police packages with lights, sirens, and the words police displayed on the side of the car send the message that the campus police agency is fully equipped and trained to render all of the police-related services the average citizen expects from his/her hometown police department. The use of smaller vehicles, including those powered by alternative means such as electricity, send the message that this is a service vehicle and is in use to assist in rendering nonpolice services. The lettering on these types of vehicles is important to stress the service versus police functions of these departments. For example, words such as campus community response unit, security service, campus watch unit, and parking lot security unit will send the message that services are the primary purpose of the vehicle.

The other universally recognized police function certain to satisfy the systemwide college or university administrator is accountability. Accountability means that a call for service can be traced from its inception through all of the important steps thereafter. The campus police chief should be able to document how long it took his/her receiving agency, through the dispatcher, to process the call. It is imperative to determine if the call had to be held or was processed immediately. The availability of units or other extenuating circumstances may cause delays, whereby the reasons for the delay must be determined.

Such documentation can be easily captured and retained through a simple "run card" (complaint control card process) whereby a time clock is used to punch in the receiving and dispatch time, thus allowing for calculation of the delay time. How long did it take for the responding unit(s) to get to the scene? Time is always distorted when it comes to people waiting for an emergency response, whether it is a fire truck, ambulance, or the campus police. Therefore, the next time frame to capture is the response time, which is accomplished via the same process as the dispatch time frame. Many administrators have saved face by being able to document their police departments' response time to a call. The individual campus police officer who responded to the call is also supported with this critical documentation.

Last, how much time was spent on the call? Was the unit out of service for an extraordinary number of minutes or hours, or did the police officer return to service in a brief period of time? When citizen complaints are received, or the "boss" or the media calls, it is extremely helpful to the campus police chief to know exactly when his/her officer cleared from the incident or that the assigned unit was unavailable to respond to another call of lower priority due to being committed to the original call.

In this day and age of electronics, college students are used to seeing technology being used for a wide variety of purposes. Likewise, their parents are aware that police agencies use a number of so-called "cutting edge" techniques to make their communities safer. Such is the case with college and university administrators who look to their police chief to institute such approaches on their respective campuses. There is a difference, however, as many administrators believe the installation of electronics will totally eliminate the need for any kind of a uniform presence in the location where the CCTV cameras, card access heads, or emergency telephones are located.

It is suggested to the campus police chief that he/she use any and all kinds of electronics available to make the campus safer and to ease the need for manpower. Electronics do not call in sick, file grievances, or leave unexpectedly to take a higher paying job elsewhere in the business. They do, however, need to be properly maintained and serviced, and when some incident is detected via an electronic reporting device, a prompt and proper response is required. In other words, any electronic system needs and requires oversight.

For liability purposes, any type of an emergency electronic device on a college or university campus that is not routinely serviced and checked to verify it is working properly is a false approach to sheltering the administration from exposure to lawsuits. For example, a "blue light" phone requires an individual to simply push a button to activate an emergency call. If the device is inoperable due to failed maintenance, the college or university then becomes subject to liability as well as criticism if harm results from the inability of an individual to place an emergency call. Suggestions regarding the use of emergency electronic devices on campus include using up-to-date electronic devices; documenting all incidents of emergency electronic use; educating the campus community with regard to the location, function, and proper use of emergency electronic devices; and educating the police officers and dispatchers on what to do if the emergency equipment should fail.

The campus police chief needs to be open to the use of electronic devices, but should not come to rely totally on their use. A CCTV system in the lobby of a residence hall cannot provide CPR or first aid, cannot detect the smell of alcohol on an underage drinker, nor can it physically prevent crime. People perform such services. The electronics detect, document, and provide evidentiary proof of medical emergencies; save the image of the underage freshman for the Dean of Students; and give the investigating campus police officer a photo profile on the suspect in the crime.

The bottom line with regard to the use of electronic devices on college and university campuses is that there needs to be a harmonic balance between human personnel and electronic services. Both are important and both are needed as they serve as compliments to each other.

NONTRADITIONAL APPROACHES

The discussion thus far has focused on somewhat traditional approaches to delivering police services in a college or university setting. The following addresses the more nontraditional methods whereby police services could be provided via some unique approaches. As stated earlier, not all college and university campuses are alike. Almost every campus is unique in itself, and though some programs work well due to the physical layout of the buildings and parking areas, the identical approach on another campus, even in the same city or local region, may not work at all. There are also human factor considerations in each of these approaches. These considerations involve not only the campus police officers themselves, but also the community in which these officers work and live. The success of any police agency most often depends upon the receiver of the services, for example, does the receiver appreciate the manner of delivery of services or are other means of delivery better suited for this particular receiver and/or community?

Mountain Bike Patrols

One nontraditional approach to the delivery of police services on a college or university campus is the use of mountain bike patrols. The use of bicycles is not exactly new, and, if you are a history buff on policing, police officers riding bikes as part of their patrols dates way back in police history. However, the bike patrol officer on the college or university campus is somewhat of a new method of policing. For the most part, the use of bike patrol officers has been well received by faculty, students, staff, and visitors to college and university campuses nationwide.

The primary success of the mountain bike patrols can be attributed to the fact that the barriers between the bike patrol officer and those he or she comes in contact with are eliminated. The face-to-face contact the bike patrol officer has with an individual on campus has proven to be effective as these officers are meeting individuals on campus in a much closer manner than from behind a windshield or window of a police car. This has provided campus police departments with a positive image, as the interaction between bike patrol officer and individual is most often one-on-one, with more open communication between that officer and the individual. Although the bike patrol officer may not have performed anything other than a routine duty service during the interaction, a duty performed numerous times before, with the barriers gone, the bike patrol officer is often perceived as being friendlier, less of a threat. With this new positive image, the campus community is more apt to ask another bike patrol officer for help and assistance in the future.

The campus police chief has to consider a number of points when a campus mountain bike patrol unit is instituted. First and foremost, quality training for the bike patrol officers is a must. Being a bike patrol officer is more than simply riding a bike across campus. There are safety factors. Bike patrol officers need to receive professional instruction on such issues as how to effectively protect themselves in the areas of campus they patrol (many areas not accessible by car); how to prevent themselves from being injured; how protective equipment should be worn; how to recover from spills or wrecks; how to ride in all kinds of weather conditions; and how to properly maintain their equipment.

With regard to obtaining mountain bikes, many departments have donated bikes that become part of bike patrol units. If funding is available, the ideal situation is to purchase police bike packages, similar to police car packages. Police bikes are typically built with stronger frames, better support systems, gel seats, extra heavy duty tires, and safety equipment packages that often come within the total package. Maintenance service contracts are essential. Just as police cars need to be maintained in top condition, patrol bikes also need daily maintenance. Such a service will help the bike patrol officers address the day-to-day safety considerations they are certain to face.

When it comes to uniforms and web gear for the bike patrol officers, it is important to have these officers participate in the decision-making process. Bike patrol uniforms can be incorporated into the department's present patrol uniform. However, certain factors peculiar to the bike patrol need to be considered. For example, padded shorts in warmer weather will give comfort when riding the bike. Long pants should be fitted so the officers' legs and feet are not restricted. This same consideration also applies to the choice of boot, shoe, or sneaker.

If the campus police department issues body armor, the wearing of these vests should be considered mandatory for bike patrol officers. This is added protection should they become involved in an accident. If the bike patrol officers train with the vest on, these officers will become used to the added protection, and the concerns relative to added weight, perspiring, or feeling less mobile will undoubtedly cease.

The primary rule in selecting outer garments for mountain bike patrols is the safety features. Can the bike patrol officers be easily seen at night, in heavy rains, in fog, or at dusk or dawn? Bike patrol officers should maximize the use of reflectorized material, for example, adding reflectorized strips to the bike, helmets, outer vests, and other issued equipment. Bike patrol officers have little protection. There are no seat belts or harnesses, no steel frames to protect them from injuries. Any way to improve visibility to others will be a true investment in officer safety. Safety First!

Walk and Talk

Another program that works on college and university campuses is a version of the so-called "park, walk and talk." The basic premise of this program is to get the police officer into the community by parking the patrol car, walking through the officer's assigned neighborhoods, and talking to residents. Most police chiefs across the country have adopted some variation of this program as part of their community policing efforts. Although not unique to academic settings, the program is effective, for much the same reason as bike patrol officers are effective—eliminating the barrier between the police officer and the community he or she serves. For the campus police officer, this program involves walking the campus and actively engaging in communication with students, faculty, staff, and visitors. The mere presence of a uniformed police officer on foot inside a residence hall, academic building, or some other targeted section of the campus is a deterrent in itself.

Information is a key element to the solving of any crime. The campus police officer who is visible, walking through campus, creates the opportunity for the campus community to get to know the police officer. Effective communication can then be established between the police officer and the community. Communication includes small talk, as well as eliciting assistance and guidance. Effective communication also provides the campus police officer the chance to gain the confidence of the campus community, whereby a professional relationship can be established. Through this type of relationship, the campus police officer will be seen as a valuable resource to the campus community, in both emergency and nonemergency situations, whereas individuals within the campus community will be seen as a valuable resource to the campus police officer in obtaining information regarding criminal activities on campus.

This type of professional relationship is not unlike those being created through community oriented policing programs by city and county police departments. The campus police chief, in establishing such a program, needs to be aware of the intricacies of effective communication. Safety is a paramount concern on a college or university campus. Both campus police officers and the campus community need to feel safe with each other in order for trust to develop. With trust will come open communication, creating an effective working and living relationship, a must for preventing crime on campus.

It should be emphasized that this program will not be successful without proper planning. Some campus police officers are invariably better communicators and more "people oriented" than others. These officers should be encouraged to engage in "walk and talk" as much as possible. Administrators and faculty should also be informed of this program and encouraged to disseminate any information they receive from students to the campus police department. It is important that all members of the campus community actively engage in open communication, while ensuring confidence, trust, and anonymity to those giving information about criminal activity on campus.

Campus residence halls and dorms are monitored by student leaders and paid professionals. These individuals make for good targets of a "walk and talk" program. For open communication to occur, it is imperative that the campus police officers are trusted. The "walk and talk" program can establish this trust by presenting the campus police officers to these individuals, creating a professional relationship long before problems arise. The "walk and talk" should be used to build bridges between campus police officers and the campus community.

Directed Deterrent Patrols ("D" Runs)

No one in present-day policing would classify Directed Deterrent Patrols or "D" Runs as a new way of preventing crime. This program has shown success in municipal applications across the country and is being implemented on college and university campuses nationwide. How the program is implemented is the basis for its success. As planning is a key factor in any crime prevention program, the planning of when to implement "D" Runs is the key to its success. The timing of "D" Runs is paramount to preventing crime. On the college or university campus, timing relates to when on campus and where on campus crime is occurring.

Crime data collection and assessment is another factor in implementing "D" Runs on campus. In order for "D" Runs to be successful, it is imperative to know exactly when and where, on campus, crime is occurring. This allows for the planning of specific patrols to be targeted to specific areas and at specific times on campus, thus the philosophy of the "D" Runs. Planning includes an in-depth examination of reports generated, calls for service made, and arrests undertaken in a specific geographic area on campus. The examination should include the separation of crime data by streets, campuses, buildings, athletic fields, gathering spots, and so forth.

Once data are separated by type of crime, location, day of week, and time of day, the optimum time to establish directed patrols, "D" Runs, can be identified. To ensure this program's success, the campus police officers actively engaged in "D" Runs should be able to remain in their target areas during their entire shift, unless an emergency situation arises. In other words, this is a committed time assignment and should be given a priority level over routine patrols. These assignments should come from the campus police chief, who in turn should ensure that supervisors, officers, and dispatchers are all working together for the success of the program.

The remaining key to the success of the Directed Deterrent Patrol program is ensuring the assigned campus patrol officers are thoroughly briefed on their assignments, including the importance of these assignments in the prevention of crime. Without all involved understanding and subscribing to the concept of "D" Runs, the program cannot succeed, on any level or on any campus, in preventing crime.

Rape Aggression Defense

Another crime prevention program shown to work on college and university campuses is a proactive program designed to heighten awareness to females, called Rape Aggression Defense, or R.A.D. for short. This program originated on the campus of The Tidewater Academy, located in West Harwich, Massachusetts. It has been successfully implemented at many institutions of higher education across the country, especially those on the eastern seaboard.

As the title indicates, the program addresses the potential female victim of sexual assault and what defenses she can utilize to protect herself at the onset of a physical attack. The actual instructional block is twelve hours and provides a unique "hands on" approach to protection. During the course of instruction and in a controlled environment under the watchful eyes of certified R.A.D. instructors, students are put in a position to actually use physical force to fend off an attacker. This portion of the program involves the use of a so-called "redman's outfit," worn by the actor playing the attacker. The student is taught defensive moves that will defeat or discourage the completion of the attack. Although this course is designed for women, instructors and students may be both male and female.

The success of this program rests on how it is presented to the campus community. Regardless of the history and amount of crime occurring on campus, crime does occur, and everyone in the campus community is a potential victim. Although the campus may seem like a sheltered, secure place, students, faculty, and staff spend many hours in activities away from campus. The information and training supplied in this course can be used anywhere and at any time. In fact, anyone who has undergone this training can call upon the teachings long after he/she has left the secure confines of the campus. As such, the campus police department should promote this program as a lifelong learning experience, one that everyone should pursue.

CONCLUSION

There are several ways of tailoring or packaging crime prevention programs to a particular campus community. First, lines of open communication must be established. Communication between the campus police department and the college or university administration is essential in promoting and establishing a variety of crime prevention programs on campus. Communication between the campus police officers and the campus community—students, faculty, staff, and visitors—also must be established. It is imperative that the campus police chief understands the vital link between the department and the campus community, as both need each other to establish a secure campus community.

Second, any crime prevention program will require funding. Whether it be hiring more police personnel, obtaining the most up-to-date equipment and technology, or presenting specific crime prevention programs to the campus community, the college or university administration must be willing to take any measures to ensure the safety of the campus community. This includes presenting crime prevention programs to the students, faculty, and staff at no charge so every individual has the opportunity to gain the valuable information contained in such programs.

The college or university administration should also consider enlarging the public safety net to protect the students, faculty, and staff when they are off-campus. This can be accomplished by having the campus police department join forces with the local city or county police departments to establish specific patrols in and around campus property.

Third, the campus police chief should keep abreast of current crime prevention trends, techniques, and programs. Although many college and university campuses and their communities are relatively crime-free, crime can occur anywhere, at any time. The more prepared for crime an individual or community is, the more likely crime can be prevented.

Any crime prevention program must be specifically fit for the college or university campus community. Acquiring this fit involves decisions made by the campus police chief in conjunction with the administration to ensure the campus community is the safest it can possibly be. After all, the college experience is supposed to be the most exciting part of any young adult's life. This can only be true in a secure, safe environment.

7

Crime Prevention in Public Housing

Brian McDonough

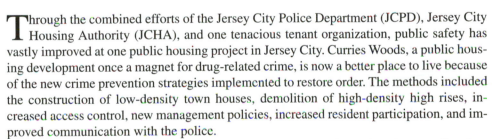

Through the combined efforts of the Jersey City Police Department (JCPD), Jersey City Housing Authority (JCHA), and one tenacious tenant organization, public safety has vastly improved at one public housing project in Jersey City. Curries Woods, a public housing development once a magnet for drug-related crime, is now a better place to live because of the new crime prevention strategies implemented to restore order. The methods included the construction of low-density town houses, demolition of high-density high rises, increased access control, new management policies, increased resident participation, and improved communication with the police.

Efforts to make Curries Woods and other public housing safer places to live date back to the 1960s when policy makers found that some high-rise public housing projects built in the late 1950s were social and security disasters (Annan & Skogan, 1992). Curries Woods housing project was no exception.

Curries Woods' towering buildings and rust color cement bricks stood isolated from the neighboring residential community that has one- and two-family homes. This complex consisted of seven buildings, twelve- and thirteen-story units housing more than two thousand five hundred tenants. Most of the residents living in the 712 apartment units were unemployed and dependent on public assistance. Not only were the residents poor, many were casualties of the drug and crime wave that plagued the project in the 1970s and 1980s. Many young adults who lived at the site succumbed to drug overdoses, the "crack" fad of the 1980s, and AIDS (acquired immune deficiency syndrome). With crime and drug activity growing and the cost of vandalism mounting, the Housing Authority was unable to provide the safe and decent housing it once did.

Curries Woods was built in 1959 and developed on a 9.8 acre of land located near a railroad. It was accessible from two main streets, Heckman Drive and Merritt Street. The streets were open to the public, accessible by car and on foot. Vehicle traffic came and went through the site without interference, as did the residents and nonresidents who walked in and out of the buildings. The inability of the JCHA and Jersey City Police Department to distinguish residents from nonresidents and public space from semi-private space made it very difficult to hold crime and drug offenders responsible for their actions.

Over the years, the physical neglect and declining standard of life took a toll on the residents, management, and police. It was not until JCHA began receiving federal funding to demolish its high rises and replace them with town houses that the site showed evidence of improvement. Up-to-date renovations include the demolition of four high-rise buildings, a renovated high rise with increased access control for the elderly and disabled, a reconfiguration of community streets into cul-de-sacs, a portable guard booth staffed by residents to control vehicle access, and the development of more than one hundred town houses.

The JCPD patrols the new community regularly. As a supplement to the on-duty patrols, off-duty police officers investigate complaints of narcotic-related activity, monitor problem-oriented offenders, and engage in resident-sponsored youth programs.

In this chapter, I discuss the myriad of crime prevention strategies implemented in Curries Woods that aided in the transformation of a crime infested high-rise project into a more secure, gated, town house community. These strategies included community redesign using Crime Prevention Through Environmental Design (CPTED) techniques, resident screening and eviction enforcement policies, resident monitors as part of the newly formed Curries Woods Tenant Task Force, a community policing program that includes both on- and off-duty police officers, and an after-school program.

CURRIES WOODS RENOVATION

Phase I

The first sign of renewal was the renovation of 3 Heckman Drive into 3 "New" Heckman Drive. The building was converted from ninety-six large family units to ninety-one smaller occupant units. Six lower level apartments were converted to accommodate the physically handicapped, and the rest of the apartments were reduced in size to house senior citizens and disabled persons.

Since relocating a number of young adult residents and installing self-locking doors, apartment buzzers with an intercom, surveillance cameras, glass panels to the lobby and ground floor, a reduced sized lobby, and a wrought iron fence around the building to protect the ground level windows, the building's security has improved. These techniques have increased access control and reduced the number of crowds that often congregated in the lobby.

When Curries Woods residents were surveyed in 1995, loitering, drinking, and drug activities were three of the most common problems occurring in the lobby area. Since then, crowd gatherings have been eliminated and the all day and night pedestrian activity that once occurred has been reduced.

Unlike the former building, which had three entrances accessible to the public, this building has only one entrance. The latter two exits are for emergency use only. In order to gain access into the renovated building, a nonresident is required to stop at the resident monitor's desk to sign the visitor's book and record his/her name and destination.

On-duty resident monitors sit inside a glass-enclosed office across from the building's two elevators in sight of the incoming and exiting pedestrian traffic. The use of residents to maintain foyer and lobby area surveillance increases resident ownership and promotes resident involvement to maintain building safety. Closed circuit television has also been installed in each resident's apartment and the manager's office to widen the use of video surveillance. An easily accessible on-site manager's office during day and evening hours promotes daily business activity as well as the use of the community room and laundry room, and reduces the opportunity for criminal and deviant behavior.

An additional measure to reduce criminal opportunity was the installation of windows around the building to enhance natural surveillance and bring more light onto the floors. The extensive use of windows adds more natural light to the floor halls, and, during the night hours, the street lamp illuminates the landings nearest the elevators. The widening of the hallways from the bottom floor up has brought increased lighting to the floor. The increased hall space eases pedestrian movement and reduced close public contact when walking. The combination of well-lit floors, wider halls, and large windows increases visibility inside the building.

The additional windows also provide the residents an opportunity to observe their cars while parked in front of the building or sit and wait for a family member who is coming in a car. Parking in front of the building increases car surveillance and decreases the risk of auto theft. It also helps the manager to more easily identify resident cars and to remove those belonging to nonresidents. For increased safety, every parking space is marked off to ease congestion and to provide adequate room for turning or backing.

Parking for the disabled is situated directly in front of the building to shorten the walking distance to and from the building. The sidewalk is accessible for wheelchair usage and is much narrower than the previous sidewalks in front of the old high rises. The wider sidewalks drew larger crowd gatherings and caused more passageway obstructions.

Entry into the building is limited only through the front center door. Except in cases of an emergency, there are three other doors that serve as fire exits. Two are located on each side of the building in the front, and a third exit is located in the back of the building. The emergency doors in the front open out away from the building to an alcove area that is enclosed with a seven-foot high gate. The gate can be opened by anyone who exits the alcove. Once opened manually, hydraulic pressure forces the gate to close when the push bar is released.

The reconstruction of 3 New Heckman Drive for seniors, the disabled, and small-sized families has significantly reduced criminal opportunity and deterred unwanted visitors. The additional windows provide an increase in surveillance using natural light and candlelight. The increase in access to the building entrance has separated the public from semiprivate areas and restricts nonresident entrance. The increase in the presence of resident monitors promotes building pride and develops tenant responsibility and accountability.

Phase 2 (Town House)

The second phase of the restoration project included the construction of town houses to re-place the obsolete, high-rise buildings and a reconfiguring of the roadway to wind through the town houses. Resident monitors hired by the JCHA staff the new guard booth just out-side the town house entrance to monitor incoming and outgoing vehicle traffic.

The "New Curries Woods" community now has more than ninety town houses. Most of the town houses have two or three bedrooms, with less than ten of the units having four bedrooms to accommodate the few larger-sized families. The houses are attached, eight houses per lot. Each home has a small garden in the front where residents can plant flow-ers and grow vegetables. In front of each house is a one- or two-step walkup porch with a roof overhang that can shield residents during inclement weather. The overhang has an ex-terior lamp that brightens the home's exterior and illuminates the address numbers on the front door. The number markings make it easier and faster for police and emergency per-sonnel to locate the house in time of emergency.

In the front of each home is a garden area, protected by a five-foot-high wrought iron fence. Residents are allowed to plant their own flowers and grow their own vegetables within the protected areas. It gives the residents an opportunity to showcase their creativity, enrich their pride, and socialize with their neighbors. Every year the Housing Authority sponsors a garden contest that recognizes the best appearance, most diverse, and best-maintained garden.

Small areas considered open for public use and commonly used by kids playing tag are laden with green sod. A subcontracted landscaper meticulously manicures the lawn. At the lawn's edge, a few residents tend to the plants that are watered daily in the spring and summer to maintain growth and beauty.

In the rear of each home is a patio where the residents can barbecue and host small family gatherings. JCHA has provided the residents a small storage shed to store barbecue grills and garden tools. Residents are expected to keep their patios neat and orderly. In the rear, between the homes, is an enclosed communal playground widely used by the chil-dren. The playground is a safe haven for the kids and parents who feel more secure know-ing their small children are within sight. Entrance to the playground is limited to one footpath that winds in and around the town houses.

Boundaries for the site were established using wrought iron fencing to limit site entry and to direct pedestrian circulation and activity. Almost all land space once heavily used with foot traffic has been eliminated. There are two narrow public footpath entrances leading into the site. Smaller-sized cement sidewalks run alongside the town houses to deter large crowd gatherings and increase private space.

Heckman Drive, a two-way thoroughfare once accessible to the public from both sides of the site, has been eliminated and replaced with a cul-de-sac. Curved curb road-ways have replaced the straight curved roads to reduce traffic speed. Parking spaces have been designated with hash marks, and no parking signs are posted in prohibited parking areas. Most residents are able to park their cars in front or near their town houses.

Residents who park overnight are now required to affix a JCHA sticker to their ve-hicle bumper. Each household is limited to two vehicles and is required to show proof of a State of New Jersey registration and insurance to the site manager. A rectangular-shaped blue and gold sign at the vehicle entrance proclaims the "New Curries Woods." Vehicle access is limited to residents and short-term visitors who are picking up and disembarking passengers. All vehicles entering the complex must stop at the entry-monitoring booth, and all occupants must identify themselves and their destination. Inside the booth is a Curries Woods' resident monitor who observes and records all visitors and vehicles.

The booth is situated atop an elevated bed of concrete enabling the monitor to oversee the driver, vehicle, and its occupants. Once the driver and vehicle have been identified, the gate attendant opens the wooden gate barrier for the resident or visitor to enter. Once inside the gate, conspicuous speed limit signs are posted to caution drivers to proceed slowly.

The parking sticker policy and gate entering monitoring station have increased the identification of resident cars and unauthorized visitations. Any visitor who is planning to stay longer than a drop off or pickup is encouraged to park in the visitor parking area. In addition to monitoring incoming traffic, the guards also are able to observe the outside visitor parking area located just outside the entry monitoring station.

The resident monitors have been trained by the JCPD to be the "eyes and ears of the community." The residents are trained to identify suspicious conditions and person(s), how to distinguish resident vehicles from nonresident vehicles, indicators of drug activity, what to do if they observe a crime or suspicious activity, and what to say when they call the police. With the increased resident involvement, the opportunity for crime and drug activity is minimal. The Curries Woods Tenant Task Force received national recognition from the Office of Housing and Urban Development at its second annual National Conference on Resident Involvement for its gate entry monitoring security initiative and for using resident monitors.

"ONE STRIKE AND YOU'RE OUT"

JCHA now conducts a thorough background review of tenants relocating to the new town houses and evicts those tenants who engage in criminal and drug activity. On March 28, 1996, President Clinton announced the "One Strike and You're Out" policy for public housing authorities (PHAs) to ensure those who engage in illegal drug use or other criminal activities are prohibited from living in public housing.

Every resident of Curries Woods relocating to a town house is now required to meet placement eligibility standards which include a criminal history background review and require he/she be without any past evictions for drug-related criminal activity. The residents who violate this lease agreement are subject to eviction, even prior to the criminal disposition.

The "One Strike" has two components. The first component is that PHAs conduct a comprehensive background check on all applicants, work with courts and police agencies to gain access to criminal records, and develop a criteria to screen for drug-related violations and other criminal activity. The second component of the policy suggests PHAs adopt clear lease provisions prohibiting drug-related violations and criminal activity and maintain strict enforcement of those provisions. A violation of the "One Strike" lease agreement is treated as serious.

When the JCHA learns a tenant or a member of the household is arrested on or off the premises or a crime was committed on the premises by a resident guest, it initiates civil eviction proceedings. The action may result in the eviction of a leaseholder or a stipulation agreement that bans the resident offender from the premises. In determining whether to evict a resident based on a pattern of use of a controlled dangerous substance or a pattern of abuse of alcohol, JCHA may take into consideration the offender's participation in a supervised drug or alcohol rehabilitation program and current sobriety.

Success of the "One Strike and You're Out" policy is attributed to working efforts of the JCPD and JCHA management. The JCPD's Housing Unit Office liaison, on a daily basis, forwards the names of individuals who are arrested on and off JCHA property. At times, residents erroneously provide the police with wrong addresses to evade "One Strike" action. However, through ongoing communication between police, residents, and managers, the violators are often located.

The JCHA legal staff is promptly provided confidential police reports to assist them in the preparation of civil eviction proceedings. Although JCHA is not required to grant the tenant a grievance hearing, every leaseholder is provided an opportunity to present a defense at the administrative hearing. If a tenancy case cannot be resolved fairly, the case proceeds to tenancy court, and the JCHA subpoenas expert police witnesses to testify against criminal and narcotic law violators in court.

Two of the more recent crime initiatives initiated by the JCPD in public housing has been the drug offender restraining order application and the identification of parolees who are looking to return back to public housing after spending time in prison. The drug offender restraining order was recently legislated by the State of New Jersey to target those offenders who habitually ply their drugs at or around the same location, more specifically public housing sites. For example, if an individual is caught selling drugs at or around any of the public housing family sites, the police officer making the arrest will apply for a drug restraining order to prohibit the return of that offender to that same location for at least two years.

The only affirmative defense to thwart the application is a plea by the defendant that he or she is a bona fide resident or has legitimate business at the site, such as the rendering of medical support and/or children living at the site. If that is the case and the court finds justification, then the judge can place conditions on the offender to disrupt any continued drug activity.

Preventing the return of violent offenders and drug dealers to public housing has been a goal of the Jersey City Police Department, Jersey City Housing Authority, and New Jersey Parole Bureau (NJPB). Working closely with the NJPB, the JCPD and JCHA have been able to temporarily deny parole to those inmates who list a public housing address as a place of refuge after prison. Those who are denied are required to resubmit their parole application with an address that is outside of public housing. It is not that the JCHA wants to deny parole to someone who has adequately served his/her time, but rather wants to be able to provide safe and decent housing without repeating the failures of yesteryear. Proactive management and proactive policing are the keys to the prevention of criminal opportunity.

POLICE PARTNERSHIP

The Jersey City Police Department, Jersey City Housing Authority, and the Curries Woods Tenant Task Force have established a working partnership to maintain a safe and secure public housing family development. Through a medium of public contacts and public meetings, on- and off-duty police officers hired by the JCHA meet with residents daily to familiarize themselves with neighborhood concerns and gain a better understanding of their work environment.

Community Service Officers Doreen Daly and Jay Cook, in the two years they have been assigned to the new community, have come to know most of the community members by name and the youth by their nicknames. In contrast, when the high rises were standing on Heckman Drive, the police rarely got to know the tenants, except those who violated the law. In patrolling the high-rise buildings, the officers conducted a method of patrol that was considered by some tenants to be too aggressive while being considered by some police to be consistent with safe operational procedure. In the high-rise buildings, the officers rode a urine and feces infested elevator to the top floor so they could descend the stairwell and check each floor landing, looking for anyone who was loitering or committing a drug violation. Many arrests, which included the confiscation of drugs and guns, were made as a result of this patrol.

Although the arrests were considered to be of high quality, the amount of time consumed walking the stairwells and hallways to conduct the patrol was time-consuming. In the new complex, the officers are able to increase their patrol area coverage, reduce the time it takes to make a perimeter inspection, and promote an effective police presence through the use of bicycles. With the use of bicycles, the officers now have a means to patrol areas that normally wouldn't be patrolled on foot or in a car. Behind the town houses are patios and a toddler playground. Officers riding their bikes on the public walkway that winds between the town houses offers the residents a heightened sense of security, as the officers can be seen patrolling an area hidden from the passing public.

During the winter months, bicycle officers wear sweatshirts and long pants. In the summer, the officers wear blue-collar golf shirts and shorts. The officers like this attire because it is much cooler and more comfortable than the traditional wool pants, cotton shirts, and eight-point hats. The bicycle is an added tool for the police which symbolizes a healthier and better conditioned police officer. The bike has given the officers a means to reinforce public confidence, which is much less intimidating than a patrol car or on foot, walking and swinging a nightstick.

The friendlier attitude of the police image is consistent with fewer drug crime complaints. In 1997 and 1998, there were less than twenty-five incidents of drug-related activity, compared with 1989 and 1990 that had more than two hundred-fifty drug-related offenses (JCPD Records 2000). Because there are fewer arrests, the Community Service Officers spend most of their time patrolling the grounds, talking with residents, and attending meetings. However, there are times when the officers are summoned to resolve disputes and diffuse tense situations.

Because the officers have come to know most of the tenants as a result of meetings they attend, situations are often resolved without arrests. At the meetings, hosted by the Curries Woods Tenant Task Force, residents often ask questions that pertain to domestic violence, personal safety, and crime prevention. The quest for crime prevention information has increased since the residents relocated from their apartments and moved into town houses. The residents' main concerns are how best they can secure their personal property using personal identification markings, as well as how best to secure their premises when they are away at business or on vacation.

Although crimes of this nature rarely occur in the Woods, residents sometimes leave their unlocked bicycles in the backyard. Management often sends out notices reminding the residents that although thefts are rare, it is important to protect their valuables and to maintain a safe and clean environment that is not inviting to intruders. Site Manager Carol Tyler is very instrumental in policing the site through her own management tactics. She conducts frequent inspections of the family development property to ensure there are no hazards present that will jeopardize resident safety or debris that will give the site a neglectful appearance.

JCHA management often requests the police as part of their duties to inform them when they come upon unattractive conditions that need to be removed. If the condition is cited and it cannot be removed and resolved without a warning, a city ordinance is issued by the police to the leaseholder for failure to maintain a sanitary environment.

As a supplement to the on-duty police, JCHA has hired a police lieutenant who serves as the Site Based Officer (SBO) and three other police officers who work as rotating officers to patrol Curries Woods in an off-duty capacity. The off-duty police officers supplement the community policing patrols and, when necessary, arrest those are who are in violation of narcotic and criminal law statutes. Because the amount of drug crime has remained constant, the SBO officer and his rotating officers have been devoting more time to drug abuse prevention and youth oriented programs to promote positive police community relations.

The off-duty officers sometimes escort the Woods kids to college and professional basketball games, amusement parks, and the Liberty Science Center, a state of the art science education facility in Jersey City, New Jersey. For the kids, this is a big treat because most are insulated from the community due to their limited means of income. Another treat for the kids is the bicycle recovery program sponsored by SBO Lieutenant William Costigan, who repairs donated used bicycles to give to children unable to afford one.

In addition to the off-duty policing element, the Public Housing Drug Elimination Program (PHDEP) funds an after-school program, a targeted intervention program that includes social service assistance and a young adult "We Care" basketball league. The basketball league is coordinated by two police officers who organized league games between Jersey City police officers and young adults from the various public housing sites. Throughout the year, the officers organize youth leagues at the Jersey City Boys and Girls Club. The "We Care" basketball league promotes better police community relations through a process of interaction on the basketball court rather than through the criminal justice process. The interaction on the court instead of in the courthouse demonstrates to the younger residents that police are individuals like themselves, with human traits, rather than just enforcers of the law who carry a badge and gun.

The officers also make it a point to visit JCHA's after-school program which is open for all public housing children between the hours of 3:00 P.M. and 8:00 P.M. Monday through Friday. Many children are unsupervised during these hours and more likely to engage in criminal and disorderly behavior because of their inappropriate use of leisure time. The after-school program is staffed by New Jersey state certified school teachers who provide homework assistance, individual tutoring, antidrug workshops, arts and crafts, special field trips, and DARE athletic programs sponsored by the Hudson County prosecutor and Jersey City Police Department.

COMMUNITY POLICING IN CURRIES WOODS

The efforts of management, residents, and police have created a community-policing model that was cited in 1998 by the Housing and Urban Development (HUD) Office as a PHDEP "Best Practice." This model was initiated in 1995 when JCPD and JCHA joined together to solve crime and disorder problems across its three low-rise and three high-rise public housing sites. The working partnership included the development of problem-solving site teams evaluated by Lorraine Green of Rutgers University Criminal Justice Studies Program, in cooperation with the National Institute of Justice. The "site team" included JCHA representatives, a social service liaison officer, resident leaders, and on-duty and off-duty police officers.

The site teams collectively identified and analyzed drug, disorder, and violent crime problems in the six largest public housing sites. I served as the coordinator of the site-based teams. The most common problems identified at all six sites were drug offenses and disorderly activities which include loud radios, loitering, and violent crime. Each site team was asked to identify individual problems in its respective public housing sites, and then, as a team, they analyzed and prioritized target problems prior to implementing tactical responses. The more common strategies suggested and implemented to suppress this activity were arrest, issuance of summons, interviewing the problem offender, evicting the offender's family, and improving access control to the site.

A finding of the study indicated that high-rise public housing sites have a greater proportion of common areas with drug and disorder problems than low-rise sites. This was particularly acute at Curries Woods, as this site still had five high-rise buildings standing during the time of the study.

Since the adoption of CPTED strategies, the JCPD, JCHA management, and Woods residents are making considerable progress in the reduction of crime, suppression of open market drug activity, and the improvement of police-resident communications. To improve communication with the residents and their knowledge of the criminal justice system, JCPD conducted a Citizen Police Academy (CPA) for the Curries Woods residents. The academic curriculum of the CPA consisted of a shortened and condensed version of the police recruit training conducted in the New Jersey Police Academy. In a short period of time, the resident students were exposed to real-life scenarios often encountered by police officers and informed of the JCPD's policies and procedures that guide the officer's decision-making process. Seasoned detectives were on hand to describe interview and interrogation methods commonly used when interviewing suspects and witnesses, locating and collecting evidence, and locating missing persons.

The CPA is one of the most notable accomplishments to the Community Policing Program and for residents of Curries Woods. Throughout the ten-week program, the resident students who attended the classes received professional instruction from experienced police officers in the areas of arrest, search and seizure, methods of patrol, investigation, traffic safety (use of police radar, vehicle, and pedestrian safety), the Juvenile Justice System, and domestic violence.

Parents who attended the class were most inquisitive of Jersey City's curfew municipal ordinance which requires all children not accompanied by an adult or guardian to be in the house by 10:30 P.M. The resident students were told the purpose of the curfew is to protect the children from becoming crime victims and to reduce daytime truancy. The parents also learned of the after-school programs available to Jersey City children between the hours of 3 P.M. and 8 P.M. when most children are thought to be unsupervised and likely to engage in misdirected behavior.

Domestic violence became a topic that hit close to home for the resident students as most either knew a victim of domestic violence and/or have witnessed an assault among family members. The resident students were told of the requirements of police officers, when they respond to a domestic violence call, to make the victim aware of social services available to victims of domestic violence. The resident students were also informed that the police have less discretion when dealing with many serious crimes, such as domestic violence, than they have when dealing with minor offenses, such as traffic violations.

New Jersey is very strict when it comes to domestic violence. In this state, every police officer is mandated by the New Jersey Attorney General's Domestic Violence Policy to arrest all domestic violence offenders if the victim exhibits any indication of bodily injury and/or when the police officer observes manifestations of an internal injury suffered by the victim. And, if there is probable cause to believe an offender violated a court-issued restraining order, the offender must be arrested.

The resident students were also given an opportunity to view Polygraph and Breathalyzer demonstrations, presented by nationally recognized experts. These instruments are most often used in criminal and traffic investigations. The instructors encouraged the resident students to participate in the field demonstrations to increase their understanding of the instruments and dispel any myths suggested by the media. The resident students were taught that they are the "eyes and ears" of the community, and they need to sharpen their skills as observers and reporters of criminal activity. Each resident needs to know that when he/she does call the police, certain information is asked by the operator so the police can properly investigate.

The resident students were given a personalized tour of the JCPD's Central Communication Room. It was an opportunity for the resident students to observe police dispatchers and call-takers operating highly technical Computer Aided Dispatch systems when handling emergency and nonemergency complaints on an hourly basis. A tour of the radio room demonstrated to the resident students the importance of civilian involvement, accurate reporting, and proper deployment of police resources.

On January 25, 1999, twenty-five residents who volunteered their time to attend the classes received a certificate of graduation from then Police Chief William Thynne and Housing Authority Executive Director Robert Rigby. Success of the program was measured by the very high level of attendance and a larger than anticipated level of response by the residents. As suggested by Jersey City Police Department's Public Safety Director Michael Moriarty, "training civilians to assist police in reducing crime increases the effectiveness of our community-oriented policing efforts." As a result of the success of the CPA at Curries Woods, the program has been implemented in other housing projects throughout Jersey City.

CONCLUSION

As shown in this chapter, it is possible to turn a crime-ridden public housing project into a much sought-after residence. It takes the commitment of the city, local police officers, and the residents. Only by working together can positive changes be made.

Crime prevention is a major component of any successful public housing renovation project. In order to revive and rejuvenate a public housing area, crime must be reduced, with the ultimate goal of elimination. Public housing residents play as big a role in crime prevention as police officers. Residents must be aware of crime and be willing to report the crime. Effective communication between residents and the local police is essential; trust is a must. Any community can become crime free, but it doesn't happen by chance.

REFERENCES

ANNAN, S. AND SKOGAN, W. (1992). *Drugs and Public Housing: Toward an Effective Police Response*. Washington, DC: Report to the National Institute of Justice: Police Foundation.

JERSEY CITY POLICE DEPARTMENT. (2000). Records maintained by the Public Housing Unit.

8

Shadows of the Street

Policing, Crime Prevention, and Gangs

Gordon A. Crews

❖

Historically, youth gangs and their activities have been a recurrent and visible indication of disorder in any given society. In essence, changes in gang structure often parallel the structural changes in a society. For example, many argue that gangs have become more violent as a result of increased violence in American society in general; others say that youth have become more attracted to gangs due to the increased pessimism and alienation being felt by American youth in general.

In trying to understand the complexities of gangs in America, several problems become immediately apparent. One of the first problems to present itself in any examination of gangs is that there is no accepted standard definition as to what constitutes a "gang." Generally, state and local jurisdictions tend to develop their own definitions to meet their needs or personal agendas. Researchers and lawmakers do the same.

There are several concepts that seem to be part of almost all existing definitions. The following criteria have been widely used in gang definitions (Crews & Montgomery, 2001; Knox, 2000; Shelden, Tracy, and Brown, 2001; Wooden & Blazak, 2001).

- Some type of formal or informal organizational-type structure
- Identifiable leadership
- Identified with a territory
- Recurrent interaction with other members
- Engaging in serious, violent, or criminal behavior

127

These criteria are increasingly used to distinguish gangs from other law-violating youth groups and other collective youth groups.

Another issue becoming apparent is that there is no national reporting system as to the extent of gang activity in the United States (Knox, 2000). Therefore, precise information is unavailable. Most police agencies cannot generate the necessary data to distinguish reported gang crimes from other types of youth crimes. From what is known, it appears gang violence is growing across the United States (Crews & Montgomery, 2001; Knox, 2000; Shelden, Tracy, and Brown, 2001; Wooden & Blazak, 2001). Surveys over the past several decades have been reporting gangs in more and more cities. The gang problem is also increasing from the standpoint of more violent offenses, more serious injuries, and use of more lethal weapons. However, it is unclear whether the growth in youth violence in general is directly related to gangs.

The body of literature relating to juvenile gangs in the country is massive (i.e., Crews & Montgomery, 2001; Knox, 2000; Shelden, Tracy, and Brown, 2001; Wooden & Blazak, 2001; Yablonsky, 2000). There are many views and opinions relating to this pressing problem. The following are the most often-cited gang characteristics as found in gang research:

- Members are typically young teenage males of similar ethnic or racial backgrounds. Loyalty and adherence to a strict gang code (i.e., the gang is more important than anything) is mandatory.
- Cohesiveness among members increases as recognition from society increases. Loyalty and camaraderie are solidified by participation in group activities that are often antisocial, illegal, violent, and criminal. Goals, identified roles, and responsibilities are clearly established and defined (they are often unspoken but are understood by all members).
- The chain of command is hierarchical.
- Identification with a local territory (often referred to as gang turf, hood, or barrio) is commonplace in the neighborhood, as well as on the school campus.
- Recruitment is an ongoing process, especially at school.

Characterizing "modern" gangs, since the 1980s, is not a simple task because they are more diverse and complex than gangs of earlier times. In addition, modern gangs are distinguishable from gangs of the past in the following manner (Crews & Montgomery, 2001; Knox, 2000; Shelden, Tracy, and Brown, 2001; Wooden & Blazak, 2001; Yablonsky, 2000):

- Younger active members (some as young as eight- or nine-years-old)
- Evidence of ethnic and racial crossover in multiethnic neighborhoods
- An insurgence of female gangs
- Established cliques or sets in suburban communities
- Acquisition of large sums of money from illegal drug markets and prostitution
- Rampant use of drugs and alcohol
- Violent membership
- Use of sophisticated communications devices and automatic weapons

- Employment of guerrilla warfarelike tactics
- Total disregard for human life as evidenced by the senseless deaths of innocent victims

OVERVIEW OF GANGS IN AMERICA

Gang culture among young people, in itself, is nothing new. Indeed, there is evidence that youth gangs have been a major part of the urban cultural landscape since at least the fourteenth and fifteenth centuries (Knox, 2000). Since the late twentieth century, however, gangs have taken on a different character and have moved into areas unimagined in the past (Crews & Montgomery, 2001). Most significantly, they are spreading from inner cities to the suburbs. Although gang activity has been stabilizing in urban areas, it has increased significantly in rural areas. At the same time, gangs have become a growing problem in public schools, which historically have been considered "neutral turf" (Crews & Counts, 1997). It is no secret that gangs and their antisocial activities have been increasing at alarming rates in communities and on school campuses nationwide. From the 1920s to the present day, gang activity has not only increased and intensified, but it has done so with notoriously senseless crime and violence (Knox, 2000).

Little empirical research has documented organizational operation of drug trafficking networks by gangs (Yablonsky, 2000). However, significant involvement of gang members in drug distribution has been demonstrated. Few drug trafficking gangs, trafficking cliques within gangs, and gangs established specifically for drug distribution purposes have been identified by the police. Also, research-to-date has provided little support for the idea that increased homicides and weapons use associated with drug trafficking can be attributed directly to gangs (Crews & Montgomery, 2001). Many of the inner-city homicides may be a result of turf battles, not drug violence.

Studies of established gangs in "chronic" gang cities since the 1920s have documented long delinquent gang careers (Knox, 2000). However, recent studies have found that most juveniles stay in the gang for no more than a year. Their delinquency levels are much lower both before and after joining the gang. To some extent, gang problems are characterized by an ebb and flow pattern. Street gang patterns reflect not only chronic social problems associated with race, social class, and immigration, but also rapidly changing contemporary conditions related to the economy, weapon availability, drug markets, and the arrangement of street gang territories (Crews & Montgomery, 2001).

Characteristics of Gangs

Researchers agree that most gangs share certain characteristics (i.e., Crews & Montgomery, 2001; Knox, 2000; Shelden, Tracy, and Brown, 2001; Wooden & Blazak, 2001; Yablonsky, 2000). Although there are exceptions, gangs tend to develop along racial and ethnic lines and are typically 90 percent male. Gang members often display their membership through distinctive styles of dress—their "colors"—and through specific activities and patterns of behavior. In addition, gangs almost universally show strong loyalty to their neighborhood, often marking out their territory with graffiti. All these representations, of course, can be visible in the schools and on most city streets.

However, the specifics of gang style (Crews & Montgomery, 2001; Knox, 2000; Shelden, Tracy, and Brown, 2001; Wooden & Blazak, 2001; Yablonsky, 2000) and activity can vary tremendously from gang to gang, and can even change rapidly within individual gangs. For instance, African American gangs tend to confine their activities to their own communities, although the Bloods and the Crips, two gangs originating in Los Angeles, now have members nationwide. In contrast, Asian gangs often travel hundreds of miles from home in order to conduct their activities. In addition, African American and Hispanic gangs are much more likely to display their colors than are Asian gangs. Anglo gangs are often made up of white supremacists. Gangs can also vary tremendously in numbers and age ranges of members.

The Impact of Gangs on Schools

Despite their high profile in the media, relatively few young people join gangs (Crews & Counts, 1997). Even in highly impacted areas, the degree of participation has rarely exceeded ten percent. In addition, it has been reported that less than two percent of all juvenile crime is gang-related. Such low numbers, however, may camouflage the impact that the presence of gangs has on a school. For one thing, they play a significant role in the widespread increase of violence in schools. Because gangs are, by definition, organized groups, and are often actively involved in drug and weapons trafficking, their mere presence in school can increase tensions. It can also increase the level of violence in schools, even though gang members themselves may not be directly responsible for all of it; both gang members and nongang members are arming themselves with increased frequency. Students in schools with a gang presence are twice as likely to report that they fear becoming victims of violence than their peers at schools without gangs. Moreover, schools with gangs are significantly more likely to have drugs available on campus than those without gangs.

Far from remaining neutral turf, schools not only suffer from gang-related violence "spilling over" from the streets, but also are themselves rapidly becoming centers of gang activities, functioning particularly as sites for recruitment and socializing (Crews & Counts, 1997). Gang members see school as a necessary evil at best and at worst as a form of "incarceration." Although many gang members acknowledge the importance of the educational objectives of school, school is much more important to them as a place for gathering with fellow gang members for socializing and other more violent activities. Significantly, even those gang members who have been suspended or have dropped out of school can often be found on campus with their associates, effectively using the school as a gang hangout rather than as an educational institution. Finally, gangs can spread unexpectedly from school to school as students transfer from gang-impacted schools to gang-free schools, causing an unintentional spillover of gang activity in the new school.

Youth Involvement in Gangs

Gangs take root in communities for many reasons, but the primary attraction of gangs is their ability to respond to a child's needs that are not otherwise being met (Crews & Montgomery, 2001; Knox, 2000; Shelden, Tracy, and Brown, 2001; Wooden & Blazak, 2001; Yablonsky,

2000). They often provide youth with a sense of family and acceptance otherwise lacking in their lives. In addition, gangs may form among groups of recent immigrants as a way of maintaining a strong ethnic identity. Understanding how gangs meet these needs prepares communities to better respond to them.

Four factors are primary in the formation of juvenile gangs (Crews & Montgomery, 2001). First, youth experience a sense of alienation and powerlessness because of a lack of traditional support structures, such as family and school. This can lead to feelings of frustration and anger, and a desire to obtain support outside of traditional institutions. Second, gang membership gives youth a sense of belonging and becomes a major source of identity for its members. In turn, gang membership affords youth a sense of power and control, and gang activities become an outlet for their anger. Third, the control of turf is essential to the well-being of the gang, which often will use force to control both its territory and members. Finally, recruitment of new members and expansion of territory are essential if a gang is to remain strong and powerful. Both "willing" and "unwilling" members are drawn into gangs to feed the need for more resources and gang members.

DEVELOPING A REALISTIC AND DISTINCTIVE GANG PREVENTION PROGRAM

Police officials must be realistic in their approach to gangs and may be required to decide whether to concentrate their efforts on preventing or reducing gang-related activity (Alpert & Piquero, 1998; Champion & Rush, 1997; Cox, 1996). The term prevention implies that methods can be employed to remove evidence of gangs and negative gang activities in a community. Reduction implies that methods can be employed to lessen the effect of negative gang activities. The suggested prevention strategies in the following discussion also have relevance as reduction strategies.

Police officials who deny the presence of gangs limit their options to confront gangs realistically and effectively (Crews & Montgomery, 2001). It is widely recognized that many police officials are victims of the "ostrich syndrome" when they become defensive and ignore critical problems in their communities. In denying negative situations, such as gang activity, officials exacerbate the problem. Reluctance by officials to address the gang issue is primarily due to a lack of knowledge about gangs. Once officials acquire the knowledge and transcend the denial stage by adopting a realistic perspective, they can initiate, maintain, and evaluate solution strategies.

Officials who are most successful in their efforts to confront negative gang activities are those who develop a "site-specific" approach to the problem (Crews & Montgomery, 2001). In doing so, a distinctive leadership style can emerge that permits officials to possess a certain mentality (attitude) about gangs. Similar to the gang mentality of most gang members, which in essence holds that nothing is more important than the gang and members are willing to do whatever the gang demands, so too must police officials adopt a "positive community mentality." Officials must believe that nothing is more important than providing a safe environment for citizens, and be willing to do whatever is necessary to prevent or reduce the negative effects of gang activity in their jurisdiction.

Taking a distinctive approach encourages the development of an organizational framework for the development of the jurisdiction's gang prevention program (Crews &

Montgomery, 2001). There are various ways to organize site-specific solution strategies, and officials must decide what is most beneficial for their jurisdiction. Regardless of the organizational design, constant revisions of strategies will always be necessary. They should be adaptable because of the ever-changing behavioral patterns of gangs. The following sections discuss three categories of solution strategies: operational strategies, alternative behavior strategies, and engagement strategies.

Operational strategies direct the operation or processes of a program or initiative (Dunham & Alpert, 1997). Initially, the police leader sets the tone for change and employs key personnel to assist with operational or organizational tasks. Later this core group (including the police leader) may be expanded to a team that will assume responsibility for all eventual gang prevention efforts. Development of this process will depend on the individual situations in each jurisdiction.

Alternative behavioral strategies are designed to turn around the negative behavior of gang members and to prevent them from engaging in disruptive activities (Crews & Montgomery, 2001). Defining gang activities, identifying and documenting gangs and members, building interpersonal relationships with members, involving members in community activities, and providing educational alternatives are proven effective solution strategies. Utilization of these strategies may require police personnel to alter their attitudes about and behavior toward the gangs. Accepting the gangs in a community is a positive way of involving members in the daily activities of the community experience. Assimilation of members into the mainstream of the community reduces recruitment by minimizing the lure and mystery of the gang.

Engagement strategies are designed to involve different groups of people in the antigang program processes (Crews & Counts, 1997). Members of school staffs, families, and community agencies have an inherent vested interest in the education and socialization of American youth. Collaboration among these groups with the police to influence and provide alternative avenues for gang members is successful and necessary. Staff development training sessions, staff and department meetings, student assemblies and parent conferences at schools, advisory council and other parent/teacher group meetings, neighborhood watch and other community meetings are but a few vehicles that police officials can use to disseminate information about antigang efforts.

The Roles of Police Officers and Police Agencies

The fundamental purpose of policing is to protect the community from criminal activities (Dunham & Alpert, 1997). Protection is achieved through a combination of suppression and preventive activities. The police need to address emerging and chronic youth gang problems distinctively. Police organizational arrangements to deal with the youth gang problem should vary depending on the scope and seriousness of the problem and available departmental resources.

In communities confronted by emerging youth gangs, the police department may not necessarily need to organize a specialized gang unit but instead establish a gang detail or designate one or more officers as gang specialists (Crews & Montgomery, 2001). Other possibilities include assigning a crime analysis officer to identify chronic or serious juvenile gang offenders and requiring patrol officers in areas of high gang activity to focus their attention on these youth.

In some jurisdictions, community relations, narcotics, and juvenile divisions may actually take on specialized functions to deal with gangs (Crews & Montgomery, 2001). Generally, in larger communities where the gang problem may be more serious and sophisticated, a specialized gang unit should probably be established. In some very large cities, specialized gang units may also be decentralized and placed in areas of need. In all cases, common definitions of the youth gang problem and ways to deal with it should characterize police policy and procedures. Special attention should be paid to leaders and to hard-core, repeat, and violent gang offenders.

The police agency should adopt an approach that combines suppression of youth gang criminal acts through aggressive enforcement of laws, with community mobilization involving a broad cross-section of the community in combating the problem (Knox, 2000). Development of social intervention activities, though maybe secondary in importance, should still be pursued. Useful interventions might include referring juveniles prone to gangs to youth service agencies, counseling such youth in collaboration with school guidance programs, and assisting community-based agencies in targeting youth gang members for job development.

The role of the police agency in controlling and reducing gang crime should include investigation, intelligence, suppression, community relations, and training (Knox, 2000). Of special importance is investigation of gang crimes to obtain information and evidence useful in the prosecution of youth involved in gang crimes; maintaining standardized, updated information on gangs, gang members, and gang incidents; concentrating surveillance on gang leaders and other hard-core members; targeting special locations, particularly selected schools, for special patrol; prevention and control of those circumstances in which youth gang crises are likely to arise; training criminal justice and community-based agency staff and local citizens in gang recognition and appropriate intervention procedures; and assessment of the effectiveness of police policies and procedures in relation to youth gang crime.

The top administrator of the police agency must be involved in determining gang policy and should insist on the officers' consistent and complete implementation of orders and procedures (Knox, 2000). The exercise of community leadership and a recognition of the scope of the gang problem will help elected leaders, agencies, and groups in the community deal with it openly and adequately. Where gang problems are emerging, administrators should not minimize the scope of the problem to protect the perception of the community but should actually call attention to incidents of gang crime. In contexts where gang problems have become chronic, the administrator should withstand pressures to simply increase the level of suppression and support the development of a comprehensive community approach targeted to both youth prone to gangs as well as other gang members.

Finally, special training is necessary for police officers assigned to deal with gang crimes (Crews & Montgomery, 2001). Knowledge from diverse fields must be integrated into the policing mission. General information is required regarding such topics as the causes of gangs, their identification and nature, and the roles police should play with each type of agency or community group in addressing the problem. Police strategies and programs should be evaluated on a regular basis. Assessments should use measures of policing outcome, internal organization, and community relations.

A strong-targeted police presence has traditionally been seen as essential to any department's mission of stemming violence in its particular community (Cox, 1996).

Targeting high-incidence areas and deploying the same officers to those areas for an extended period of time was considered essential. Effective suppression is still based on gathering and organizing intelligence information on youth gangs and their members. Police officers must be specifically trained and experienced to recognize gang problems in their jurisdiction. The police must also be able to communicate with gang members in a positive way.

Police agencies must ensure that judges are aware of the gang affiliations of defendants before sentencing (Knox, 2000). These efforts will result in large numbers of gang members being imprisoned. In many areas, targeted suppression, in combination with other justice and community interventions, cause a reduction in gang violence. Many departments have tactical and crime specialist officers. The tactical officers, in uniform or plain clothes, are given directed missions on a day-to-day basis. The gang crime specialists do more investigative follow-up of crimes. They write gang histories and prepare cases for trial. A monthly report is prepared based on statistics including type of crime, location of crime, and district of occurrence. Most gang crime units work closely to assist the district commander with information on gangs and to supplement the commander's personnel in a given situation.

Many gang units use a central records division to determine whether a person arrested is on probation or parole (Knox, 2000). If so, the proper authority is notified. The unit notifies the corrections department when a leader or core gang member is being incarcerated. In turn, the prison authorities are expected to notify the gang unit when a high-ranking gang member returns to the community or a potential gang problem may occur with that person's release. It must always be remembered that both suppression and social intervention programs in combination are most often needed to stop gang violence.

Community Police Responses

It should be no surprise that police can provide children and families with a sense of security and safety through rapid, authoritative, and effective responses at times of danger (Alpert & Piquero, 1998; Champion & Rush, 1997). It is sad, however, that most children's contacts with police officers arouse more negative feelings than positive. For example, the arrival of officers after a violent event can reinforce a child's sense of being unprotected and the feeling that those in charge provide too little help, too late. For many children, particularly those in impoverished inner cities, the police are seen as representatives of a dominant, insensitive culture and quickly become targets of children's anger toward a hostile and uncaring society.

Community policing (Alpert & Piquero, 1998; Champion & Rush, 1997; Cox, 1996) provides officers with opportunities to minimize these negative experiences and instead offer children positive models for identification. Police officers who take on a consistent, authoritative presence in their neighborhoods are potential heroes for young people for whom there are all too few prosocial adult models. Generally, community policing places individual officers on long-term assignments in specific neighborhoods and encourages them to work with community residents to analyze and solve problems before they erupt in lethal violence. Under this philosophy, children and families come in contact with officers in a wide variety of helping roles, well beyond the context of such traditional police functions as making arrests or executing search warrants.

As community policing integrates officers within their communities, they become known as individuals, rather than by role, and they come to know the people they serve as individuals. These strategies allow officers to develop relationships and assume roles in children's lives that would not be possible in a more impersonal, reactive policing system. As figures of authority, police officers are also in a position to broker services for families and to coordinate the responses of other institutions. The assumption of such expanded roles in the lives of children also imposes new burdens on police officers and requires new modes of training and operational support.

The central focus on relationships between police and community members has also resulted in other examples of policing success (Crews & Montgomery, 2001). When officers know the community, they recognize that the majority of citizens are law abiding and represent potential partners for a better neighborhood. This frees officers to focus more effective enforcement efforts on the small number of career and violent offenders.

Gang Violence Reduction Strategies

Fortunately, many progressive communities are implementing a combination of prevention, intervention, and suppression strategies to address their gang problem (Crews & Montgomery, 2001). An effective antieffort must be based on sound theory and work closely with the juvenile justice system. Policy and programs must be based on appropriate targeting of both institutions and youth and also their relation to each other at a specific time and place, for example, when the youth is entering the gang or ready to leave it and/or at the stage the gang problem is developing in the particular institution or community.

Conclusive evaluations of these types of strategies are still needed, but the following common elements appear to be associated with sustained reduction of gang problems: Community leaders must recognize the presence of gangs and seek to understand the nature and extent of the local gang problem through a comprehensive and systematic assessment of the gang problem. The combined leadership of the justice system and the community must focus on the mobilization of institutional and community resources to address gang problems.

Those in principal roles must develop a consensus on definitions (e.g., gang, gang incident, etc.), specific targets of agency and interagency efforts, and interrelated strategies—based on problem assessment, not assumptions. Research supports that coordinated strategies should include the following (Crews & Montgomery, 2001; Knox, 2000; Shelden, Tracy, and Brown, 2001; Wooden & Blazak, 2001; Yablonsky, 2000):

- Community mobilization (including citizens, youth, community groups, and agencies)
- Social and economic opportunities, including special school, training, and job programs (These are especially critical for older gang members who are not in school but may be ready to leave the gang or decrease participation in criminal gang activity for many reasons, including maturation and the need to provide for family.)
- Social intervention (especially youth outreach and work with street gangs directed toward mainstreaming youth)

- Gang suppression (formal and informal social control procedures of the justice systems and community agencies and groups)
- Community-based agencies and local groups to collaborate with juvenile and criminal justice agencies in surveillance and sharing of information under conditions that protect the community and the civil liberties of youth
- Organizational change and development (the appropriate organization and integration of the discussed strategies and potential reallocation of resources among involved agencies)
- Any approach to be guided by concern not only for safeguarding the community against youth gang activities but also for providing support and supervision to present and potential gang members in a way that contributes to their prosocial development.

CONCLUSION

There is a myriad of issues surrounding the issue of gangs in America. The field of gang research is filled with controversies and conflicts. Researchers cannot agree on a definition of what a gang is, much less what should be done about issues related to gang behavior. Until some consistency or collaboration develops in the study of gangs, it will be plagued with problems.

Fortunately, there is a light at the end of the tunnel—and it may not be a train! Police officers have found they can make a difference. Through careful, site-specific, community-based efforts, positive changes can be made. Many jurisdictions have realized they do have the light needed to drive away many of the "shadows of the street."

REFERENCES

ALPERT, G. P., & PIQUERO, A. (1998). *Community policing: Contemporary readings*. Prospect Heights, IL: Waveland Press, Inc.

CHAMPION, D. J., & RUSH, G. E. (1997). *Policing the community*. Upper Saddle River, NJ: Prentice Hall.

COX, S. M. (1996). *Police: Practices perspectives problems*. Boston, MA: Allyn and Bacon.

CREWS, G. A., & MONTGOMERY, R. H., Jr. (2001). *Chasing shadows: Confronting juvenile violence in America*. Upper Saddle River, NJ: Prentice Hall.

CREWS, G. A. & COUNTS, M. R. (1997). *The evolution of school disturbance in America: Colonial times to modern day*. Westport, CT: Praeger.

DUNHAM, R. G., & ALPERT, G. P. (1997). *Critical issues in policing*. Prospect Heights, IL: Waveland Press, Inc.

KNOX, G. (2000). *An introduction to gangs*. Peotone, IL: New Chicago School Press, Inc.

SHELDEN, R. G., TRACY, S. K., & BROWN, W. B. (2001). *Youth gangs in American society* (2nd ed.). Belmont, CA: Wadsworth Publishing.

WOODEN, W. S., & BLAZAK, R. (2001). *Renegade kids, suburban outlaws: From youth culture to delinquency*. Belmont, CA: Wadsworth Publishing.

YABLONSKY, L. (2000). *Juvenile delinquency: Into the 21st century*. Belmont, CA: Wadsworth Publishing.

9

Policing Domestic Violence

Susan T. Krumholz

Police action cannot by itself stem the tide of violence against women. It can, however, stop perpetuating and reproducing it.

Elizabeth Stanko

❖

In the past thirty years, domestic violence has emerged as a significant social issue in need of a social response (Dobash & Dobash, 1979; Gelles & Cornell, 1990; Martin, 1987; Schecter, 1982). Awareness grew out of the feminist movement of the 1970s (the so-called Second Wave of Feminism) and became known as the Battered Woman's or Shelter Movement. This movement began as an effort to empower women to help themselves and one another escape violence inflicted by the men with whom they were intimate. As the movement grew, visibility of domestic violence increased, and some of the old attitudes and stereotypes began to change (Lentz, 1999). But increased visibility did little to reduce the incidence of domestic assault. Recent statistics illustrate the extent of the problem that continues to exist. In a large scale survey of American women, 25 percent reported having been raped or physically assaulted by an intimate, 1.5 percent in the previous twelve months (Tjaden & Thomas, 1998).

The view emerged that women's experiences with violence in their homes would not be recognized as a serious social problem until the law took the problem seriously (Lentz, 1999; Schecter, 1982). As with other matters of violence, the problem of domestic violence was deemed best addressed by the criminal justice system (Buzawa & Buzawa, 1996; Parnas, 1967; Pleck, 1989). The police are the frontline in that system, and so the burden has fallen on the police to develop new and better methods of enforcement (Bell, 1985; Berk, Loseke, Berk, and Rauma, 1980; Buzawa & Buzawa, 1992).

In the past two decades, new laws covering domestic violence have been passed in every jurisdiction in the United States (Collins, 1995; Davis & Smith, 1995). Changes brought about by these new laws include the widespread availability of Civil Protection Orders (Collins, 1995), waiving the probable cause requirement for arrest in instances of misdemeanor domestic disturbances, requiring that police provide affirmative assistance to complainants, and mandating that police make an arrest (Lyon, 1999).

Local police departments, in attempting to comply with these changes, developed their own administrative tools for enforcement. The result is a significant amount of procedural variation. Some jurisdictions have mandatory arrest policies which, for some, arrest is not mandatory, but preferred. Some departments have specialized units, others a designated officer, still others handle domestic complaints as any other disturbance or assault call. Some departments work closely with community programs serving battered women; others are very insular. Some departments see their role as neutral enforcers of the law; others see themselves as advocates for the victims of crime.

An abundance of research has focused on the role of arrest in deterring the reoccurrence of violence (i.e., Bourg & Stock, 1994; Buzawa & Buzawa, 1993; Dunford, Hunizinga, and Elliot, 1990; Finesmith, 1993; Hirschel & Hutchinson, 1992; Manning, 1993; McCord, 1992; Meeker & Binder, 1990; Sherman & Berk, 1984; Sherman & Cohn, 1989; Sherman, Smith, Schmidt, and Rogan, 1992; Stark, 1993; Zorza, 1994). Research has looked at the effect of officer attitudes on enforcement (Black, 1980), and the effect of training on those attitudes (Ferraro & Pope, 1993; Sgarzi, 1991). Research has been done as well on several "model" programs where the criminal justice system works closely and cooperatively with battered women's groups and other community agencies (Edleson, 1991; Salzman, 1994; Soler, 1987; Steinman, 1991; Tolman & Weisz, 1995).

DOMESTIC VIOLENCE DEFINED

Domestic violence has become the term of art most commonly used to define what has been described as "violence between heterosexual adults who are living together or who have previously cohabited" (Buzawa & Buzawa, 1996, p. 4); the occurrence of one or more of the following acts between family or household members: (1) attempting to cause or causing physical harm; (2) placing another in fear of imminent serious physical harm; (3) causing another to engage involuntarily in sexual relations by force, threat, or duress by family or household members (Massachusetts General Law ch. 209A §1); (4) "violence committed by those individuals one is more likely to trust and have continuing social relations with" (Miller & Welford, 1997, p. 17); or (5) "the pattern of violent acts and their political framework, the pattern of social, institutional, and interpersonal controls that usurp a woman's capacity to determine her destiny and make her vulnerable to a range of secondary consequences—attempted suicide, substance abuse, mental illness and the like" (Stark, 1993, p. 656). Despite the common use of the term "domestic violence," it has been objected to on several grounds, and alternative labels have been suggested.

"Domestic" is a sterile term which barely enables one to imagine the human element, the victim. Straus, Gelles, and Steinmetz (1980) choose the terms "marital conflict" or "marital violence" to describe what they were observing. This terminology also lacks a sense of the person involved and is too narrowly focused, as it refers to conflicts that occur only within marriage. More significantly, it fails to recognize the gendered nature of such violence. Similar objection has been made of the term "spouse abuse," which "obfuscate[s] criticism of the traditional patriarchal family" (Daniels, 1997, p. 2).

Some have preferred the use of terms such as "violence between intimate partners" (Browne, 1987), or simply "battering." These terms, too, have been objected to by those who wish to remind us that violence against *women* by their *male* partners is the most common form of intimate violence (Dobash & Dobash, 1979; Schecter, 1982). The term "wife battering," suggested early on by such pivotal works as *The Battered Woman* (Walker, 1979) and *Violence against Wives* (Dobash & Dobash, 1979), though identifying the primary victim of violence, also offers too narrow a focus for current purposes. And though the term "woman battering" may satisfy much of the criticism, it too has been denounced for stressing the biological over the relational (Martin, 1987) and for ignoring the men in heterosexual and homosexual intimate relationships who are themselves victims of violence.

As "domestic violence" is the most generally recognized terminology in both law and the literature on policing, it will be used, with some reservation, for the remainder of the present chapter as the principal terminology to describe those acts of violence committed within an intimate relationship.

SOCIAL AND LEGAL CHANGES

Early History—The Bad Old Days

Evidence offered by researchers indicates men have beaten their wives for centuries (Pleck, 1989). Martin (1987) suggests such beatings were condoned from the moment humankind discovered men played a role in the creation of a child. Men quickly assumed the power that women, as bearers of children, had held, and "the strictest fidelity was demanded of the wife in order to guarantee and authenticate the husband's fatherhood" (p. 4). So began patriarchy, "a system of male authority which oppresses women through its social, political and economic institutions" (Humm, 1990, p. 159). The feminist view of violence proposes that violence is an extension of patriarchy, or men's need to maintain their control over women (Dobash & Dobash, 1979).

The emergence of patriarchal religions, Christianity and others, reinforced the role of man as the head of the family. Women were not to be trusted. They were "inferior, childlike and mindless . . . suitable only for conjugal duties" (Martin, 1987, p. 6). It was man's duty to assure his wife, as his children and livestock, obeyed or he was to use "reasonable chastisement" (Lentz, 1999) to assure obedience. This, according to the Dobashes (1979), made women the "appropriate victims" of family violence.

Under the legal doctrine of coverture, when a man and woman married, they became one person, that person was the man. A woman forfeited her right to own property, to make contracts, or even to retain her own wages. The doctrine carried with it the implicit, and sometimes explicit, understanding that the woman's actions were the man's responsibility, and the burden fell upon him to monitor those actions. If force were necessary, the law would tolerate it, as long as no severe injury resulted (Lentz, 1999).

The Puritans who settled much of New England brought with them the humanitarian belief that it was immoral for a husband to beat his wife. This prohibition became a part of the Massachusetts Bay Colony Criminal Code. The prohibition did not, however, extend to what was considered to be "reasonable" punishment, punishment that did not leave scars or do permanent injury (Pleck, 1989). And when cases were brought to trial, judges often inquired as to the wife's responsibility in inciting the violence (Lentz, 1999). Consequently, no one was ever convicted (Pleck, 1989).

During the nineteenth century, a middle-class consensus began to emerge that a resort to violence was plebian, and therefore unacceptable (Pleck, 1989). This was reinforced by the cult of domesticity (see Humm, 1990, p. 55) which became prominent at the end of the century (Lentz, 1999). Neither of these influences was sufficient to counter the belief in the sanctity of the home (Steinman, 1991). The "curtain rule" (1874 North Carolina court decision as cited in Browne, 1987, p. 167) was relied upon to justify the failure to provide legal or social remedies (Kurz, 1992).

By the late nineteenth century, a public debate about women's social and legal status had begun (Lentz, 1999), and the stage was set for women to speak. North Carolina became the first state in the new nation to curtail a man's right to whip his wife, rejecting the argument that provocation could be a justification for beating (*State v Oliver*). The Court qualified the prohibition, however, suggesting that for the protection of the family, courts should not intervene "unless there existed permanent injury or extreme violence" (Lentz, 1999, p. 18).

In the early 1900s, the interspousal immunity rule appeared in court decisions. This rule prevented one spouse from testifying against the other. It also assured that battered women could not bring tort actions against their husbands (Finesmith, 1993). Women were thus silenced, and it would take almost a century before the voices of the victims of intimate violence would be heard.

The Second Wave of Feminism and Wife Beating

Dobash and Dobash (1979) pinpoint the emergence of women's struggle against the abuse by their male partners as a societal problem, to a march of five hundred women and children in Chiswick, England, in 1971. Schecter (1982) stated it seems as if the issue of battered women "came out of nowhere" in the early 1970s. Steinman (1991) notes that in 1971, the first hotline for battered women was established, and the first shelters followed. Prior to this time, few were even aware that such a problem existed. Even the women being abused, most of whom accepted or resisted the violence in silence, were not aware of the others who shared their experiences. It is generally agreed that the women's movement, or the so-called Second Wave of Feminism, of the late 1960s, brought women together in record numbers. They began to share their own experiences, and to recognize the extent to which those experiences where shared (Dobash & Dobash, 1979; Pleck, 1989; Schecter, 1982).

Along with the discovery of child abuse and the increasing public awareness of the violence being done to women in their homes, changes in the criminal justice system played a role in the emergence of domestic violence as a social problem. The emphasis on the victim (Fagan, 1988) and the public and political mood of law and order (Gelles, 1993; Pleck, 1989) increased demands for more protection for victims and more aggressive actions by the police. Fagan (1998) suggests rapid legal change was made in an effort by some lawmakers to avoid the larger issue of male power and domination.

Even with recognition there is not agreement. Two prominent approaches to domestic violence are identified in the literature: feminist and social control or the "family violence perspective" (Breines & Gordon, 1983; Fagan, 1988). The feminist view focuses on men's use of violence to control women. The purpose of such violence would be to maintain the existing social order. Feminist theorists emphasize the fact that women are the usual victims, and their primary goal is protecting the women. The social control view employs the social work model of family systems to illustrate how the family interactions result in violence. Social control theorists often refer to mutual combat, suggesting use of violence is similar for men and women. Family violence is viewed as resulting from a breakdown in social order. Although all theorists share the goal of reducing the amount of violence in the family, feminist theorists fear that social control policies will ignore the larger issues of inequality and the distribution of power (Breines & Gordon, 1983; Fagan, 1988; Kurz, 1992).

The Law Changes

In the United States, domestic violence is now recognized as a crime in all fifty states and the District of Columbia. Prior to the mid-1970s, this was not the case. Domestic violence was viewed as a private matter and legal protections were limited to a handful of unusually brutal cases (Pleck, 1989). Police officials maintained an explicit "hands-off" policy, and prosecutors were discouraged from actively pursuing cases (Parnas, 1967). One of the limited options available to women, civil injunctions, carried no criminal penalty and therefore little protection. In addition, civil injunctions applied only to women who were married to their abuser, and often were available only to women who had filed for divorce or legal separation (Zorza, 1992). It was primarily the work of feminist legal scholars who made domestic violence the subject of extensive reforms.

A series of court cases and the publication of the first book on the subject of woman battering set the stage for the legal changes to come. In 1976, two class action lawsuits were filed on behalf of women on opposite sides of the country. The first, *Scott v Hart*, was filed against the police chief of Oakland, California, "on behalf of black victims of domestic violence who were getting less adequate police responses than were white victims" (Zorza, 1992, pp. 54–55). The complaint alleged a denial of equal protection pursuant to the Fourteenth Amendment. The second case, *Bruno v Codd*, was filed "on behalf of married battered women against the New York City Police Department and the New York Family Court" alleging failure to protect (Zorza, 1992, p. 57). Both cases culminated in consent decrees, agreements between the parties detailing the manner in which the problems would be remedied.

Eight years later, in the landmark case of *Thurman v City of Torrington, Connecticut*, the Court found the city's police policy of inaction made it negligent for failing to protect Tracy Thurman from the violence of her husband. She and her son were awarded $2.3 million. In conjunction with the *Scott* and *Bruno* cases, *Thurman* alerted police departments nationally to their potential liability if they did not review their policies, formal and informal, addressing domestic violence.

Policing—A First Look

As domestic violence gained visibility in the public domain, pressure began to intensify over the inadequate response of policing. At the same time, the societal attitudes toward crime and the response to crime were changing. Politicians and the public began to demand stricter enforcement, more actions were deemed criminal (criminalized), minimum or mandatory sentences became the norm, and time served was increasingly punitive (Gelles, 1993). In a political climate that favored control, it became possible for battered women's advocates and social conservatives to become allies in demanding police action in instances of domestic violence (Walker, 1993).

Oregon was the first state to require police to arrest in the case of domestic assault, having passed its Abuse Prevention Act in 1977 (Zorza, 1992). By 1983, thirty-three states and the District of Columbia had passed legislation permitting warrantless arrests, and forty-three states had new laws pertaining to orders of protection for battered women (Ferraro, 1989). The next year, the Task Force on Family Violence, representing the U.S. Attorney General (Hart, 1984), issued a report recommending that police agencies "establish arrest as the preferred response" (Ferraro, 1989).

The impact that the legal changes had on policing domestic violence has been called into question by many researchers. In the early 1980s, Finesmith (1993, p. 75) found that "less than twenty-five percent of the jurisdictions surveyed . . . require full enforcement of the law." And as recently as 1985, Bell (1985) reported that many departments instructed officers not to arrest offenders in domestic disputes unless there is significant injury.

Yet the laws continued to change, and by 1992, arrest was mandatory in fourteen states and many cities and towns (Buzawa & Buzawa, 1996). The 1992 numbers reflected a growing recognition of the problem of domestic violence. Forty-seven states and the District of Columbia had statutes allowing for warrantless arrests (Buzawa & Buzawa, 1996). Some of the other statutory changes have included requiring police to provide women with information about legal options and available services, providing transportation for the victim to a safe location, making violation of protective orders a criminal offense, and adding surcharges on marriage licenses and/or divorce decrees to help support services for battered women (Buzawa & Buzawa, 1996; Ferraro, 1989).

Federal Law

Although the federal government played a role in funding research and recommending policy, little was done to address domestic violence in federal law until passage of the Violence Against Women Act (VAWA) in 1994 (42 USCA § 13931). Prior to passage of VAWA, the legislature had defeated several pieces of legislation aimed at domestic violence, and passed only two. Buzawa and Buzawa (1996) offer a glimpse into the Congressional Record, which suggests some of the powerful criticism: "Senator Jesse Helms critiqued providing any federal support to domestic violence shelters because they constituted 'social engineering,' challenging the husband's place as 'head of the family' (126 Cong. Rec. 24, 120, 1980)" (p. 129). The two pieces of federal legislation addressing domestic violence were the Family Violence Prevention and Services Act of 1984, which provided limited grant money to shelter programs and for police training programs, and the Victims of Crime Act of 1984, which provided money for victims of crime (Brooks, 1997).

The VAWA was first presented to Congress in 1990, where it was not well received. When the VAWA was reintroduced by Senator Biden in 1994, it meet with much more limited resistance. Some have suggested the ongoing spectacle of the O. J. Simpson murder trial and the shift in public opinion about domestic violence affected the bill's passage (Brooks, 1997). The VAWA was finally passed as part of a larger crime bill which provides $1.62 billion over six years to fund a wide range of programs, including items from public park improvements to education for judges. In addition to the funding, the act contains provisions that provide some protection for battered immigrant women and their children, and a "Civil Rights Remedy for victims who can prove that the violence inflicted upon them was motivated by their gender" (Brooks, 1997, p. 77).

Although the legislation passed, "the fact that VAWA was ultimately consolidated into a crime bill placed many feminists in the awkward position of mobilizing around a measure with which they did not agree" (Brooks, 1997, p. 79). To further complicate the legitimacy of the VAWA, on May 15, 2000, in the case of *US v Morrison* (120 S.Ct. 1740), the Supreme Court overturned that part of the Violence Against Women Act which allowed rape victims to sue attackers in Federal Court. At the time of this writing, the Violence Against Women Act, initially funded for five years, awaits reauthorization.

POLICING DOMESTIC VIOLENCE

In the twentieth century, the traditional police response to cases of domestic violence has been dominated by their "overriding goal to extricate (themselves) with 'real' police work" (Buzawa & Buzawa, 1992). The typical police response was to do nothing, or to respond with minimal action. Roy (1977) reminds us that barely two decades ago "the underlying criminal justice system's response is the covert toleration of wife beating as indicated in the policy and personal attitudes of police, prosecutors, and judges" (p. 138).

The attitudes and policies found in most police departments encouraged a "do nothing" response from officers (Bowker, 1982). Parnas (1967) identifies "several very practical reasons for a nonarrest policy," including:

1) the victim doesn't really want the offender arrested, but wants some immediate assistance;
2) the parties couldn't afford it if the offender loses work;
3) this behavior is culturally appropriate (therefore acceptable) in the disputants' culture;
4) the offender may retaliate with more severe violence; and
5) arrest may harm the family structure. (pp. 930–931)

That most domestic violence cases were classified as misdemeanor assaults also discouraged police action. Until recently, police officers were unable to arrest without a warrant unless they had actually witnessed the incident. No matter how warranted, the officer could not make an arrest unless the victim swore out a complaint before a magistrate, a process victims often found confusing, intimidating, and expensive (Zorza, 1992). This restriction reinforced the police response of doing nothing by prohibiting police from taking independent action, and forcing them to rely instead upon the perseverance of the victim. The victim's failure to follow through with the complaint process was read by police as indicative of the severity, or lack thereof, of the abuse (Buzawa & Buzawa, 1996).

Compounding the problem of police acting on domestic violence calls, promotion in police departments has historically been based on arrest and conviction rates. As officers were restricted in their ability to arrest, and cases were rarely prosecuted, domestic calls received low priority (Berk et al., 1980).

The individual officer approached domestic violence calls with personal beliefs about the right of men to dominate women (Berk et al., 1980; Zorza, 1994). Many officers regarded domestic violence incidents as private disputes that should be settled by the parties involved. Researchers suggested officers viewed wife abuse as "normal" and perceived the victim as not seriously concerned about the violence (Field & Field, 1973). Departmental policies discouraged incursions into the "right of men to exercise their authority" over women (Berk et al., 1980).

The historical view supported by officers and administrators alike—that the role of police is to enforce the law and not provide social services—provided no incentive to act. The training officers received did little to undermine the negative stereotypes of domestic violence (Sgarzi, 1991). Domestic violence calls were explained to officers as an unproductive use of time because they were unlikely to result in arrest, so they were instructed to attempt to exit the situation as soon as possible (Buzawa & Buzawa, 1992). In addition, officers were told repeatedly that domestic calls held the most potential dangers for the officer (Bowker, 1982; Field & Field, 1973; Parnas, 1967). Given the plethora of factors discouraging police involvement in domestic violence, it is no surprise that the most frequent police response to domestic calls was to do nothing.

In 1966, Morton Bard embarked on an experimental project with the New York City Police Department (Bard, 1974). He observed that much police work involved "noncrime" functions, including policing events that could be classified as domestic violence such as "family fights" or "family disturbances" (p. 150). Bard believed the officers were not properly trained to respond when called upon to act outside their traditional roles. He was interested in determining what could be done if police officers were trained by, and consulted with, psychologists.

Two precincts were selected: the 30th was be the site of the experiment, the 24th was used for comparison. A group of officers were selected from the 30th precinct to form a unit known as the Family Crisis Intervention Unit (FCIU). The unit officers received intensive training, then divided into small teams and returned to their patrol duties. These patrol teams would be known as "family motor patrol."

The officers in the family motor patrol would perform regular patrol duties, but were on call to respond to family disputes throughout the precinct. Bard believed it was essential to the success of the project that the officers not be exclusively assigned to family violence cases. That, he suggested, would negatively affect morale, and not encourage other officers to accept the experiment (Bard, 1974).

The operational phase of the project lasted twenty-three months. At the end of the experiment, Bard (1974) collected data and evaluated the project's success. He found the 30th precinct "intervened on 1,388 occasions with 962 families," whereas the 24th precinct "recorded 492 interventions with 484 families" (p. 180). Bard concluded the experiment participants were more motivated to record incidents, and that the "chronically disordered families" felt more comfortable accessing services. Other data, such as an increase in the rate of family homicides, were more difficult to explain.

The finding from Bard's evaluation that received the most publicity (Liebman & Schwartz, 1973) was that this model contributed to reducing injuries to police officers. Bard based this finding on data that showed that no FCIU patrolmen were injured during the nearly two-year experiment. During that same time period, two regular patrol officers in the 30th precinct and one officer in the 24th precinct were injured (Bard, 1974).

Liebman and Schwartz (1973) evaluated the New York Family Crisis Intervention Unit project along with thirteen other such projects. Based upon their review of the data, they had several criticisms of Bard's conclusions. First, the fact that repeat calls were higher for the 30th precinct than for the comparison precinct was wrongly interpreted as a positive result if their overall goal was to reduce chronic violence in families. Second, the 30th precinct had more family homicides, and actually experienced an increase in such homicides, whereas family homicides declined in the comparison precinct. Third, both general assaults and family assaults appear to follow the same patterns as homicides. Fourth, Bard's finding that FCIU members had fewer than expected injuries was based on insufficient data.

Hirschel, Hutchinson, Dean, and Mills (1992) agree there was little evidence to support the view that crisis intervention and mediation reduced abuse, though they also suggest the subject was poorly researched. Three reasons they cite for the failure of crisis intervention and mediation are (1) the police officers didn't appreciate the changes being required of them; (2) the officers were generally ill-equipped for what was being asked of them; and (3) the police misapplied the lessons learned, using "techniques designed for situations involving verbal abuse . . . [in] situations involving physical assaults" (p. 262).

THE ROLE OF SOCIAL SCIENCE RESEARCH

Barely twenty years ago, in a report prepared for the Police Executive Research Forum, Nancy Loving (1980) noted "the lack of relevant and reliable information about how the police actually handle spouse abuse and wife beating calls" (p. 38). Two decades later, there is an abundance of such research.

Training and Police Attitudes

The importance of training in shaping police officers' attitudes has been a key area of research among academicians. Just what kind of impact training can have on policing remains controversial.

With the development of police academies, officers are generally taught by men who become instructors "not because of their academic ability or interest in teaching, but because of their advancing age or temporary disability, or because they were on leave or special duty restriction pending departmental investigation" (Zorza, 1992, p. 49). The implication is apparent. As long as police receive their education in isolated circumstances, from those ill-prepared to be teaching, it is unlikely that anything new (assuming "new" is the desired lesson) will be taught. On domestic violence, this training simply served to reinforce traditional notions of masculinity and entitlement. A presentation might consist of a reading from the formal department policy, followed by anecdotes from the instructor's own experience. These stories may reflect the view that domestic violence is a private matter, or that it is not a crime for a husband to keep his wife in line (Walker, 1993). The instructor's prejudices often undermined the policy itself (Buzawa & Buzawa, 1996).

Indeed, the emphasis in training for intervention in domestic disputes was on the risk to the officer. In a study of Chicago police in the 1960s, Parnas (1967) found when patrol officers were asked what they recalled from their domestic dispute training, almost all recalled the need to protect themselves.

In the late 1960s, Morton Bard began working on the project to establish Family Violence Intervention Teams in the New York City Police Department, bringing together psychologists, social workers, and police officers. It would be the job of the mental health workers to train the select group of police officers in crisis management. In many ways, this project altered police training. Reporting in 1970, Bard predicted police officers would abandon their isolationist stance and introduce method-appropriate education. To some extent, his project moved policing in the directions he predicted.

In the introduction to the section on innovation in training, Snibbe and Snibbe (1973) note these new techniques—crisis intervention and counseling, for example—would "contribute significantly to the re-evaluation of the role of police officers" (p. 406). Increasingly, the methods they described have found their way into police training programs, but the reevaluation the authors predicted has yet to materialize on a broad scale. In the same publication, Danish and Ferguson (1973) report on reasons why police may not take the trainings to heart. First, police have a mandate to maintain the social good, even at the cost of the individual. Second, results of personality tests given to police recruits suggest that the recruits may not be suitable for these new roles, generally lacking in trust and tolerance, for example.

Formal in-service training was rare prior to the 1980s (Buzawa & Buzawa, 1996). Loving (1980) suggests training programs addressing domestic disputes must contain, at minimum, training on the nature of the problem, department policy and agency procedure, how to use referrals, as well as personal considerations such as fear, stress, and the officers' own marriages. Whether such training is effective is still a subject of disagreement.

Pearce and Snortum (1983) found that officers who had received training appeared better prepared to deal with crisis situations. Although not specifically addressing domestic violence calls, this training consisted of fifty-six hours of classroom time, and covered safety factors, methods for diffusing violent situations, techniques in information gathering, mediation skills, and referral sources. Officers indicated they felt training was interesting and practical. Disputants revealed higher satisfaction with trained officers, and trained officers used referrals more than untrained officers.

Sgarzi's (1991) research contests Pearce and Snortum's findings. In a study that focused specifically on the impact of training on the policing of domestic violence, Sgarzi used a pre- and posttest design to explore the effect training would have on new police recruits' attitudes toward domestic violence. Using the *Inventory of Beliefs about Wife Beating* and the *Attitude towards Women* scales, she tested the beliefs of new recruits before and after they received a six- to eight-hour training on domestic violence. She found that the training had no significant impact on the attitudes of the officers about domestic violence or the victims of domestic violence. However, the training did impact the recruits' attitudes toward the offender. Following training, officers felt more strongly that the offender should be punished. Sgarzi was unable, however, to generalize her findings beyond the specifics of this particular training program. In addition, Sgarzi is testing attitude alone. To evaluate the significance of training, additional research needs to be done on the effect training has on performance.

Two studies, one conducted by Bourg and Stock (1994) and the other by Mignon and Holmes (1995), suggest that training does make a difference in the enforcement of mandatory or proarrest policies. Bourg and Stock examined domestic violence arrest statistics for a police department with a proarrest policy, but little training and no coordinated community approach to domestic violence. They found that less than one-third of domestic violence cases in this jurisdiction culminated in arrest. Although not comparing these arrest rates to similar rates in jurisdictions with more training, they nonetheless concluded that these arrest rates were low, and that lack of adequate training could be at least partially responsible (see Black, 1980).

In a random sample study of twenty-four Massachusetts police departments, Mignon and Holmes (1995) found rates of arrest similar to those found by Bourg and Stock (about one-third) occurred in domestic violence cases. Mignon and Holmes found training was a significant factor in determining the likelihood of arrest. Specifically, they found officers with one hour of domestic violence training were most likely to arrest. Surprisingly, an officer was less likely to arrest if he/she had three and a half or more hours of training. Mignon and Holmes suggest this interesting finding might be explained by the fact that Massachusetts had recently revised its domestic violence laws. Officers with only one hour of training were likely to have been recently trained, therefore learning the new laws. Officers with more training may have received their training over time, and were not as likely to have been exposed to the new laws. This is only speculation, however, and suggests this issue needs to be further investigated.

More recently, Buerger (1999) has voiced skepticism about the model of education employed in police training to open minds or change beliefs and attitudes. As increasing numbers of police officers are educated outside the department, for example, in the university/college classroom, it will be interesting to consider whether it is the model of training or the individuals being trained that are more intransigent.

Arrest as Best Response

Arrest and Situational Factors.   Early research on the policing of domestic violence explored the relevance to situational factors on the likelihood of arrest. These factors included relational distance, who initiates the complaint, extent of the injury, race, marital status of the parties, and the presence of weapons, witnesses, alcohol, or the offender (Bell, 1985; Berk et al., 1980; Black, 1980; Buzawa, Austin, and Buzawa, 1995; Smith & Klein, 1984; Worden & Pollitz, 1984).

Black, in *The Manners and Custom of Police* (1980), applied the principal that the amount of law in any situation is inversely associated with the relationship of the individuals to police work. He made several observations, of which the following stand out as most significant: "The police are more likely to comply with complainants [requests] as the relational distance between the disputants increases. The police are more conciliatory as the parties to the dispute are more intimate, and they were more penal as the parties are more relationally distant" (p. 187).

Berk et al. (1980), using a sample of 430 domestic violence cases, tested each for fifteen variables, from marital status to property damage. They found the police decision to arrest was based not on factors that might build a solid case (i.e., property damage), but on situational factors. Specifically, they found four variables to be significant. Arrest is more likely to occur if (1) there is evidence of the man's use of alcohol; (2) if both parties are present; (3) the female victim agrees to sign the complaint; or (4) there are allegations the woman was violent. Arrest is less likely to occur if the female victim calls the police, leading the researchers to speculate that if the victim is capable of calling the police, the incident is not yet serious.

Worden and Pollitz (1984) replicated Berk et al.'s study, though improving the quality of the sample by taking data from trained observers, rather than the officers' incidence reports. They also applied an attitudinal distinction, dividing police into crime fighters and problem solvers. The researchers found officers from both categories arrest based on their assessment of the circumstances, thus supporting Berk et al.'s findings.

Smith and Klein (1984) modeled their research on the sociological theories presented by Black (1980). The sixteen variables included source of complaint and presence of alcohol, as well as poverty level and offender demeanor. Findings confirm that situational factors play a role in police decision making. Additionally, Smith and Klein found that police were more likely to arrest an offender who shows disrespect, and were more likely to arrest generally in poor neighborhoods.

Bell (1985) focused specifically on the role of the victim-offender relationship in determining police action in domestic disputes. Although the percent of complaints that resulted in official police action was low, Bell found police are more likely to act if the complainant is the wife than a stranger, thus contradicting Black's findings. This contradiction, however, can be explained by such factors as the implementation of domestic violence laws which occurred between the timing of the two studies (early 1970s versus early 1980s) and the differing major focus of the two studies. Regardless of these contradictions, Bell's results do support the proposition that when victims initiate complaints, police are more likely to arrest, supporting earlier works cited above.

In the most recent in this line of studies, Buzawa, Austin, and Buzawa's (1995) findings contradict those of Bell (1985), and support the findings of Black (1980). Even though arrest rates were low for all categories of assault, arrest was more likely in cases of stranger assault than domestic assault. The preferences of strangers were more likely to be considered by police than were preferences of intimates. Buzawa et al. (1995) suggest, in conclusion, that the practice of limited police action in domestic violence must be continuously challenged.

Mandatory and Proarrest

In 1984, the results of the Minneapolis Domestic Violence Experiment were published by Lawrence Sherman and Richard Berk (Sherman & Berk, 1984). Funded by the National Institute of Justice and arising from an interest in general deterrence research, the Minneapolis Domestic Violence Experiment was the first controlled, randomized test of effectiveness of arrest for any offense (Sherman, 1992). The experiment attempted to examine the deterrent effect of arrest for misdemeanor domestic assault. It examined three randomly assigned treatments: arrest, separation (ordering the offender out of the house), and advising or mediating (in any way the officer saw fit, as long as it was not separation or arrest). The efficiency of each treatment was measured by follow-up interviews with the victims and review of police department records of calls to the same address during the following six months.

Sherman and Berk (1984) found that within the six-month follow-up period, the arrested offenders had the lowest recidivism rates (10 percent) against the same victim, compared with 19 percent recidivism for those offenders advised and 24 percent for those removed from the scene. This was interpreted to mean that arrest appeared to prevent repeated domestic violence more effectively than either separation or mediation. This led the researchers to recommend that states change laws prohibiting police from making warrantless arrests in misdemeanor domestic violence cases, and that some form of proarrest policy be implemented (Sherman, 1992).

The results of the Minneapolis Domestic Violence Experiment have come under a great deal of scrutiny, and have been broadly criticized. Criticism includes challenges to the methodology, both the internal and external validity of the study (Binder & Meeker, 1992; Elliot, 1989; Fagan, 1988; Gelles, 1993; McCord, 1992; Sherman & Cohn, 1989), questions about the assumptions made by the researchers and the researchers' biases (Lerman, 1992; McCord, 1992; Wright, 1985; Zorza, 1994), and concerns about the uses made of the data (Gelles, 1993; Meeker & Binder, 1990; Zorza, 1994).

Some question the extent to which the action of the officers was truly based upon random assignment. The officers may have excluded nonarrest cases from the study, may have avoided domestic violence calls, or may have reclassified calls as simple assaults or disturbances to avoid triggering an assigned response (Gelles, 1993; Sherman & Cohn, 1989). Sherman (1992) himself has raised questions about the sample, suggesting the sample size was insufficient to test the different effects arrest had on different groups, and that most of the cases in the study were completed by a few officers in just two precincts. The six-month follow-up period has also been criticized (Gelles, 1993). Perhaps if follow-up had been longer, the results would have been different. And, as the experiment was limited to recidivism against the same victims, it did not consider that perhaps the offender assaulted other victims (Gelles, 1993). Arrest might merely have displaced the offender's abuse. Wright (1985) criticizes the time frame and the researcher's understanding of the legal process. She notes that arrested offenders were likely to spend the six months of the study engaged in court proceedings, and that it is not unusual for "a defendant refrain . . . while a charge is pending" (p. 225).

In the Minneapolis Experiment, the amount of time the offender spent in jail was almost always at least one night (Sherman & Cohn, 1989). Researchers do not address variations in time held. Therefore, in other cities where offenders may be immediately released following arrest, or held for longer than one night, recidivism rates may be different, so the results were not necessarily generalizable (Meeker & Binder, 1990). The follow-up interviews themselves may have affected the outcome of the experiment, serving as deterrents to assaults during the timeframe of the experiment (Sherman & Cohn, 1989). Also, the experimental model itself is criticized for not accurately testing the effects of mediation as a response, as the officers involved in the experiment had no special training in mediation intervention (Loving, 1980; Stratton, 1990). Finally, the study was used to create large-scale changes in the policing of domestic violence (Gelles, 1993). This occurred despite the fact that the researchers acted without a clearly established theoretical basis for the deterrent effects of arrest (Elliot, 1989).

In response to questions concerning the validity of the Minneapolis Experiment's results, the National Institute of Justice funded six replication studies (Omaha, NE; Charlotte, NC; Milwaukee, WI; Colorado Springs, CO; Miami, FL; Atlanta, GA). The first of these studies was conducted in Omaha, NE. Researchers here attempted to address some of the problems with internal validity found in the Minneapolis Experiment (Dunford, Hunizinga, and Elliot, 1990). The findings in Omaha allowed researchers to conclude that arrest by itself did not deter recidivism any more than did the response of mediating or separating. The Omaha findings also suggested victims whose abusers were arrested were not in any greater risk of subsequent violence than were those where mediation was the assigned response. Of particular note, researchers in the Omaha experiment measured the effect of offender absence. If an offender was not present when police arrived, they might, based on random assignment, issue a warrant for arrest or take no action. Where no warrant was issued, offenders were twice as likely to commit another act of domestic abuse (11.8 percent to 5.4 percent).

The Charlotte, NC study found essentially the same results as those found in Omaha. Researchers concluded the results of the experiment were "decisive and unambiguous, clearly indicating that arrest of misdemeanor spouse abusers is neither substantially nor statistically a more effective deterrent to repeat abuse than either of the other two police responses examined" in their study (Hirschel & Hutchinson, 1992, p. 115).

The Milwaukee replication study (also conducted by Sherman) was the only study done in a city that could be characterized as a "northern industrial-urban Black ghetto" (Gelles, 1993, p. 580). Responses available to the police were different in Milwaukee than in the previous studies. Here, the three possible responses were: standard arrest (an average of eleven hours in custody), a short arrest (an average of three hours in custody), or no arrest but a warning from the police. The Milwaukee findings indicated the impact of arrest differed by employment status. Offenders who were employed at the time of the arrest were less likely to recidivate than those who were unemployed. There were also differences in the experiment's results between standard and short arrest. Short arrest lessened the likelihood of recidivism in the short term, but increased the risks over the long term. Standard arrest did not have an impact on long-term recidivism.

Sherman (1992) draws the following conclusions from the research on the use of arrest by police as a response to domestic violence: (1) arrest reduces the incidence of domestic violence in some cities, but increases it in others; (2) arrest reduces domestic violence among employed people, but increases it among the unemployed; and (3) arrest reduces domestic violence in the short run, but can increase it over the long run. The research results pose a dilemma.

> A policy of arresting employed persons but not unemployed persons would punish employment. A policy of not arresting all may erode the *general* deterrent effect of arrest on potential spouse abusers. Yet a policy of arresting all offenders may simply produce more violence [among some offenders] (Sherman et al., 1992, p. 688).

In a subsequent study, Friday, Metzgar, and Walters (1991) found arrest was most effective for those who had no prior contacts with the police. This result suggests, as do the results of the Minneapolis replications studies, that the deterrent effect of arrest may be related to one's stake in conformity (Sherman et al., 1992). There is an additional irony here, in the fact that these findings suggest those most likely to be deterred by arrest are also those (first offenders) least likely to be arrested (Friday, Metzgar, and Walters, 1991, p. 210).

The largely conflicting results from the replication studies further challenged the conclusions of the Minneapolis Experiment, and raised the level of criticism. Although taking differing positions on the police response to domestic violence, Zorza (1994), Gelles (1993), Manning (1993), Bowman (1992), Lerman (1992), McCord (1992), and Meeker and Binder (1990) were all among the numerous critics of the domestic violence arrest experiments.

McCord (1992) begins her critique by examining the narrow perspective taken by the researchers regarding the effects of intervention. In many of the studies, McCord notes evaluation of the impact of arrest on recidivism only looked at offenders who revictimized the same victims. There is no effort to look for other victims of the same offender. In Milwaukee, where researchers did look at recidivism rates for acts against any victim, the incidents had to occur within the jurisdiction to appear in the data. McCord argues prior research has shown that multiple victimization is common, and those who are violent in one relationship tend to be violent in others. Thus, much is being missed by the narrow focus of these experiments.

McCord (1992) criticizes the time frame employed by the researchers. Even the one-year time period after initial arrest used in the replication studies (versus the six-month follow-up of the Minneapolis Experiment), is insufficient to take into account what is known about the dynamic nature of relationships. The offender and victim may have a so-called honeymoon period (Walker, 1979), or may separate immediately following the arrest incident, only to have the cycle of violence recur at a later time. Nor do any of these studies consider that, though violence may cease, abuse, both verbal and emotional, and control, may continue. Threats may replace action. The very definition of abuse used in the studies may be too narrow. Last, the studies fail to consider the effect of arrest on the victim's welfare (McCord, 1992).

The second thread of criticism put forth by McCord (1992) is that shallow consideration is given to process. She suggests an analysis of domestic violence occurrences needs to occur, one that examines beyond whether the offenses are felonies or misdemeanors. For example, interventions by the police may have a differing impact on people who have differently experienced the criminal justice system. McCord cites studies showing that beliefs, attitudes and situational factors are likely to influence actions of police, suspects and victims, thus they will certainly affect the overall interaction. None of these distinctions are made in the arrest experiments. McCord's final criticism of the arrest experiments is that they fail to examine consequences of alternatives to arrest, other than mediation (or what police may do at the scene) and separation.

Other criticism focuses not on the arrest experiments, but on the mandatory or presumptive arrest polices that have resulted. Binder and Meeker (1992) question the constitutionality of mandatory arrest policies in domestic violence cases. The justification for incarceration before trial is allegedly based on dangerousness of the defendant, and the potential that the defendant will flee the jurisdiction of the court. The intended purpose of arrest and detention in domestic violence cases is to deter recidivism through punishment versus arrest and detention because of the danger these offenders pose to the victim. This, they state, violates due process.

Manning (1993) suggests the whole notion of testing the impact of arrest rests on an inherent fallacy, what he refers to as "the preventive conceit." Manning challenges the assumption that arrest has any impact on deterring crime. He contends that arrest is not supported by any known theory, and any stated connection between arrest and rearrest is based on "a series of rather dubious methodological and operational definitions and arbitrary measurement decisions" and that considering arrest out of context is meaningless (p. 640).

Gelles (1993) suggests arrest may actually disempower the victim. Many victims want the violence to stop at the moment of intervention, but do not want the offender arrested. According to this argument, mandatory arrest may actually disempower the victim, as it removes the choice of whether to request arrest. The victims may then choose not to call the police in the event of further violence, as they now believe the police will again arrest the offender despite their wishes.

Martin's (1987) research describes the manner in which mandatory arrest policies have encouraged the arrest of the victim, along with the offender. Her conclusion is that if the police are mandated to arrest upon a reasonable allegation of abuse, they may be unable (or unwilling) to ascertain who is the aggressor. Saunders' (1995) study, which provided officers with vignettes and measured their response, confirms Martin's findings. Saunders found that some officers were likely to arrest the victim, and speculated that "the findings might have been even stronger under conditions of mandatory arrest because of many officers' resistance to such policies" (p. 149).

Bourg and Stock (1994) found that in a police department with a proarrest policy, but little domestic violence training, 8.4 percent of the arrests made were of women, in contrast to cited studies indicating only 3 percent to 5 percent of women fit the description of batterer. A Michigan study conducted in 1996 found a woman was arrested in over 12 percent of the domestic violence calls (Lyon, 1999, p. 271). Miller (1994), citing Hamberger and Potente (1994), describes a jurisdiction where, in the aftermath of a new mandatory arrest law, "women experienced a 12-fold increase in arrests whereas men experienced only a 2-fold increase" (p. 190).

In her feminist critique of the arrest experiments, Bowman (1992) faults them for being too simplistic. By reducing the victim to a statistic, she says, researchers fail to consider how arrest might empower the victim, and so the experiments draw conclusions based on a very limited picture of the arrest event.

The narrow approach taken by domestic violence experiment research draws criticism, as does the narrow approach of quantitative studies (Bowman) and social scientists generally (Zorza, 1994). Lerman (1992) goes so far as to challenge the usefulness of any social science research in determining policy when she states, "The entire system would grind to a halt if policy initiatives were contingent upon empirical proof of their effectiveness" (p. 239).

Lerman's (1992) criticism includes examining arrest in a vacuum, without consideration of training, prosecution, the response of the mental health community, the punishment or treatment provided, and researchers failing to state their biases, thus presenting themselves as objective. Lerman concludes the replication studies make a compelling argument for more enforcement, as there appears to be "a high likelihood of repeat assaults" (p. 239).

Zorza (1994) reiterates the concern of Lerman and others that the researchers considered arrest, without examining the subsequent action of prosecutors and courts. "While . . . the police can probably sabotage the effectiveness of . . . [the system] by failing to arrest offenders," the message that domestic violence is unacceptable must come from the system as a whole (p. 972). The researchers did not take into consideration the likelihood an arrest would be followed by prosecution, that prosecution would result in conviction, or what sentence, if any, might be imposed.

Zorza (1994) is also concerned that the studies "ignored that fact that domestic violence, unchecked, usually escalates in frequency and severity" (p. 930). The measurement of successful intervention, then, might be a reduction in the escalation of violence. Zorza also challenges the usefulness of the domestic violence policing studies for determining policy, as they do not examine the effect nonarrest has on the victims and their families.

Zorza concludes that, though there may be reason to oppose mandatory arrest, such reason cannot be found in the present studies.

As much as there is criticism of the Minneapolis Experiment and the replication studies, so too is there disagreement about the interpretation of the results. For example, is a mandatory or proarrest policy a step forward in the policing of domestic violence? Much of the feminist literature suggests it is. Stark (1993) summarizes the prominent supporting arguments. First, if as Stark suggests, battering is rooted in sexual inequality, then everything about the violence, including the response, reflects the power of men over women. Battering denies women their civil rights. A proarrest policy, on the other hand, aids women in their effort to achieve greater equality by redistributing justice on behalf of women.

Second, mandatory arrest law is a method of controlling and directing police behavior. Policy dictates what the police are expected to do if certain criteria exist, and they can then be held accountable if they fail to take the required action. Stark (1993) contends that, though there has been much resistance to the limits on police discretion resulting from the mandatory domestic violence arrest laws, arrests for domestic assault did increase by 70 percent between 1984 and 1989, an increase he attributes to changes in domestic violence laws (pp. 660–661). Police discretion in these matters is no longer politically expedient.

Third, mandatory arrest of offenders of domestic violence does provide immediate protection for the victim. Mandatory arrest gives the victim time to consider her options, to get an order of protection, and to make arrangements to leave if she chooses to do so.

Fourth, Stark (1993) states, "making battering the only crime in which police discretion is removed acknowledges a special social interest in redressing the legacy of discriminatory treatment of women by law enforcement" (p. 662). Mandatory arrest assures police service is available to women on a more equal basis.

Finally, a proarrest policy makes clear that domestic violence is a crime. Finesmith (1993) suggests that what the public observes as the police response affects what they expect that response should be. A clear message is thus sent to the abuser, the victim, and the community that domestic violence will not be tolerated. This, then, strengthens and reinforces informal social controls (Lerman, 1992).

Alternatives to Arrest

Although most of the research on police response to domestic violence has focused on the use of arrest, arrest is only one of the possible responses employed by police. Studies have found that arrest rates for domestic violence incidents range from 12 percent to 40 percent of all cases seen by police (Walker, 1993). Whether arrest might be appropriate under the circumstances, it appears that in the majority of domestic calls, police employ alternatives to arrest. These alternatives include mediation, making referrals, separation, or simply doing nothing. McKean and Hendricks' (1997) review of the research on arrest and domestic violence lead them to conclude the majority of domestic calls to which police respond are disturbances, not assaults. If this observation is correct, then the police need to have a range of responses available, or their only choice is to do nothing.

Mediation, or what has been called mediation in research on policing, includes a variety of different verbal responses. Officers may talk to the offender and the victim in a sympathetic or unsympathetic manner (Walker, 1993). They may discuss what action the victim would like taken, may order the parties to be quiet, or may threaten arrest. Police may refer the offender to professional help, or the victim to social service or legal aid agencies. Most studies prior to the 1990s indicate that referrals are rarely used, even though recent changes in many state and local statutes mandate officers to provide victims with information regarding referrals to social and legal services. In a study conducted by Walker (1993), referral was used in only 4 percent of cases.

Separation may be used by police as a method of defusing a situation. However, absent arrest, if the offender is a legal resident of the property at which the incident occurs, the police have no legal authority to force the offender to leave. Walker (1993) reports that separation is used in as much as 40 percent of all domestic violence calls, and in most instances, people do comply with such requests from the police. Finally, many police officers continue to use the response of taking no action at all (Ferraro, 1989).

Although separation and mediation have been evaluated in terms of deterrence, it is not yet clear whether they are more or less effective alternatives than arrest. Studies find that one significant problem with police acting to mediate or separate is they have not received specific training in how to do so in domestic violence situations (Loving, 1980; Stratton, 1990).

In an early study on police referrals, Dolon, Hendricks, and Meagher (1986) found that police officers most often refer victims and offenders to other criminal justice agencies, rather than to agencies that provide social services. In their study, police referrals occurred as follows, reported from most referrals to least: prosecuting attorneys, courts, mental health care facility, shelters, legal aid attorneys, drug and alcohol services, Alcoholics Anonymous (AA), hospitals, family services, church or minister, welfare department, Salvation Army, and the YWCA. Police officers, in this study, reported that referrals to prosecuting attorneys and the courts were the most effective.

Belknap and McCall (1994) state the belief that police response to domestic violence needs to be refocused, to extend beyond whether to arrest. Research should include referrals to social service agencies that may be useful to victims, offenders, and children living in abusive environments.

In an attempt to apply these suggestions, Belknap and McCall (1994) conducted an extensive study of police use of referrals in domestic violence situations. They surveyed officers in a large Midwestern metropolitan area in the late 1980s, analyzing the response of 324 police officers to a questionnaire. They examined the number and types of referrals given by police, and the way in which the police officers' personal characteristics were related to the referrals they give. Officers reported making referrals in the following ways: victims' hotlines—44.3 percent; private complaint programs—14.2 percent; battered women's shelters—10.5 percent; clergy—9 percent; court—7.1 percent; and miscellaneous referrals—6.5 percent (pp. 230–231).

One-third of the officers reported they "rarely" referred victims to battered women's shelters. Among officers with less experience, the shelters were the referral they "usually" gave. Officers on first and second shifts were more likely to report they "usually" referred victims to shelters than officers on the third shift. Educated officers were more likely than those less educated to refer women to court or to victims' hotlines. Younger officers were more likely than older officers to refer women to private complaint programs. The variable Belknap and McCall found to be most significant in predicting the type of referral given was the type of department: sheriff's office deputies were more likely to refer to AA or welfare, whereas local police officers were more likely to refer to a shelter (p. 234).

Mills (1998) suggests that as an alternative to mandatory arrest, there could be a requirement of mandatory action. This reflects a growing trend to expect officers to be sensitive to the needs of individual victims, and to tailor their response accordingly (Sherman, 1992). Police might respond that left to their own discretion, that is exactly what they do (see Black, 1980). More research needs to be done on the various interventions available to police, and on their relative effectiveness in protecting the victim from present and future harm.

Impact of Research on Law and Policy

The Minneapolis Domestic Violence Experiment had a profound impact on policy in regard to the policing of domestic violence (i.e., Gelles, 1993; Meeker & Binder, 1990). After the public release of the findings of the Minneapolis Experiment, police departments across the nation began to adopt mandatory or presumptive arrest policies for instances of domestic violence. The U.S. Attorney General's Task Force on Family Violence, which drew heavily on the Minneapolis findings, came to the conclusion that family violence should be recognized and responded to as serious criminal activity by police departments and other criminal justice agencies (Gelles, 1993).

Sherman and Cohn (1989) surveyed police departments in 1985 and 1986 to assess the impact the Minneapolis study had on department policy and action. They found that two-thirds of the departments were aware of the study and knew the results; few departments had a policy of arrest in 1984; nearly half of the departments reported that by 1986 arrest was the policy for domestic violence calls; and one-third of the departments reporting said the study's results influenced their policy (pp. 124–125). As of 1995, forty-seven states and the District of Columbia have enacted laws allowing police to arrest with probable cause in cases of misdemeanor domestic violence. Arrest is mandatory in fourteen states (Buzawa & Buzawa, 1996). Subsequent criticisms of the Minneapolis Experiment, results from six "replica" studies, and further analysis of the negative aspects of mandatory or presumptive arrest policies have led to suggestions that policy makers and lawmakers reacted too quickly to Sherman and Berk's (1984) conclusions.

The question of just what should be the role of the researcher in publicizing his or her results, and the research itself in developing criminal justice policy, has become a much debated issue in the aftermath of the domestic violence police studies (Gelles, 1993; Meeker & Binder, 1990; Sherman, 1992; Sherman & Cohn, 1989). Although the research community agrees, in general, to the dissemination of research and to the significance of working with policy makers, there is concern about the manner and scope of such publicity.

According to Binder and Meeker (1992), there should be a correlation between the certainty one has in his/her conclusions and the amount of "active advocacy" done to promote policy change. They suggest that, given the concerns Sherman and Berk had about both the internal and external validity of their data, they went too far in orchestrating the release and dissemination of their data so as to maximize its impact on policy. It should be noted, however, that it is a rare instance indeed when social science research receives adequate consideration in policy debates (Buzawa & Buzawa, 1996).

CURRENT TRENDS IN POLICING DOMESTIC VIOLENCE

Domestic Violence Units

The first units within police departments to focus on crimes occurring within the family were the Family Crisis Units (Loving, 1980) established in the 1960s in New York City. At the time little, if any, mention was made of the abuse of women at the hands of their partners. Attention focused instead of the abuse of children, as every jurisdiction in the country identified child abuse as a crime and mandated reporting by 1970. As society's understanding of the issue of domestic violence evolved, police specialization in the area increased. The wave of units established in the late 1970s and early 1980s referred to themselves as Family Crisis Units, Domestic Service Units, or Domestic Violence Squads. The most commonly used designation at present is the Domestic Violence Unit. In some departments, large and small, rather than establishing a unit, a single officer has been given the responsibilities associated with carrying out the enforcement of domestic violence within that city or town.

Based on their evaluation of fourteen Family Crisis Intervention Units, Liebman and Schwartz (1973) offer several suggestions for what they believe would make a specialized unit, specifically one designed to address domestic violence, successful. Of their recommendations, six seem to be particularly pertinent to the present inquiry.

1) There must be clear support and involvement from the top of the hierarchy.
2) There must be reasonable goals and realistic expectations for the unit.
3) A token program does not appear to be worthwhile. "There is no evidence that small demonstration projects are stepping stones for department-wide training; rather, these programs remain outside the mainstream of departmental activity and disintegrate rather rapidly."
4) Management must assure that those officers who participate are neither "locked in" nor do they form "an elite 'clique.'"
5) Management should be included in planning, and involved in all stages of development and training. This will help secure its cooperation.
6) There must be a long-term plan for the unit, which extends beyond the current grant or particular personnel involved. (pp. 464–468)

Little research has been published since the early 1980s on the effectiveness of Domestic Violence Units. Some examples from the recent literature of specialized units in other contexts, nevertheless, offer useful insights into the functions of contemporary Domestic Violence Units. Levin and McDevitt (1993) state some conscientious police departments have established bias or "hate" crime units to respond to bias-motivated violence. They report these units, especially Boston's Community Disorders Unit, are successful in achieving their goal of reducing bias-motivated violence. In fact, they report that, according to the FBI, having a bias crime unit or designated officer is necessary for properly policing bias-motivated crime. The unit or officer is better trained and, therefore, better able to recognize bias-motivated crimes, thus providing the victims with more help.

Walker and Katz (1995) don't fully agree with Levin and McDevitt's optimism about the bias crime units. Although they believe the units can be successful in large cities, they turned their attention to midsize communities. They found that bias crime units existed in 13.1 percent of the cities in their study (p. 38). (This compared unfavorably with the Law Enforcement Management Administrative Statistics estimate of 35 percent.) Where there were units, they found tremendous variation. Units were located in different places within the departments. The number of officers assigned and the manner of assignment varied. Some offered specialized training; others sent officers to outside seminars. The procedures and activities varied as well. Those departments with special procedures addressing bias-crime, or a designated officer, had just as much variation. They conclude the departments do not show much of a commitment by simply having a unit or special procedure. Walker and Katz sum up the findings by saying, "there is far less . . . than meets the eye" (p. 42).

Kraska and Kappeler (1997) examined the rapid growth in Police Paramilitary Units (PPUs) or SWAT Teams. They found that, although these units were originally created in the 1960s and 1970s to respond effectively to urban riots and large demonstrations, they are now becoming increasingly common in small departments nationwide. These units evolve into elite, militaristic enclaves, provided with highly evolved weaponry and plenty of military equipment. And although these units were conceived to be rapid response units, "most PPUs proactively seek out and even manufacture highly dangerous situations" (p. 12). They found the militarism of these units becomes infectious, spreading throughout the department.

It is indeed interesting to note the contrast found here between the officers' acceptance, even admiration, of the PPU as compared with their less than favorable attitudes toward Bias Crime Units. Several factors appear to contribute to this contrast. Bias Crime Units are often less aggressively supported by the police administrators (Walker & Katz, 1995), and less appealing to the militaristic nature of policing than are the PPUs (Kraska & Kappeler, 1997). Bias crimes require no special equipment, and the victims are often judged as contributing to their own situation (for example, by "acting gay"). The PPUs, on the other hand, are glamorous and high profile, the weaponry and special outfits are tangible, and the victims are deemed to be "innocent victims" while the offenders are considered undeniably "bad."

Domestic Violence Units, and the enforcement of domestic violence laws, share many characteristics of Bias Crime Units, including jurisdictional variation, uncertainty of mission, and ambivalence about the victim. It appears the problems facing Bias Crime Units are similar to those confronted by Domestic Violence Units, many of the concerns being the same as those voiced by Liebman and Schwartz nearly thirty years ago.

Model Programs

One alternative has been the integrated model programs. In most instances, these are coordinated efforts that include the district attorney's office, the local police department, and the community, often represented by grassroots women's groups and/or the local shelter. An early example of such a coordinated response is the Santa Barbara Family Violence Program, evaluated by Berk et al. (1980). This program was primarily championed by the district attorney's office, which then drew in the local police and the county sheriff. Community groups were not directly involved, though the district attorney, as an elected official, represented a community where grassroots feminist organizations wielded some power. A Family Violence Unit (FVU) was established within the district attorney's office. The goals of the FVU were to improve the reporting practices of the police by instituting an educational program, and to prosecute cases more aggressively.

In their evaluation of the FVU, Berk et al. (1980) concluded the FVU was successful in educating police. They based their conclusion on the finding that the number of domestic violence incidents documented and the adequacy of that documentation increased gradually over the sixty weeks of the study. The FVU itself succeeded largely because of its independence from the rest of the district attorney's office. It achieved this by being housed at a distinct location and having its own, distinct line of funding (therefore not being seen as in competition with other priorities of the office). They attribute the FVU's success with police personnel to the diplomatic manner in which the district attorney approached the local police and the county sheriff's office, acknowledging their efforts and suggesting how they might cooperate. Additionally, according to Berk et al., "the very existence of the meetings [between the District Attorney's office staff and the police] *probably* legitimized the problem of domestic violence for police officers and *perhaps* communicated that improved performance was going to be expected" (1980, p. 213; italics added).

Steinman (1991) studied the impact of a coordinated program in Nebraska. A special task force, known as the Domestic Violence Coalition, DVC, was created in 1985, bringing together shelter representatives, advocates for women, the local police chief, the county sheriff, representatives from the courts, lawyers, corrections, and a men's anger control program. Together, they developed policies and procedures to address the process from police response to offender treatment. Steinman compared police action and rates of recidivism for a period prior to 1985 with those during a time after implementation of the DVC's policies. He found that "arrest was related to significantly less re-offending when the enforcement of arrest policies was coordinated with other criminal justice responses" (p. 235).

The Community Intervention Projects, or CIPs, arose from a combination of community pressures and interest on the part of the police (Edleson, 1991). Duluth, MN was one of the first cities to establish a CIP, "a coordinated community response to domestic violence that included mandatory arrest and treatment" (Sparks, 1997, p. 44). Over twenty CIPs operate in Minnesota alone. Another CIP, the San Francisco Family Violence Project, was established in 1980 as a demonstration project (Soler, 1987).

According to Edleson (1991), the CIPs are founded on a shared set of assumptions about battering. First, no one has the right to use violence against another, except in self-defense. Second, social norms have allowed men to use violence to maintain control in the family. Third, if society has allowed the violence to continue, then the systems representing that society must provide the response. Although the operating philosophy represents a feminist construct of battering, the operational model is much the same as that described by Berk et al. earlier.

Other examples deserve mention. London, Ontario, where the police and community work closely together, has been the subject of much study (Bowman, 1992). Similar model programs exist in Quincy, MA (Salzman, 1994), Newport News, VA (Police Response to Incidence of Domestic Emergency or PRIDE), and DuPage County, IL (Toman & Weisz, 1995). Results of evaluations done in these jurisdictions hold promise that a coordinated effort can reduce recidivism and produce greater levels of victim satisfaction (Bowman, 1992) and can ultimately reduce the rate of domestic homicides (Salzman, 1994).

Since the passage of the Violence Against Women Act in 1994, funding has been provided for new collaborative efforts to begin, and for those projects to be evaluated on an ongoing basis. One such project, the Alexandria Domestic Violence Intervention Project, reports improved attitudes of police officers, leading to an increase in arrests and a reduction in revictimization (Orchowsky, 1999). As more of those evaluations are published, police and communities will be better able to assess the value of this model.

CONCLUSION

Although feminists were the first to recognize the severity and extent of domestic violence and the failures of the criminal justice system to respond effectively, there has also been a history of concern about reliance upon the police and courts. Martin (1999) summarizes that concern when she writes, "The use of a social control response to address a complex and entrenched social problem is both problematic and ineffectual" (p. 416). She and others have begun exploring alternatives, such as those found in models of restorative justice.

Whatever directions we move toward in the future, it seems certain the police will continue to have an important role in matters of immediate safety for victims. As such, the work of the police in this arena will continue to be researched, reviewed, and rewritten.

REFERENCES

BARD, M. (1974). Training police as specialists in family crisis intervention. In R. W. Kobetz (Ed.), *Crisis Intervention and the Police* (pp. 149–187). Chicago, IL: Dayton.

BELKNAP, J., & McCall, K. D. (1994). Woman battering and police referrals. *Journal of Criminal Justice, 22*(3), 223–236.

BELL, D. (1985). Domestic violence victimization, police intervention, and disposition. *Journal of Criminal Justice, 13*(6), 525–534.

BERK, R. A., LOSEKE, D. R., BERK, S. F., & RAUMA, D. (1980). Bringing the cops back in: A study of efforts to make the criminal justice system more responsive to incidents of family violence. *Social Science Research, 9,* 193–215.

BINDER, A., & MEEKER, J. (1992). Arrest as a method to control spouse abuse. In E. S. Buzawa & C. G. Buzawa (Eds.), *Domestic Violence: The Changing Criminal Justice Response* (pp. 129–140). Westport, CT.: Auburn House.

BLACK, D. (1980). *The manner and customs of police.* New York: Academic Press.

BOURG, S., & STOCK, H. V. (1994). A review of domestic violence arrest statistics in a police department using pro-arrest policy: Are pro-arrest policies enough? *Journal of Family Violence, 9*(2), 177–189.

BOWKER, L. H. (1982). Police services to battered women—Bad or not so bad? *Criminal Justice and Behavior, 9*(4), 476–494.

BOWMAN, C. G. (1992). The arrest experiments: A feminist critique. *The Journal of Criminal Law & Criminology, 83*(1), 201–208.

BREINES, W., & GORDON, L. (1983). The new scholarship on family violence. *Signs, 8*(3), 490–531.

BROOKS, R. (1997). Feminists negotiate the legislative branch: The violence against women act. In C. R. Daniels (Ed.), *Feminists Negotiate the State: The Politics of Domestic Violence* (pp. 65–81). Lanham, Maryland: University Press of America.

BROWNE, A. (1987). *When battered women kill.* New York: Free Press.

Bruno v. Codd, 90 Misc.2d 1047, 396 N.Y.S.2d 974 (Sup. Ct. 1977).

BUERGER, M. E. (1999). Police training as pentecost: Using tools singularly ill-suited to the purpose of reform. *Police Quarterly, 1*(1), 27–63.

BUZAWA, E., AUSTIN, T. L., & BUZAWA, C. G. (1995). Responding to crimes of violence against women: Gender differences versus organizational imperatives. *Crime & Delinquency, 41*(4), 443–466.

BUZAWA, E. S., & BUZAWA, C. G. (Eds.). (1992). *Domestic violence: The changing criminal justice response*. Westport, CT: Auburn House.

BUZAWA, E. S., & BUZAWA, C. G. (1996). *Domestic violence: The criminal justice response* (2nd ed.). Thousand Oaks, CA.: Sage.

COLLINS, M. E. (1995). *Mahoney v. Commonwealth*: A response to domestic violence. *New England Law Review, 29*(4), 981–1010.

DANIELS, C. R. (Ed.). (1997). *Feminists negotiate the state: The politics of domestic violence*. Latham, Maryland: University Press of America.

DANISH, S. J., & FERGUSON, N. (1973). Training police to intervene in human conflict. In J. R. Snibbe & H. M. Snibbe (Eds.), *The Urban Policeman in Transition* (pp. 486–506). Springfield, IL.: Charles C. Thomas.

DAVIS, R., & SMITH, B. (1995). Domestic violence reforms. *Crime and Delinquency, 41*(4), 541–552.

DOBASH, R. E., & DOBASH, R. (1979). *Violence against wives: A case against patriarchy*. New York: The Free Press.

DOLON, R., HENDRICKS, J., & MEAGHER, M. S. (1986). Police practices and attitudes toward domestic violence. *Journal of Police Science and Administration, 14*(3), 187–192.

DUNFORD, F. W., HUNIZINGA, D., & ELLIOT, D. S. (1990). The role of arrest in domestic assault: The Omaha police experiment. *Criminology, 28*(2), 183–206.

EDLESON, J. L. (1991). Coordinated community responses. In M. Steinman (Ed.), *Woman Battering: Policy Responses* (pp. 203–219). Cincinati, OH: Anderson.

ELLIOT, D. S. (1989). Criminal justice procedures in family violence crimes. In L. Ohlin & M. Tonry (Eds.), *Family Violence* (pp. 427–480). Chicago: University of Chicago Press.

FAGAN, J. (1988). Contributions of family violence research to criminal justice policy on wife assault: Paradigms of science and social control. *Violence and Victims, 3*(3), 159–186.

FERRARO, K. J. (1989). The legal response to woman battering in the United States. In J. Hanmer, J. Radford, & E. A. Stanko (Eds.), *Women, Policing, and Male Violence* (pp. 155–184). London: Routledge.

FERRARO, K. J., & POPE, L. (1993). Irreconcilable differences: Battered women, police and the law. In N. Z. Hilton (Ed.), *Legal Responses to Wife Assault: Current Trends and Evaluation* (pp. 96–123). Newbury Park, CA.: Sage.

FIELD, M. H., & FIELD, H. F. (1973). Marital violence and the criminal justice process: Neither justice nor peace. *Social Service Review, 47*, 221.

FINESMITH, B. K. (1993). Police response to battered women: A critique and proposals for reform. *Seton Hall Law Review, 14*(1), 74–108.

FRIDAY, P. C., METZGAR, S., & WALTERS, D. (1991). Policing domestic violence: Perceptions, experience, and reality. *Criminal Justice Review, 16*(2), 198–213.

GELLES, R. J. (1993). Constraints against family violence: How well do they work. *American Behavioral Scientist, 36*(5), 575–585.

GELLES, R. J., & CORNELL, C. P. (1990). *Intimate violence in families* (2nd ed.). Newbury Park, CA.: Sage Publications.

HAMBERGER, L. K., & POTENTE, T. (1994). Counseling heterosexual women arrested for domestic violence: Implications for theory and practice. *Violence and Victims, 9*, 125–137.

HART, W., Chairman. (1984). Attorney general's task force on family violence (final report). U.S. Department of Justice.

HIRSCHEL, J. D., & HUTCHINSON, I. W. (1992). Female spouse abuse and the police response: The Charlotte, North Carolina experiment. *Journal of Criminal Law and Criminology, 83*(1), 73–119.

HIRSCHEL, J. D., HUTCHINSON, I. W., DEAN, C. W., & MILLS, A.-M. (1992). Review essay on law enforcement response to spouse abuse: Past, present and future. *Justice Quarterly, 9*(2), 247–283.

HUMM, M. (1990). *The dictionary of feminist theory.* Columbus, OH.: Ohio State University Press.

KRASKA, P. B., & KAPPELER, V. E. (1997). Militarizing American police: The rise and normalization of paramilitary units. *Social Problems, 44*(1), 1–38.

KURZ, D. (1992). Battering and the criminal justice system: A feminist view. In E. S. Buzawa & C. G. Buzawa (Eds.), *Domestic Violence: The Changing Criminal Justice Response* (pp. 21–38). Westport, CT.: Auburn House.

LENTZ, S. A. (1999). Revisiting the rule of thumb: An overview of the history of wife abuse. *Women & Criminal Justice, 10*(2), 9–27.

LERMAN, L. G. (1992). The decontextualization of domestic violence. *Journal of Criminal Law and Criminology, 83*(1), 217–240.

LEVIN, J., & McDEVITT, J. (1993). *Hate crimes: The rising tide of bigotry and bloodshed.* New York: Plenum Press.

LIEBMAN, D. A., & SCHWARTZ, J. A. (1973). Police programs in domestic crisis intervention: A review. In J. R. Snibbe & H. M. Snibbe (Eds.), *The Urban Policeman in Transition* (pp. 421–472). Springfield, IL.: Charles C. Thomas.

LOVING, N. (1980). *Responding to spouse abuse and wife beating: A guide for police.* Washington, D. C.: Police Executive Research Forum.

LYON, A. D. (1999). Be careful what you wish for: An examination of arrest and prosecution patterns of domestic violence cases in two cities in Michigan. *Michigan Journal of Gender and Law, 5*(2), 253–298.

MANNING, P. K. (1993). The preventive conceit: The black box in market context. *American Behavioral Scientist, 36*(5), 639–650.

MARTIN, D. (1987). The historical roots of domestic violence. In D. J. Sonkin (Ed.), *Domestic Violence on Trial* (pp. 3–20). New York: Springer Publishing Company.

Massachusetts General Law, Chapter 209A.

McCORD, J. (1992). Deterrence of domestic violence: A critical view of research. *Journal of Research in Crime and Delinquency, 29*(2), 229–339.

McKEAN, J., & HENDRICKS, J. (1997). The role of crisis intervention in the police response to domestic disturbances. *Criminal Justice Policy Review, 8*(2/3), 269–294.

MEEKER, J. W., & BINDER, A. (1990). Experiments as reform: The impact of the Minneapolis experiment on police policy. *Journal of Police Science and Administration, 17*(2), 147–153.

MIGNON, S. I., & HOLMES, W. M. (1995). Police response to mandatory arrest laws. *Crime and Delinquency, 41*(4), 430–442.

MILLER, S. L. (1994). Expanding the boundaries: Toward a more inclusive and integrated study of intimate violence. *Violence and Victims, 9*(2), 183–194.

MILLER, S. L., & WELLFORD, C. F. (1997). Patterns and correlates of interpersonal violence. In A. P. Cardarelli (Ed.), *Violence Between Intimate Partners: Patterns, Causes, and Effects* (pp. 16–28). Boston: Allyn and Bacon.

MILLS, L. G. (1998). Mandatory arrest and prosecution policies for domestic violence. *Criminal Justice and Behavior, 25*(3), 306–318.

ORCHOWSKY, S. J. (1999). *Evaluation of a coordinated community response to domestic violence: The Alexandria domestic violence intervention project* (NCJ No. 179974). National Institute of Justice.

PARNAS, R. (1967). The police response to the domestic disturbance. *Wisconsin Law Review, 1967*(4), 914–960.

PEARCE, J., & SNORTUM, J. (1983). Police effectiveness in handling disturbance calls: An evaluation of crisis intervention training. *Criminal Justice and Behavior, 10*(1), 71–92.

PLECK, E. (1989). Criminal approaches to family violence. In L. Ohlin & M. Tonry (Eds.), *Family Violence* (pp. 19–57). Chicago: University of Chicago Press.

ROY, M. (1977). Some thoughts regarding the criminal justice system and wife-beating. In M. Roy (Ed.), *Battered Women: A Psychological Study of Domestic Violence*. New York: Van Nostran.

SALZMAN, E. (1994). The Quincy District Court domestic violence intervention. *Boston University Law Review, 74*, 329–364.

SAUNDERS, D. G. (1995). The tendency to arrest victims of domestic violence. *Journal of Interpersonal Violence, 10*(2), 147–158.

SCHECTER, S. (1982). *Women and male violence: The visions and struggles of the battered women's movement*. Boston: South End Press.

Scott v. Hart, No. C-76–2395 (N.D, Cal., filed Oct. 28, 1976)

SGARZI, J. M. (1991) *Attitudes of new police recruits concerning domestic violence: A pre- and post- test design*. Dissertation, Boston College School of Social Work.

SHERMAN, L. W. (1992). *Policing domestic violence: Experiments and dilemmas*. New York: The Free Press.

SHERMAN, L. W., & BERK, R. A. (1984). The specific deterrent effects of arrest for domestic assault. *American Sociological Review, 49*, 261–272.

SHERMAN, L. W., & COHN, E. G. (1989). The impact of research on legal policy: The Minneapolis domestic violence experiment. *Law & Society Review, 23*(1), 117–144.

SHERMAN, L. W., SMITH, D. A., SCHMIDT, J. D., & ROGAN, D. P. (1992). Crime, punishment, and stake in conformity: Legal and informal control of domestic violence. *American Sociological Review, 57*(October), 680–690.

SMITH, D. A., & KLEIN, J. R. (1984). Police control of interpersonal disputes. *Social Problems, 31*(4), 468–481.

SNIBBE, J.R., & SNIBBE, H.M. (1973). The urban policeman in transition. Springfield, IL: Charles C. Thomas.

SOLER, E. (1987). Domestic violence is a crime: A case study-San Francisco Family Violence Project. In D. J. Sonkin (Ed.), *Domestic Violence on Trial* (pp. 21–35). New York: Springer.

SPARKS, A. (1997). Feminists negotiate the executive branch: The policing of male violence. In C. R. Daniels (Ed.), *Feminists Negotiate the State: The Politics of Domestic Violence* (pp. 35–52). Latham, Maryland: University Press of America.

STARK, E. (1993). Mandatory arrest of batterers: A reply to its critics. *American Behavioral Scientist, 36*, 651–680.

State v. Oliver, 70 N.C. 44 (1874).

STEINMAN, M. (Ed.). (1991). *Women battering: Policy responses*. Cincinnati, OH.: Anderson Publishing Co., Criminal Justice Division.

STRATTON, N. R. M. (1990). The domestic violence response team. In J. A. Brown, P. C. Unsinger, & H. W. More (Eds.), *Law Enforcement and Social Welfare: The Emergency Response* (pp. 21–49). Springfield, Ill.: Charles C. Thomas.

STRAUS, M.A., GELLES, R.J., & STEINMETZ, S.K. (1980). Behind closed doors: Violence in the American family. New York: Doubleday.

Thurman v. City of Torrington, Conn., 595 F.Supp. 1521 (Dist. Conn. 1984).

TJADEN, P., & THOENNES, N. (1998). *Prevalence, incidence, and consequences of violence against women: Findings from the National Violence against Women Survey.* Washington, DC: National Institute of Justice and Centers for Disease Control and Prevention.

TOLMAN, R. M., & WEISZ, A. (1995). Coordinated community intervention for domestic violence. *Crime & Delinquency, 41*(4), 481–495.

VIOLENCE AGAINST WOMEN ACT, otherwise know as Title IV of the Violence Crime Control and Law Enforcement Act, 42 USCA §13931 (1994).

WALKER, L. (1979). *The battered woman.* New York: Harper and Row.

WALKER, S. (1993). *Taming the system: The control of discretion in criminal justice, 1950–1990.* New York: Oxford University Press.

WALKER, S., & KATZ, C. M. (1995). Less than meets the eye: Police department bias-crime units. *American Journal of Police, XIV*(1), 29–48.

WORDEN, R. E., & POLLITZ, A. (1984). Police arrests in domestic disturbances: A further look. *Law and Society Review, 18*(1), 105–119.

WRIGHT, C. (1985). Immediate arrest in domestic violence situations: Mandate or alternative. *Capital University Law Review, 14*(2), 243–268.

ZORZA, J. (1992). The criminal law of misdemeanor domestic violence, 1970–1990. *Journal of Criminal Law & Criminology, 83*(1), 46–72.

ZORZA, J. (1994). Must we stop arresting batterers?: Analysis and policy implications of new police domestic violence studies. *New England Law Review, 28*(4), 929–99.

10

Perspectives on Crime Prevention

A Capstone View

M. L. Dantzker

Deborah Mitchell Robinson

The concept of preventing crime has existed since the earliest beginning of the establishment of formal social rules or laws. However, it did not become a true police objective until the formalization of modern policing with the London Metropolitan Police Department (LMPD) whose main objective was crime prevention through preventive patrol (Dantzker, 2000). Since the establishment of the LMPD, crime prevention, "the police agency's ability to prevent criminal activity before it occurs," has continued to be a major objective of today's police agencies (p. 67).

When discussing crime prevention or proactive deterrence, we are referring to the ability of the police to eliminate completely those factors that could lead to crime (Dantzker, 2000). This is in contrast to the more recognized function of crime suppression, that is, the attempt to stop crime prior to or during its commission. Unfortunately, the police have not necessarily been successful at either prevention or suppression.

However, reality dictates that the failure not be placed solely on the police, but on society's shortcomings as well. As Hunter, Mayhall, and Barker (2000) have noted, "[C]rime prevention has become a household phrase, although not necessarily a household effort" (p. 40). That is, people spend considerable time talking about preventing crime, but often little is actually done to accomplish this task. The outcome is usually to charge the police agency with the task of crime prevention.

Many of the crime prevention programs currently being developed and implemented have their origins in the Crime Prevention Through Environmental Design (CPTED) model proposed by C. Ray Jeffery in 1971. As "all human behavior is a function of the interaction of the individual human with his or her environment" (Robinson, 1998b, p. 45), the CPTED model differs from other models by "focusing on the physical environment" (Robinson, 1998a, p. 32). This is an important aspect as it promotes the idea that all individuals can participate in and are responsible for crime prevention.

Many of the programs developed by police agencies have a CPTED component. These include Neighborhood Watches, Operation Identification, Police Auxiliary Volunteers, Community Crime Watches, and Crime Stoppers (Hunter, Mayhall, and Barker, 2000). Perhaps one of the most current attempts to improve crime prevention efforts has been through various implementations of community oriented policing, a major component of which is the renovation and rejuvenation of the physical environment to reduce and prevent crime.

Yet, despite all these efforts, crime continues to exist and, at times and in some places, grows. This results in continuing efforts by the police and society to look for ways to improve upon crime prevention. One such way to improve is through knowledge. Thus, the purpose of this text.

Although unable to cover everything there is to write about crime prevention, this text is presented as a myriad of helpful information to students and practitioners. It begins through an effort to describe the evolution of crime prevention.

HISTORICAL ASPECTS OF POLICING AND CRIME PREVENTION

In Chapter 1, C. Frank Simons takes us on a journey of the evolution of crime prevention. He begins with a brief discussion of what makes an action a crime, reminding us of the difference between crimes that are "evil in themselves"—*mala in se*—and those that are prohibited by statute—*mala prohibita.* From here, Simons advises there are two main elements within the process of crime prevention: (1) the identification of unacceptable behavior and the creation of criminal prohibitions, and (2) enforcement.

Borrowing from an historical approach, Simons suggests the approach to crime prevention requires three main criteria: (1) developing a strong police force; (2) organizing of an active group of citizens; and (3) initiating action to remove some of the causes of crime and conditions in which it flourishes. Furthermore, Simons identifies what may be perceived as the cornerstones of crime prevention: citizen involvement, community policing, and the understanding of the causes of crime. Ultimately, he concludes that crime is always with us and the best approach is to avoid being a victim, that is, being vigilant in how we live our lives.

In examining crime prevention, it is found that enforcement plays a major role. John R. Pike and Laura S. Gaultney explore how cooperation and coordination can improve crime prevention strategies. They identify nine areas impacting successful enforcement initiatives.

The first area is turf protection. It is relatively commonplace for a police agency to want to handle its own problems, that is, handling anything that happens within its own jurisdiction or "on its own turf." Even though this is an understandable position, as Pike and Gaultney suggest, seeking and accepting assistance would allow for more resources to be applied toward the problem. For example, the Dallas (TX) Police Department has worked for years with local private security firms on projects that ultimately provide the DPD with more "eyes" in the community.

A second area the police agency should address is pride, which is associated with turf protection. Many police agencies do not want to ask for assistance, believing that their personnel can handle "any situation." However, this may not always be the case, and pride could result in the inability to solve certain crimes, let alone prevent them.

Sharing information or intelligence dissemination is another way to improve crime prevention strategies. Most police agencies collect a plethora of information that could be useful to other agencies and sharing this information could conceivably assist other agencies in their crime prevention efforts. For example, data collected about a gang in one city, when shared with neighboring cities, could possibly assist those neighboring cities in preventing the formation of a gang within its community.

Although it is perhaps common sense, the fourth area identified by Pike and Gaultney is ethics and professional courtesy between agencies. Basically, what they advise here is that the application of basic principles, morals, and values when dealing with other agencies can go a long way in improving crime prevention efforts.

Because it is a mainstay of community policing, issues related to public relations and trust have received more and more attention in recent years. Building a trusting relationship with the community is paramount to the police agency. This trust can lead to improved cooperation and provision of information regarding potential or already committed crimes, as well as assistance in improving the community environment so as to prevent crime.

The next three areas include resource indexing, combining resources, and crossing jurisdictional boundaries. Perhaps a weakness for many police agencies is not knowing what is available within their jurisdiction as a resource. Victim aide, school, or other social service programs that may impact crime prevention exist in many communities, yet few police officers or community members are aware of them. Resource indexing supports compiling and disseminating a comprehensive list of all the resources available in the community. This, according to Pike and Gaultney, should be followed-up with a means of bringing resources together, such as task forces or community action groups. Finally, crossing jurisdictional boundaries or working with other agencies can influence crime prevention, for example, creating a countywide crime stoppers program and creating a task force comprised of individuals from all the agencies within the jurisdiction.

The last item Pike and Gaultney offered was a Reverse 911 system. This is where the police agency can send out messages or inquiries to businesses and residents. Keeping the community posted on crime and events and being able to seek information is important to crime prevention. Reverse 911 can be a useful tool in this arena.

Overall, Pike and Gaultney recognize that crime prevention is not just a one-step program, nor can it be approached simplistically. It requires cooperation and coordination among police agencies and community members. Addressing the nine areas they identify could go a long way toward improving crime prevention strategies.

Probably one of the more interesting debates in crime prevention is the choice of private security over public security. According to available data, there are approximately 1.5 million private security officers in the United States, in comparison to less than six hundred thousand sworn public police officers. Some cities have eliminated their local public force, only to replace it with a lesser expense private security force. In Chapter 3, Pamela Ann Sexton-Alyea explores this interesting and often controversial debate of public versus private security and whom do we trust.

Sexton-Alyea begins her discourse with an historical overview, reminding us how public security development has existed throughout the development of modern man. Early public security included the building of walls and moats to protect the village and went on to the creation of constables, watchmen, and "bobbies." When these creations did not quite meet the requirements for crime prevention, private security was created with the establishment of the Pinkerton and Wackenhut private security firms.

After the historical perspective, Sexton-Alyea discusses the issue of when to choose public over private security. In her discussion, she examines the similarities and differences between the two entities. The similarities include recognizable uniform and badge, being skilled to compel obedience, and being liable for actions. Differences include (1) financial—where private is profit oriented; (2) employers—for private is usually specific clients; (3) specific functions performed—where private security is charged with preventing crime, protecting assets, and reducing losses; and (4) statutory power—where private police are charged with regulating noncriminal conduct not under the authority of public security. Despite the differences, Sexton-Alyea notes that both have complimentary roles, and there are more restrictions on private than on public security.

Another aspect facing both entities is how they are projected by the media. As Sexton-Alyea indicates, private security in not projected in a very positive light. Then again, seldom is public security. Along with media problems, she enlightens us about litigation and lawsuits, again offering a comparative discussion. She advises that lawsuits against private security mostly stem from assaults, battery, false imprisonment, defamation, intentional infliction of emotional distress, and invasion of privacy. Lawsuits against public security often stem from brutality and violations of constitutional rights.

Finally, Sexton-Alyea suggests five areas that should be considered when debating or considering whether to choose public or private security. The first is the issue of armed versus unarmed. The majority of private security officers do not carry weapons. Second, the salary for private security is often much lower than public security salaries, and you often get what you pay for. Third, the level of education for private security is often less than that of public security, although a high school education is commonplace for both entities. Fourth, the number of guards needed will affect choice. Last, the issue of union versus nonunion can be influential in the finally choice.

Ultimately, Sexton-Alyea doesn't favor one over the other, but suggests bridging the gap and interfacing between public and private security. The issue shouldn't be which one to choose, but making good use of both entities in a combined manner best suited for the community (a sentiment offered by Pike and Gaultney).

POLICING AND CRIME PREVENTION IN THE ACADEMIC SETTING

The first three chapters of this text helped set a foundation for crime prevention. Beginning with Chapter 4, we see more specific applications of crime prevention.

During the late 1990s, a spate of violent events within and around our nation's schoolyards focused the spotlight on the safety of our children in school. How to prevent any type of crime, violent or otherwise, has become of vital interest and importance. This is evidenced by the fact that the federal government has made millions of dollars available to school systems for crime prevention purposes. One way of addressing crime prevention in elementary and secondary schools has been through environmental design. In Chapter 4, Matthew B. Robinson introduces to us Crime Prevention Through Environmental Design or CPTED.

Robinson begins by advising that contrary to popular belief, crimes in our schools are not increasing and students are relatively as safe as ever. Then again, he suggests that more recent surveys may indicate otherwise, contending that crime may become a major issue if it is not addressed. As to what can be done, he starts with a discussion of crime control (suppression) versus crime prevention, claiming that the United States is miserable at crime control and needs to concentrate on crime prevention.

According to Robinson, crime prevention activities can be classified as primary, where efforts are on eliminating that which produces crimes; secondary, where the focus is eliminating problems in specific or particular areas; and tertiary, where efforts are on eliminating problems after crime has occurred. This last approach, he indicates, is most common in schools.

So what is CPTED? Robinson clarifies that CPTED focuses on settings and techniques to reduce crime. He explains that CPTED means changing factors in any environment to (1) prevent or reduce crime; (2) to reduce fear of crime and perceptions of crime risks; (3) to increase the aesthetic quality of an environment; and (4) to increase the quality of life for law-abiding citizens, especially by reducing the propensity of the physical environment to support criminal behavior.

Robinson discusses several levels of analysis or approaches where CPTED is applicable—individual, group, school, community, and social. The individual level includes programs that focus on the individual's behavior; the group level focuses on behavior as it stems from groups; and the school level approaches include a variety of strategies and techniques. The main focus of these three levels appears to be on the physical environment—for example, clean and fenced school yard, controlling access, and so on, but it also includes discipline codes, mentoring, school uniforms, and so forth. The community approach includes helpful programs that involve community members, for example, after-school programs, while the social level is where government is involved, for example, through grants such as "Cops in Schools." In closing, Robinson advocates that the most effective approach to preventing school crimes would be a comprehensive crime prevention program that would include all levels or approaches.

Since the mid-1980s, policing has attempted to address crime prevention through community policing. Again, with school crime having been in the spotlight, it is conceivable that eventually community policing would be introduced into our schools. In Chapter 5, Michael S. Dorn explains how community policing in a county school system in Georgia has become a model for community policing in schools nationwide. Dorn's offerings are based on the success of community policing in the Bibb County, GA, school system. Through Dorn's efforts, this school system went from one whose policing history had been *scandalous* to one of the most respected policing agencies in the country. Although changes in both the school and school police administrations were key to the improvements, he suggests that community policing was the main motivation, and its implementation into the school system created a better, prouder, more efficient crime prevention system.

The Bibb County Model, as referred to by Dorn, had ten key components for its success. These components are (1) standardized reporting; (2) involvement of the community in the problem-solving process; (3) careful and considerate selection of department personnel; (4) ongoing employee development; (5) empowerment; (6) keeping the department in touch with the pulse of the community; (7) providing personnel with the best available equipment; (8) development of a comprehensive salary and benefits package; (9) a human relations management style; and (10) being open-minded as an organization. He concludes that based on the success of the Bibb County Model, community policing efforts are needed in schools across the nation.

Public and private elementary and secondary schools are arenas where crime prevention is important. Another such arena is the college or university campus. In Chapter 6, James W. Rowe and Deborah Mitchell Robinson offer a brief look at several approaches which, when implemented on the college or university campus, will provide for a safe environment without the campus police officers looking like the gestapo. Rowe and Robinson suggest that there are two approaches to crime prevention on the college campus: traditional and nontraditional. The traditional approach includes the use of uniformed patrols, keeping track of time, how long it takes to respond to a call, how long on a call, the use of electronics (e.g., video cameras), and so forth. The nontraditional approaches include bike patrols; park, walk, and talk programs; directed deterrent patrols; and rape aggression defense programs. Overall, Rowe and Robinson advise that there are several positive ways to address crime prevention on college campuses.

POLICING AND CRIME PREVENTION PROGRAMS AT WORK

Schools are not the only singular environment where crime prevention efforts are needed. The remaining chapters of the text examine crime prevention strategies and programs at work. A popular trouble spot for crime in many larger cities has been public housing. Brian McDonough, in Chapter 7, provides an example of crime prevention in public housing through the exploration of efforts in a public housing development in Jersey City, NJ.

Like many public housing projects established in the late 1970s, the Jersey City public housing development Curries Woods had witnessed better days. In more recent years, it had become a hotbed for crime, to the point that the Jersey City Police Department did not like to even respond to calls there. Eventually, enough was enough, and new efforts were undertaken to change the nature of Curries Woods, with an emphasis on crime prevention. To achieve this goal, five main strategies were undertaken.

The first strategy involved CPTED. Old high rises were demolished and construction of low-density town houses took place. New fences, lighting, limited entrances, manned monitoring booths, and parking stickers were all added to improve the general environment. The second strategy was resident screening and eviction enforcement policies. Residents would now have to meet placement eligibility standards and agree to all aspects of the lease agreement, which included a "one strike and you're out" clause. Violators of the lease were evicted.

Using resident monitors was a third strategy employed. These resident monitors were part of the newly formed Curries Woods Tenant Task Force, which not only provided employment for residents, but also allowed the residents the opportunity to "police" their own.

Perhaps one of the more recognizable strategies was the implementation of a community policing program. This program placed community service officers from Jersey City PD on the premises a majority of the time. Generally on bicycle, these officers, including both on- and off-duty personnel, had more interaction with residents, allowing them to get better acquainted with those they were serving.

The last of the strategies was an after-school program. This program was a targeted intervention program that included social service assistance and a young adult basketball league. Overall, McDonough credits the variety of efforts to helping lower crime in Curries Woods. Through a variety of strategies, a once high-risk environment has become a model for safety and crime prevention.

Whether in a secondary school, in public housing, on a college campus, or in the neighborhood where you reside, gangs have left their mark and have quickly become a crime prevention target. In Chapter 8, Gordon A. Crews directs us through a discussion of policing, crime prevention, and gangs. Crews begins by offering "criteria" used in definitions of a gang. They include some type of formal or informal organized type structure, identifiable leadership, identification with a territory, recurrent interaction with other members, and engaging in serious, violent, or criminal behavior. He points out that a lack of specific measures causes speculation as to the existence and growth of gangs and gang crime. Still, he notes, evidence is increasing of a growing gang presence and gang activities on our streets. In particular, gangs are having an impact on schools despite a low number of members. Crews also suggests gangs have the ability to respond to a youth's needs and therefore may be a hard-to-resist temptation.

According to Crews, developing a realistic and distinctive gang prevention program requires two things. First, officials must recognize and admit to a gang presence, and second, site-specific approaches that are operational, include alternative behaviors, and are engagement strategy driven should be adopted. As with other writers in this text, Crews is an advocate of community policing efforts with a focus on minimizing negative experiences of youths with police officers.

Crews contends that gangs can be addressed and dealt with using specific gang reduction strategies. These strategies must include both the recognition by community leaders of gang presence and a mobilization of institutional and community resources.

Crime prevention is not for one specific crime but for the prevention of all crimes. Still, some crimes require and deserve special attention. One such crime is domestic violence, an action that has long gone unchallenged until recently. Because domestic violence impacts so many different people, its inclusion in this text with respect to crime prevention was inevitable. To address this issue, Susan T. Krumholz, in Chapter 9, looks at policing domestic violence.

To establish crime prevention for domestic violence, Krumholz begins by offering terminology and a history of domestic violence. From a policing perspective, the traditional response of police to domestic violence had been enforcement of laws, not to provide social services, and often ignoring domestic situations unless it was absolutely necessary to address them. However, in more recent years, federal and state laws have influenced how police address domestic violence. To demonstrate the changes, Krumholz provides an in-depth review of the research conducted during the past twenty years. Her discussion is divided into five main areas: training and attitudes, arrest as a best response, mandatory and proarrest, alternatives to arrest, and the impact research has had on the law and policing.

Using the extensive literature review, Krumholz acknowledges that the trends in policing domestic violence include formation of special units and various model programs. Her summation of the literature indicates that the police will continue to have an important role in matters of immediate safety for victims of domestic violence.

CONCLUSION

There will always be laws and subsequent crime. As long as there is crime, there will be a need for the police and crime prevention. Because crime reaches all levels of society, invades all environments, and is committed by a broad spectrum of offenders, its prevention will require a myriad of approaches. Therefore, much can be said and written about policing and crime prevention. Although this text only begins to cover aspects of the subject, it does provide a beginning into the exploration of a necessary and important component of our society—crime prevention.

REFERENCES

DANTZKER, M. L. 2000. *Understanding today's police.* 2d ed. Upper Saddle River, NJ: Prentice Hall.

HUNTER, R. D., MAYHALL, P. D., & BARKER, T. (2000). *Police-community relations: The administration of justice* (3rd Ed.) Upper Saddle River, NJ: Prentice Hall.

ROBINSON, D. M. (1998a). A case study of student fear of crime on a small southeastern university campus: Is it justified? In L. J. MORIARTY & R. A. JERIN (Eds.), *Current Issues in Victimology Research* (pp. 31–42). Durham, NC: Carolina Academic Press.

ROBINSON, D. M. (1998b). A comparative analysis of environmental characteristics related to criminal victimization in activity areas of interstate highway interchanges and local highway intersection. *Journal of Security Administration, 21*(1), 45–57.

JEFFERY, C. R. (1971). *Crime prevention through environmental design.* Beverly Hills, CA: Sage Publications.